Bloom's Modern Critical Interpretations

Bloom's Modern Critical Interpretations

Jane Austen's
Pride and Prejudice
Updated Edition

Edited and with an introduction by
Harold Bloom
Sterling Professor of the Humanities
Yale University

BLC BLOOM'S
LITERARY CRITICISM
An imprint of Infobase Publishing

Bloom's Modern Critical Interpretations: Pride and Prejudice, Updated Edition

Copyright ©2007 Infobase Publishing

Introduction © 2007 by Harold Bloom

Bloom's Literary Criticism
An imprint of Infobase Publishing
132 West 31st Street
New York NY 10001

Library of Congress Cataloging-in-Publication Data
Jane austen's pride and prejudice / Harold Bloom, editor. -- Updated ed.
    p. cm. -- (Bloom's modern critical interpretations)
  Includes bibliographical references and index.
  ISBN-13: 978-0-7910-9437-2 (hard cover)
  ISBN-10: 0-7910-9437-5 (hard cover)
  1. Austen, Jane, 1775-1817. Pride and prejudice. I. Bloom, Harold.
II. Title. III. Series.

  PR4034.P72J36 2007
  823'.7--dc22   2006101022

Contributing Editor: Pamela Loos
Cover designed by Ben Peterson
Cover photo © New York, The Granger Collection
Printed in the United States of America
Bang EJB 10 9 8 7 6 5 4 3 2 1

This book is printed on acid-free paper.

Contents

Editor's Note

My Introduction traces Austen's literary heritage from Shakespeare to Samuel Richardson's *Clarissa* whose heroine is the direct precursor of Elizabeth Bennet.

Stuart M. Tave, the classic exegete of Austen's irony, intimates that Elizabeth will educate Darcy into laughter, while Christopher Brooke emphasizes the natural knowledge these lovers share.

"Serious Pastoral" is invoked as a Feminist mode by Mary Jane Curry, after which Johanna M. Smith uncovers a pattern of "oppositional readings" sanctioned by *Pride and Prejudice*.

Samuel Richardson's stylistic influence upon Austen is traced by Joe Bray, while Alex Woloch attempts to set the boundaries between major and minor characters in the book.

Carole Moses centers on the difficulties presented by Austen's ironies in portraying Elizabeth, after which Emily Auerbach justly praises Austen's balance of wit and wisdom.

For Darryl Jones, *Pride and Prejudice* is a kind of fairy tale diverted into high seriousness by Darcy's letter, while Jillian Heydt-Stevenson subtly tries to show a suppressed element of Feminist ideology in the novel.

In this volume's final essay, Ashley Tauchert also stresses strands of an implicit Feminism in Austen's masterwork.

HAROLD BLOOM

Introduction

I

The oddest yet by no means inapt analogy to Jane Austen's art of representation is Shakespeare's—oddest, because she is so careful of limits, as classical as Ben Jonson in that regard, and Shakespeare transcends all limits. Austen's humor, her mode of rhetorical irony, is not particularly Shakespearean, and yet her precision and accuracy of representation is. Like Shakespeare, she gives us figures, major and minor, utterly consistent each in her or his own mode of speech and being, and utterly different from one another. Her heroines have firm selves, each molded with an individuality that continues to suggest Austen's reserve of power, her potential for creating an endless diversity. To recur to the metaphor of oddness, the highly deliberate limitation of social scale in Austen seems a paradoxical theater of mind in which so fecund a humanity could be fostered. Irony, the concern of most critics of Austen, seems more than a trope in her work, seems indeed to be the condition of her language, yet hardly accounts for the effect of moral and spiritual power that she so constantly conveys, however implicitly or obliquely.

Ian Watt, in his permanently useful *The Rise of the Novel*, portrays Austen as Fanny Burney's direct heir in the difficult art of combining the rival modes of Samuel Richardson and Henry Fielding. Like Burney, Austen is thus seen as following the Richardson of *Sir Charles Grandison*, in a "minute presentation of daily life," while emulating Fielding in "adopting a more detached attitude to her narrative material, and in evaluating it from a comic and objective point of view." Watt goes further when he points out that Austen tells her stories in a discreet variant of Fielding's manner "as a confessed author," though her ironical juxtapositions are made to appear not those of "an intrusive author but rather of some august and impersonal spirit of social and psychological understanding."

And yet, as Watt knows, Austen truly is the daughter of Richardson, and not of Fielding, just as she is the ancestor of George Eliot and Henry James, rather than of Dickens and Thackeray. Her inwardness is an ironic revision of Richardson's extraordinary conversion of English Protestant sensibility into the figure of Clarissa Harlowe, and her own moral and spiritual concerns fuse in the crucial need of her heroines to sustain their individual integrities, a need so intense that it compels them to fall into those errors about life that are necessary for life (to adopt a Nietzschean formulation). In this too they follow, though in a comic register, the pattern of their tragic precursor, the magnificent but sublimely flawed Clarissa Harlowe.

Richardson's *Clarissa*, perhaps still the longest novel in the language, seems to me also still the greatest, despite the achievements of Austen, Dickens, George Eliot, Henry James, and Joyce. Austen's Elizabeth Bennet and Emma Woodhouse, Eliot's Dorothea Brooke and Gwendolen Harleth, James's Isabel Archer and Milly Theale—though all these are Clarissa Harlowe's direct descendants, they are not proportioned to her more sublime scale. David Copperfield and Leopold Bloom have her completeness; indeed Joyce's Bloom may be the most complete representation of a human being in all of literature. But they belong to the secular age; Clarissa Harlowe is poised upon the threshold that leads from the Protestant religion to a purely secular sainthood.

C. S. Lewis, who read Milton as though that fiercest of Protestant temperaments had been an orthodox Anglican, also seems to have read Jane Austen by listening for her echoings of the New Testament. Quite explicitly, Lewis named Austen as the daughter of Dr. Samuel Johnson, greatest of literary critics, and rigorous Christian moralist:

> I feel ... sure that she is the daughter of Dr. Johnson: she inherits
> his commonsense, his morality, even much of his style.

The Johnson of *Rasselas* and of *The Rambler*, surely the essential Johnson, is something of a classical ironist, but we do not read Johnson for his ironies, or for his dramatic representations of fictive selves. Rather, we read him as we read Koheleth; he writes wisdom literature. That Jane

Austen is a wise writer is indisputable, but we do not read *Pride and Prejudice* as though it were Ecclesiastes. Doubtless, Austen's religious ideas were as profound as Samuel Richardson's were shallow, but *Emma* and *Clarissa* are Protestant novels without being in any way religious. What is most original about the representation of Clarissa Harlowe is the magnificent intensity of her slowly described dying, which goes on for about the last third of Richardson's vast novel, in a Puritan ritual that celebrates the preternatural strength of her will. For that is Richardson's sublime concern: the self-reliant apotheosis of the Protestant will. What is tragedy in *Clarissa* becomes serious or moral comedy in *Pride and Prejudice* and *Emma*, and something just the other side of comedy in *Mansfield Park* and *Persuasion*.

II

Rereading *Pride and Prejudice* gives one a sense of Proustian ballet beautifully working itself through in the novel's formal centerpiece, the deferred but progressive mutual enlightenment of Elizabeth and Darcy in regard to the other's true nature. "Proper pride" is what they learn to recognize in one another; propriety scarcely needs definition in that phrase, but precisely what is the pride that allows amiability to flourish? Whatever it is in Darcy, to what extent is it an art of the will in Elizabeth Bennet? Consider the superb scene of Darcy's first and failed marriage proposal:

> While settling this point, she was suddenly roused by the sound of the doorbell, and her spirits were a little fluttered by the idea of its being Colonel Fitzwilliam himself, who had once before called late in the evening, and might now come to inquire particularly after her. But this idea was soon banished, and her spirits were very differently affected, when, to her utter amazement, she saw Mr. Darcy walk into the room. In an hurried manner he immediately began an inquiry after her health, imputing his visit to a wish of hearing that she were better. She answered him with cold civility. He sat down for a few moments, and then getting up, walked about the room. Elizabeth was surprised, but said not a word. After a silence of several minutes, he came towards her in an agitated manner, and thus began:
>
> "In vain have I struggled. It will not do. My feelings will not be repressed. You must allow me to tell you how ardently I admire and love you."
>
> Elizabeth's astonishment was beyond expression. She stared, coloured, doubted, and was silent. This he considered sufficient

encouragement; and the avowal of all that he felt, and had long felt for her, immediately followed. He spoke well; but there were feelings besides those of the heart to be detailed, and he was not more eloquent on the subject of tenderness than of pride. His sense of her inferiority—of its being a degradation—of the family obstacles which judgment had always opposed to inclination, were dwelt on with a warmth which seemed due to the consequence he was wounding, but was very unlikely to recommend his suit.

In spite of her deeply rooted dislike, she could not be insensible to the compliment of such a man's affection, and though her intentions did not vary for an instant, she was at first sorry for the pain he was to receive; till, roused to resentment by his subsequent language, she lost all compassion in anger. She tried, however, to compose herself to answer him with patience, when he should have done. He concluded with representing to her the strength of that attachment which, in spite of all his endeavours, he had found impossible to conquer; and with expressing his hope that it would now be rewarded by her acceptance of his hand. As he said this, she could easily see that he had no doubt of a favourable answer. He *spoke* of apprehension and anxiety, but his countenance expressed real security. Such a circumstance could only exasperate farther, and, when he ceased, the colour rose into her cheeks, and she said:

"In such cases as this, it is, I believe, the established mode to express a sense of obligation for the sentiments avowed, however unequally they may be returned. It is natural that obligation should be felt, and if I could *feel* gratitude, I would now thank you. But I cannot—I have never desired your good opinion, and you have certainly bestowed it most unwillingly. I am sorry to have occasioned pain to anyone. It has been most unconsciously done, however, and I hope will be of short duration. The feelings which, you tell me, have long prevented the acknowledgment of your regard, can have little difficulty in overcoming it after this explanation."

Mr. Darcy, who was leaning against the mantelpiece with his eyes fixed on her face, seemed to catch her words with no less resentment than surprise. His complexion became pale with anger, and the disturbance of his mind was visible in every feature. He was struggling for the appearance of composure, and would not open his lips till he believed himself to have attained it. The pause was to Elizabeth's feelings dreadful. At length, in a voice of forced calmness, he said:

"And this is all the reply which I am to have the honour of expecting? I might, perhaps, wish to be informed why, with so little *endeavour* at civility, I am thus rejected. But it is of small importance."

Stuart M. Tave believes that both Darcy and Elizabeth become so changed by one another that their "happiness is deserved by a process of mortification begun early and ended late," mortification here being the wounding of pride. Tave's learning and insight are impressive, but I favor the judgment that Elizabeth and Darcy scarcely change, and learn rather that they complement each other's not wholly illegitimate pride. They come to see that their wills are naturally allied, since they have no differences upon the will. The will to what? Their will, Austen's, is neither the will to live nor the will to power. They wish to be esteemed precisely where they estimate value to be high, and neither can afford to make a fundamental error, which is both the anxiety and the comedy of the first proposal scene. Why after all does Darcy allow himself to be eloquent on the subject of his pride, to the extraordinary extent of conveying "with a warmth" what Austen grimly names as "his sense of her inferiority"?

As readers, we have learned already that Elizabeth is inferior to no one, whoever he is. Indeed, I sense as the novel closes (though nearly all Austen critics, and doubtless Austen herself, would disagree with me) that Darcy is her inferior, amiable and properly prideful as he is. I do not mean by this that Elizabeth is a clearer representation of Austenian values than Darcy ever could be; that is made finely obvious by Austen, and her critics have developed her ironic apprehension, which is that Elizabeth incarnates the standard of measurement in her cosmos. There is also a transcendent strength to Elizabeth's will that raises her above that cosmos, in a mode that returns us to Clarissa Harlowe's transcendence of her society, of Lovelace, and even of everything in herself that is not the will to a self-esteem that has also made an accurate estimate of every other will to pride it ever has encountered.

I am suggesting that Ralph Waldo Emerson (who to me is sacred) was mistaken when he rejected Austen as a "sterile" upholder of social conformities and social ironies, as an author who could not celebrate the soul's freedom from societal conventions. Austen's ultimate irony is that Elizabeth Bennet is inwardly so free that convention performs for her the ideal function it cannot perform for us: it liberates her will without tending to stifle her high individuality. But we ought to be wary of even the most distinguished of Austen's moral celebrants, Lionel Trilling, who in effect defended her against Emerson by seeing *Pride and Prejudice* as a triumph "of

morality as style." If Emerson wanted to see a touch more Margaret Fuller
in Elizabeth Bennet (sublimely ghastly notion!), Trilling wanted to forget the
Emersonian law of Compensation, which is that nothing is got for nothing:

> The relation of Elizabeth Bennet to Darcy is real, is intense,
> but it expresses itself as a conflict and reconciliation of styles:
> a formal rhetoric, traditional and rigorous, must find a way to
> accommodate a female vivacity, which in turn must recognize
> the principled demands of the strict male syntax. The high moral
> import of the novel lies in the fact that the union of styles is
> accomplished without injury to either lover.

Yes and no, I would say. Yes, because the wills of both lovers work by
similar dialectics, but also no, because Elizabeth's will is more intense and
purer, and inevitably must be dimmed by her dwindling into a wife, even
though Darcy may well be the best man that society could offer to her. Her
pride has playfulness in it, a touch even of the Quixotic. Uncannily, she is
both her father's daughter and Samuel Richardson's daughter as well. Her
wit is Mr. Bennet's, refined and elaborated, but her will, and her pride in her
will, returns us to Clarissa's Puritan passion to maintain the power of the self
to confer esteem, and to accept esteem only in response to its bestowal.

STUART M. TAVE

What Are Men to Rocks and Mountains?
Pride and Prejudice

A young lover in *A Midsummer Night's Dream* or in *Man and Superman* who finds the course of true love becoming too difficult to negotiate has the option of escaping to a country where he, or she, imagines this matter can be better ordered. But time and place are not so magically disposable in *Pride and Prejudice*. The story here is familiar: we are presented with two sets of young lovers who have problems which must be worked out, and here too are those who try to direct their lives for them, and varied clowns doing their own foolish acts, before the lovers can attain the deserved happiness we expect for them; but here their solutions cannot be sought in another world among the powers of more than mortal spirits.

As in *Man and Superman* the lovers are not interchangeable pairs, as Elizabeth points out to her kind and less perceptive sister. When Jane and Bingley have finally come together in their felicity Jane wants everybody to be as happy as she: "If I could but see you as happy!" she says to Elizabeth. "If there *were* but such another man for you!" It does not seem possible to her that there could be a second Bingley in the universe, but for Elizabeth that limitation is just as well. "If you were to give me forty such men, I could never be so happy as you. Till I have your disposition ... I never can have your happiness." She'll have to shift for herself and perhaps with very good luck she may meet with another Mr. Collins in time (III, xiii, 350). Elizabeth's time

From *Lovers, Clowns, and Fairies: An Essay on Comedies*. © 1993 by The University of Chicago.

has not been and will not be so empty and desperate as that, but certainly as she has not her sister's disposition a duplicate of her sister's fortune cannot fulfill her desires. Her sister's difficulties in the course of true love have been rather simple as she and Bingley fell in love very quickly, to say the least, and were kept apart only by the interference of others; or if there is a defect in Bingley which made him vulnerable to such interference in the happiness of himself and the woman he loves it is because, as Elizabeth says gently now, "He made a little mistake to be sure; but it is to the credit of his modesty" (350). She has had, for herself, a different opinion of Bingley's weakness and he would never be the man for her. There is certainly no sign that he has learned anything or will ever be any different. Like him Jane is not one to profit much by experience: she does not ever comprehend why the false Miss Bingley wished to be intimate with her, "but if the same circumstances were to happen again, I am sure I should be deceived again" (II, iii, 148). She and Bingley are well matched, they being two of a kind, so easy, Mr. Bennet says, every servant will cheat there (III, xiii, 348). Two of a kind is not Elizabeth's style. And if there are external problems in the matching of Elizabeth they are not what delays her happiness. Unlike the story of Jane the story of Elizabeth takes time because it takes time for Elizabeth to learn and to change, and the story is complicated further because it takes time for Darcy to learn and to change and because those processes are continually affected by one another.

We have here too, as in our previous tales, interfering elders who are busy breakers and makers of matches; and, as before, these are ineffective clownish figures with none of the power of their pretensions to arrange the fates of others. Mrs. Bennet is one of the best ever in this role, a legend for all time—that mother whose main business in life is match-making, with five daughters and slender means, but so eager and silly that she is marvellously incompetent at her business, simply by being herself. She is a grand hazard in the course of the true loves of Jane and Elizabeth; she also pushes Elizabeth as hard as she can to take that clown Mr. Collins (commending him for speaking so sensibly to Mr. Darcy and for being a remarkably clever young man, I, xviii, 101); she pushes her favorite Lydia into a danger where Lydia, the likest to her mother, succumbs, thereby immediately prostrating her mother and then quickly throwing her into ecstasy. But then in a year Mrs. Bennet has surprisingly married off three of five, a commendable, statistically remarkable, record. "Three daughters married! ... Oh, Lord! What will become of me. I shall go distracted" (III, xvii, 378): one of those great fools who succeed so well in spite of herself. Then there is that other clown, Lady Catherine—Mr. Darcy has already been forced to see that he too has relatives to blush for, "ashamed of his aunt's ill breeding" (II, viii, 173)—that other match-making mother. This one has arranged the marriage for her own daughter and nephew when they were children, and she has not been in the habit of brooking disappointment: "depend upon it I will carry my point" (III, xiv, 358). Her superb effort to break the engagement of Darcy and Elizabeth, which in fact doesn't yet exist, helps bring that match to its happy conclusion. "Lady Catherine has been of infinite use," Elizabeth says, "which ought to make her happy, for she loves to be of use" (III, xviii, 381).

But then Elizabeth and Darcy, the young lovers very like Jack Tanner in this respect, also think of themselves as superior spirits with strong confidence in their own abilities to oversee the lives of others. They know how to read minds and characters and thereby to predict conduct and to determine proper matches for their friends. What they know least is the proper marriage for themselves, knowing least their own minds and characters. Like Shaw, Jane Austen has a special delight in such interesting people, handsome and clever, and sometimes rich, the most attractive people we have ever met: those who are so bright they think they are Puck, and who must discover that they are really mortals in love, much in need of the time and place of the eye-opening experience.

Emma might have been a better example for this chapter. She has charm, the charming Miss Woodhouse, and though that is a commonplace compliment, and though there is a false charm, as it is offered in Augusta Hawkins, there is a reality in Emma's which is validated by that contrast. It is made convincing not only by what we can see for ourselves but by the denial of Mr. Knightley, early in the novel: "But I ... who have had no such charm thrown over my senses, must still see, hear, and remember" (I, v, 37). He, unlike Miss Taylor (as was) and most of those within Emma's circle, has kept his senses clear, which is not always gratifying to Emma. But it is borne in on us at the start how effective she thinks she is. If Mr. Knightley, hearing her abuse the reason she has, in breaking the match between Harriet Smith and Robert Martin, thinks it would be better to be without reason than misapply it as she does, Emma has a higher certainty of her knowledge of love and of the minds of men: men fall in love with girls like Harriet (or what Emma thinks Harriet is) and Emma confers on her the power of choosing from among many. And, playful with Mr. Knightley, as we have seen her from the start (I, i, 10), she informs him of how bewitchment works on men. "'To be sure!' she cried playfully. 'I know that is the feeling of you all.'" She knows that such a girl as Harriet is exactly what every man delights in, what at once "bewitches his senses" and satisfies his judgment. We know Mr. Knightley's senses are neither charmed nor bewitched, but Emma is certain that "Were you, yourself, ever to marry, she is the very woman for you" (I, viii, 63–64), a delightful promise. And so it is not surprising that a few pages later Emma then begins to create a play and assures Harriet that Mr. Elton's sweet verses of courtship are certainly for her: "It is a sort of prologue to the play ... and will soon be followed by matter-of-fact prose," as indeed it will be. Harriet, with a better sense of uncertainty, but now overridden, is more like the open Hippolyta—"The strangest things to take place!" To Emma it is nothing strange or out of the common course but so evidently, so palpably, desirable; what courts her pre-arrangement immediately shapes itself into the proper form. Her Hartfield, under her rule, seems to have a magic quality, seems to have "a something in the air," she says, "which gives love exactly the right direction, and sends it into the very channel where it ought to flow." She has the right text—

The course of true love never did run smooth—

and she is the right editor. "A Hartfield edition of Shakespeare would have a long note on that passage." She has her map of misreading, because under her direction, she expects, all will run smooth, and she will be distressed later to find that the text of her own play will run closer to Shakespeare's. There may be some without common sense who will not find agreeable Harriet's match with Mr. Elton, she says, but "we are not to be addressing our conduct to fools" (I, ix, 74–75). She is, like Puck, above that mortal condition. The charade of courtship found on the table was, she tells her father, "dropt, we suppose, by a fairy"; but it is so pretty, her father says, that he can easily guess "what fairy brought it." Nobody could have written so prettily but Emma, a pretty confusion that helps to define her status among the fairies. Emma only nodded and smiled (78). She can indeed laugh: Harriet may so wonder that Miss Woodhouse should not marry, "so charming as you are!" but "Emma laughed and replied, 'My being charming, Harriet, is not quite enough to induce me to marry; I must find other people charming—one other person at least.'" And, free from the charms of others, in maiden meditation fancy free, as we may offer our own quotation for the Hartfield edition, she has very little intention of ever marrying at all. "I must see somebody very superior to any one I have seen yet, to be tempted," and she would rather not be tempted. The fact is "I cannot really change for the better." If she were to fall in love that would be a different thing, but "I have never been in love; it is not my way, or my nature; and I do not think I ever shall." So she would be a fool to change such a situation as hers (I, x, 84).

We may be certain that such exemption from the human condition is not a role a young lady or man can play for long on this earth. By the end of Volume I Emma has learned that she has been in error, that she did not see into Mr. Elton's mind, though the misread signs were fairly obvious even to her unimaginative brother-in-law, that she has been foolish, wrong in taking so active a part in bringing any two people together, adventuring too far, assuming too much, making light of what ought to be serious, and, not being tricky Puck, "making a trick of what ought to be simple." She is ashamed and resolved to do such things no more (I, xvi, 137). But of course she is not done; she is still "acting a part" on a succeeding matter (I, xviii, 145); or she is rebuking Mrs. Weston for trying Emma's specialty—"My dear Mrs. Weston, do not take to match-making. You do it very ill," without seeing why Mrs. Weston's suggestion of Mr. Knightley and Jane Fairfax is so irritating to her—and then running off into ridicule of the possibility by expertly imitating Miss Bates as Mr. Knightley's prospective relative. "For shame, Emma! Do not mimic her. You divert me against my conscience" (II, viii, 225). She has some real talents in this Puckish line of acting and of mimicry and of seeing into others and directing them, but that is part of her problem since she enjoys the power and cultivates it until her limits close in on her painfully. By the late stages of her third volume the faith of Miss Smith, her most malleable creation, who is still certain that Miss Woodhouse "can see into everybody's heart" is no longer gratifying (III, xi, 404).

Emma has been a disinterested fairy, exerting her talents to be helpful, enjoying the fun of match-making. "It is the greatest amusement in the world!" But Mr. Knightley knows she is not good at it and is more likely to do harm to herself than good to others (I, i, 11–13). He is better in foretelling things than she, as she is forced to see at several times and, most painfully, when it appears that she has unwittingly brought together Harriet and Mr. Knightley. The discovery of her blindness is mortifying. She had believed herself "in the secret of everybody's feelings," had "proposed to arrange everybody's destiny," and proved to be universally mistaken: and, incompetent fairy that she was, "she had not quite done nothing—for she had done mischief" (III, xi, 411–13). Happily she is still mistaken in foretelling the results of these evils, for Harriet, that clown, will always bounce, and Mr. Knightley, that superior spirit administering the counter-charm, with no charm thrown over his senses, had doted on her, faults and all (III, xvii, 462).

But for our purposes we will stay with *Pride and Prejudice*. It's a story that enables us to follow more readily the pattern we've been working with, both in the symmetrical contrasting of the two main sets of young lovers, and in the way in which the primary couple play off one another to bring about their eye-opening changes. Elizabeth, of course, is the central and most active character, and it is the mind and fortunes of her spirit we follow in its wit and its wanderings. We pick up the bright and attractive quality of Elizabeth from the beginning, her first encounter with Darcy when, catching her eye, he makes the mistake of underestimating her powers of temptation and leaves her with no very cordial feelings towards him: she tells the story "with great spirit" among her friends; "for she had a lively, playful disposition, which delighted in any thing ridiculous" (I, iii, 12). With all the right equipment, the liveliness, playfulness, the delight in all that is ridiculous, the imagination, this young lady is a spirit who will change his vision and tell his story in another way. The result is confirmed in the final chapter when Georgiana Darcy listens with astonishment bordering on alarm at Elizabeth's "lively, sportive, manner" of talking to him, now the object of open pleasantry; by Elizabeth's instruction Georgiana's mind receives knowledge which has never before fallen in her way, how a woman may take liberties with her husband (III, xix, 388). We, not as naive as the young sister and with more opportunities for observation, have seen this spirit in its liberty, the "easy playfulness" of manner by which Darcy is caught (I, vi, 23), the continual "liveliness," "lively imagination," "lively talents" and the "spirits soon rising to playfulness" and "liveliness of your mind" Darcy learns to admire (III, xviii, 380). Others do not notice the effect of the first meeting of Darcy and Wickham, but characteristically Elizabeth sees and is astonished. "What could be the meaning of it?—It was impossible to imagine; it was impossible not to long to know" (I, xv, 73). When she arrives at Hunsford to visit Charlotte and Mr. Collins she anticipates quickly how her visit will pass, for "A lively imagination soon settled it all" (II, v, 158). If she cannot find out a secret in an honorable manner she is quite capable of "tricks and stratagems" to find it out (III, ix, 320). To the uncomprehending, like Mrs. Hurst and Mrs. Bennet, her look and manner may seem even "wild" (I, viii, 35; ix, 42), a shocking free spirit.

She has more than the manner, or the art to please by her easy playing and singing, or the lightness to run across the fields when she has an important mission, for she has the superior power of the mind reader. We see that early, just after the great spirit of her response to Darcy, as Jane, who has had better dancing, expresses her admiration for Bingley. "He is just what a young man ought to be," with sense and good humor, Jane says, "and I never saw such happy manners!—so much ease, with such perfect good breeding!" Elizabeth sees quickly what Jane is really thinking of, besides these proper social qualities. "He is also handsome," she replies, "which a young man ought likewise to be, if he possibly can. His character is thereby complete." And she gives her approval: "Well, he certainly is very agreeable, and I give you leave to like him. You have liked many a stupider person." Jane is easy to read, though no one appreciates her goodness and its weaknesses better than Elizabeth: "Oh! you are a great deal too apt you know, to like people in general. You never see a fault in any body." (Jane is the sort of girl who, in another time, might become a school-teacher because, as the happy saying goes, she likes people.) "With *your* good sense, to be so honestly blind to the follies and nonsense of others!" (I, iv, 14). When she sees Jane's smile of sweet complacency and glow of happy expression in Bingley's company, "Elizabeth instantly read her feelings." Loving sister that Elizabeth is, her own concerns of the moment give way to Jane's happiness (I, xviii, 95). But that lively mind stays sharp in its understanding of the minds of even those she loves. Jane's honest blindness to the faults of others leads her to faulty assumptions—that Bingley's sisters can only wish his happiness and if he is attached to her she cannot believe they would influence him against her, the only woman who can secure his happiness. Elizabeth knows a defective syllogism when she sees one: "Your first position is false. They may wish many things besides his happiness ..." (II, i, 136).

Elizabeth ranges more widely than her family out into the neighborhood, has rather a vocation for seeing into thoughts and characters, is therefore capable of predicting action. If Bingley says that whatever he does he does in a hurry, that he may depart Netherfield in five minutes, "That is exactly what I should have supposed of you," Elizabeth replies. "You begin to comprehend me, do you?" "Oh! yes—I understand you perfectly." He would like to take that for a compliment, "but to be so easily seen through," he is afraid, is pitiful. She can make better distinctions than that: it does not necessarily follow that "a deep, intricate character" is more or less estimable, she tells him, "than such a one as yours." She doesn't give a name to such a one as his, though shallow and simple do seem to be implied. Bingley continues immediately, "I did not know before ... that you were a studier of character. It must be an amusing study." She is a connoisseur: "Yes; but intricate characters are the most amusing. They have at least that advantage." Even in a country neighborhood, where there are few subjects, a confined society, people themselves alter so much there is something new to be observed forever (I ix, 42–43): she has a delighted sense of the effects of time on character.

It is amusing and she dearly loves a laugh. There, is a sisterly resemblance to Lydia, but Lydia is louder and more violent ("Lord! how I laughed! ... I thought I should have died.... any body might have heard us ten miles off!"), whether her enjoyment is a silly joke or a good journey to an unthinking immoral end (II, xvi, 221–22; III, v, 291). Elizabeth has a discriminating appreciation of levels and occasions. Her enjoyment is often private, as she sees into how others are making fools of themselves: she turns away "to hide a smile," from Darcy's assurance of his "real superiority of mind" (I, xi, 57); "nor could she think, without a smile," what Lady Catherine's indignation would have been if Elizabeth had been presented to her ladyship as the future

niece (II, xiv, 210); "and she could hardly suppress a smile" when Darcy later
seeks the acquaintance of some of her relatives, perhaps thinking them people
of fashion (III, i, 254). Mr. Collins's proposal brings her closer to an open
expression, when the idea of Mr. Collins, "with all his solemn composure,
being run away with by his feelings," makes her "so near laughing" that for
the moment she can't stop him (I, xix, 105). Some of these opportunities,
as with Collins, or Sir William Lucas, are rather too easy, as she knows.
"Elizabeth loved absurdities, but she had known Sir William's too long" (II,
iv, 152). It is more impressive to hear that the sensible Mrs. Gardiner, who
knows her nieces well, can say to her of Jane's disappointment in love that "It
had better have happened to *you*, Lizzy; you would have laughed yourself out
of it sooner" (II, ii, 141). Elizabeth is admirable, for she has that awareness
of herself too as object. If observant Mrs. Gardiner then points out that it
would be better if Elizabeth did not *remind* her mother to invite Wickham,
she understands immediately: "'As I did the other day,' said Elizabeth, with
a conscious smile" (II, iii, 145). If Darcy says, with some truth, that she finds
great enjoyment in occasionally professing opinions which are not in fact her
own, "Elizabeth laughed heartily at this picture of herself" (II, viii, 174).

But she is herself best able to draw for him the picture of Elizabeth
as the witty laugher. Miss Bingley is incapable of punishing what is, in her
trivial language, a shocking speech of Darcy's, but for Elizabeth "Nothing
so easy, if you have but the inclination." She knows we can all punish one
another: "Teaze him—laugh at him.—Intimate as you are, you must know
how it is to be done." Witless Miss Bingley does not know that, even her
intimacy has not yet taught her; his temper may defy teasing, "And as to
laughter, we will not expose ourselves, if you please, by attempting to laugh
without a subject. Mr. Darcy may hug himself." That absurdity will not
pass with Elizabeth, who knows that all mortals are subjects. "'Mr. Darcy
is not to be laughed at!' cried Elizabeth. 'That is an uncommon advantage,
and uncommon I hope it will continue, for it would be a great loss to *me* to
have many such acquaintance. I dearly love a laugh.'" Darcy is not prepared
to hug himself, for he knows the general principle that "The wisest and the
best of men, nay, the wisest and the best of their actions, may be rendered
ridiculous by a person whose first object in life is a joke." But Elizabeth
is as well read in eighteenth-century comic theory as he. Certainly, she
replies, there are such people, "but I hope I am not one of *them*. I hope
I never ridicule what is wise or good. Follies and nonsense, whims and
inconsistencies *do* divert me, I own, and I laugh at them whenever I
can.—But these, I suppose, are precisely what you are without." And from
there she draws him out until she must turn away to hide the smile (I, xi,
57). Her diversions are impeccable in principle and skillful in execution.

As with the family resemblance and distinction in the laughter of Lydia, her sport in exposing follies and nonsense has her father's talent but is essentially different. For one thing, he lacks depth and his range is limited to hitting easy marks. He does well with Mr. Collins, who is deserving of the ironic contempt which we enjoy, but Mr. Collins is such an obvious fool that he walks with happy cooperation into the wit-traps Mr. Bennet sets for him. Mrs. Bennet, who, in her way, appreciates her husband's ability to give what she calls "one of your set downs" (I, iii, 13), is herself the continual victim of his traps, but she, and her younger daughters too, are hardly worth the effort. Worse yet, there is a cynical disappointment in this treatment of his wife, whom he chose for foolish reasons and without accepting responsibility thereafter for the consequences of his choice. The effect is not amusing and creates a family with unhappy defects, "hopeless of remedy." He is "contented with laughing at them," and never exerts himself (II, xiv, 213). He sees into others, this man who is "a mixture of quick parts, sarcastic humour, reserve, and caprice" (I, 1, 5), but not into himself (except for one moment in his life which he knows will pass soon enough, III, vi, 299).

Elizabeth sees with a better eye. The eyes are the first thing that catch Darcy, make her an object of some interest in his eyes who had at first scarcely allowed her to be pretty and looked at her only to criticize: he no sooner made it clear to himself and his friends that she had hardly a good feature in her face "than he began to find that it was rendered uncommonly intelligent by the beautiful expression of her dark eyes." What he is beginning to see of course is a superior mind and his own "critical eye" is forced to a better discrimination (I, vi, 23). It is the first indication the obtuse Miss Bingley receives of his admiration. She thinks, watching him exchange a few words with Elizabeth, that she can read his mind, that "I can guess the subject of your reverie." Darcy knows her better: "I should imagine not." Miss Bingley assumes they think alike, that she is quite of his opinion in contempt of present company, but her conjecture, as he tells her, is totally wrong: "I have been meditating on the very great pleasure which a pair of fine eyes in the face of a pretty woman can bestow." She immediately fixes her eyes on his face and desires to know who is the lady inspiring such reflections and when he replies, with great intrepidity, that it is Miss Elizabeth Bennet she is astonished. "How long has she been such a favourite?—and pray when am I to wish you joy?" Darcy is the one who can read the mind: "That is exactly the question which I expected you to ask." This is a bit unfair to Miss Bingley, because after all it is he who had misled her and has now changed his own mind, but we don't mind anything unfair to Miss Bingley. What is of more interest to us is, first, that she is an easy read, and he is making his read by an easy generalization about what he calls "A lady's imagination," so he doesn't get much credit for that; and, second, that he is still quite ignorant of who Elizabeth is and what will be the effect, how much greater and different the pleasure and how unsuspected the pain, which she will have on him. But for us it is a pleasure to see this sign of a better vision in him (I, vi, 27). Miss Bingley continues to act blindly when Elizabeth turns up at Netherfield after the active cross-country walk—hair untidy, blowsy, petticoat six inches deep in mud as the ladies see her—and Miss Bingley whispers to Darcy that this adventure must have rather affected his admiration of her fine eyes. "Not at all," he replies; "they were brightened by the exercise" (I, viii, 36). Poor Miss Bingley cannot let it alone and is at it again in the next chapter, forcing even more precise detailed observations from Darcy. "As for your Elizabeth's picture, you must not attempt to have it taken, for what painter could do justice to those beautiful eyes?" No, Darcy agrees, "It would not be easy, indeed, to catch their expression, but their colour and shape, and the eyelashes, so remarkably fine, might be copied." It is lovely to see Elizabeth, who of course hasn't heard this, conclude the chapter by laughing at them all and refusing to spoil their picturesque grouping. "Good bye," and she runs gaily off (I, x, 53).

But the fact is those fine eyes, bright and beautifully expressive of an uncommon intelligence, and they are all of that, with their quick sight into the minds of others, are not always properly observant or accurate. They do not see Darcy and his thoughts very well, even, or especially, when she is his object. "Occupied in observing Mr. Bingley's attentions to her sister, Elizabeth was far from suspecting that she was herself becoming an object of some interest in the eyes of his friend." She notices that Darcy is attending to her conversation with others. What does he mean by listening? she asks Charlotte. Charlotte, who is an accurate observer, pretends to know no more than she sees: "That is a question which Mr. Darcy only can answer." Elizabeth is more sharp: "... if he does it any more I shall certainly let him know that I see what he is about. He has a very satirical eye," and if she doesn't begin to become impertinent herself she will soon grow afraid of him (I, vi, 23–24). But she does not see what he is about and his eye is not now satirical, and she does grow mistakenly impertinent in self-defense. Darcy deserves it all, and at the moment he doesn't himself know what he is about, but our concern is for her and her overconfidence in her sight and for the insufficient self-defense to which it leads.

Darcy is not the only young lover who gives her difficulties in understanding, because even Mr. Collins, so much simpler to see through and to escape, in some ways rather an enjoyable object, even he in his strange way does puzzle her. Mr. Collins is a wonderful clown, a gentleman and a stranger who announces himself before he arrives, in the language of his letter, with its formal pretensions to the higher literacy, its ideas of healing the breach and offering the olive branch, its ponderous sentences. He has no noun without its adjective, "valuable rectory ... earnest endeavour ... grateful respect," no word where two will do, "bounty and beneficence ... rites and ceremonies ... promote and establish," and he has the loftier diction, "subsisting," and "demean myself," with the happy ambiguity of that last. As he says, "I flatter myself...." "He must be an oddity, I think," Elizabeth says. "I cannot make him out.—There is something very pompous in his stile ... Can he be a sensible man, sir?" "No, my dear; I think not," says Mr. Bennet, "I have great hopes of finding him quite the reverse. There is a mixture of servility and self-importance in his letter, which promises well. I am impatient to see him." This polite young man's appearance fulfills the promise of his language, heavy looking, air grave and stately, manners very formal (I, xiii, 62–64). Mr. Bennet cultivates him and brings him out. When he solemnly discloses his feelings for Elizabeth she is near laughing, to be sure, but when the critical moment comes—"And now nothing remains for me but to assure you in the most animated language of the violence of my affection"—she has a problem, because he is so fixed in his form that she cannot make him understand her language. He is so confident of his understanding of the minds and motions of ladies that, "with a formal wave of the hand," he dismisses her own words of declination: "it is usual with young ladies to reject the address of the man whom they secretly mean to accept, when he first applies for their favour ..." "Upon my word, Sir," she says, she is perfectly serious in her refusal. She considers the matter finally settled and, rising as she speaks, she wants to quit the room; but no, her word cannot mean, he will speak to her again, not accuse her of cruelty at present, "because I know it to be the established custom of your sex to reject a man on the first application ..." "Really, Mr. Collins ... you puzzle me exceedingly ... I know not how to express my refusal in such a way as may convince you of its being one." But, once more, in words we have heard before in his letter (and once more earlier in the present dialogue), "You must give me leave to flatter myself, my dear cousin, that your refusal of my addresses is merely words of course." He must conclude that she wishes to increase his love by suspense, "according to the usual practice of elegant females." What can she say? "Can I speak plainer?" she asks, "... as a rational creature speaking the truth from her heart." "You are uniformly charming!" cries he. And to such perseverance in willful self-deception she can only immediately and in silence withdraw (I, xix, 106–09). Mr. Collins is the fool who sees himself as the master of language and reading of minds and as the irresistible lover. And he does play the lover with success. If he is told that his first possible choice,

Jane, is already spoken for, he can turn to Elizabeth, and when he finds that
she really is unwilling, he could turn readily to the third sister, who might
have been prevailed on to accept him. Mary had appreciated, judiciously,
the composition of his letter (I, xiii, 64), the solidity of his reflections often
struck her, and though he was by no means so clever as herself she thought
he could improve himself by such an example as hers (I, xxii, 124). But
clever Mr. Collins surprises them all by his proposal to Charlotte when even
Charlotte had little dared to hope that so much love and eloquence awaited
her so quickly. "In as short a time as Mr. Collins's long speeches would allow"
she accepted him, to the satisfaction of both (121–22). He runs his course in
three days, not quite as fast as Puck in one night switches lovers around, but
a creditable performance for a mortal playing both roles. (And really in not
much more time than the whole of *A Midsummer Night's Dream*.)

For Mr. Collins, that unchangeable clown, time can have no
meaning—and he has done remarkably well for himself. He appears very
fortunate in his choice of a wife, Darcy says. Yes indeed, Elizabeth can
confirm; "his friends may well rejoice in his having met with one of the very
few sensible women who would have accepted him, or have made him happy
if they had" (II, ix, 178). Fortunate Mr. Collins has found a sensible woman
for whom time has no meaning; to the bright-eyed Elizabeth's astonishment
it is her intimate friend, a character she discovers she has never understood.
Charlotte had never deceived her. Charlotte had been quite clear in advice
about Jane's slowness with Bingley: "if she were married to him tomorrow,
I should think she had as good a chance of happiness, as if she were to be
studying his character for a twelve-month." Charlotte needs no time, no
affection, no movement in feeling or knowledge; knowing does not advance
felicity in the least and "it is better to know as little as possible of the defects
of the person with whom you are to pass your life." Elizabeth, we know
already, delights in anything ridiculous: "You make me laugh, Charlotte; but
it is not sound. You know it is not sound, and that you would never act in this
way yourself" (I, vi, 23). Charlotte knows quite well how she would act and
does not lose the opportunity of "fixing" her man (21). "You are uniformly
charming," Mr. Collins had declared to Elizabeth, and we can assume that
he used the same uniformity with Charlotte, but Charlotte's own eye cannot
be and has no need to be charmed. If Mr. Collins entreats her to name the
day that is to make him the happiest of men, the lady feels no need to trifle
with his happiness. "The stupidity with which he was favoured by nature,
must guard his courtship from any charm that could make a woman wish
for its continuance; and Miss Lucas, who accepted him solely from the
pure and disinterested desire of an establishment, cared not how soon that
establishment were gained" (I, xxii, 122). It is a long time before Elizabeth

becomes at all reconciled to the idea of so unsuitable a match; she had always felt Charlotte's opinion of matrimony was not exactly like her own, "but she could not have supposed it possible that when called into action, she would have sacrificed every better feeling to worldly advantage." It is a most humiliating picture. And to this is added the distressing conviction that it is impossible for her friend to be tolerably happy in that lot she had chosen (125).

When she visits Mr. and Mrs. Collins at Hunsford she "looked with wonder" at her friend who can have so cheerful an air with such a companion. Charlotte knows how to manage that air, by wisely not hearing or seeing her husband. It costs only a faint blush, because it is certainly "not unseldom" when such wisdom is not possible, and Elizabeth, seeing her composure in bearing with her husband, has "to acknowledge that it was all done very well" (II, v, 156–57). By the time the visit ends Elizabeth sees Charlotte more clearly, in that friend's acceptance of a permanent diminishment of life. "Poor Charlotte!—it was melancholy to leave her to such society!—But she had chosen it with her eyes open." Charlotte does not seem to ask for compassion. She keeps busy: her home and housekeeping, parish and poultry and all their dependent concerns "had not yet lost their charms" (II, xv, 216). Charlotte is no blind lover, makes her choice with her eyes open, takes the consequences and does as well as can be done with them. The charm that needs no time was not in love but in the home, the parish and the poultry; and yet they too, it seems, like all charms, may be not fixed but subject to time.

Elizabeth is never liable to the charm that needs no time as it appears in the grave and stately air of clownish Mr. Collins, but there is another stranger who has an air and to whom she is blind. It takes little or no time, she later realizes, "a first interview ... and even before two words have been exchanged" (III, iv, 279). Wickham charms her. Her first sight of him comes when she is walking in Meryton with her sisters, so that her vision is merged for that moment with Kitty's and Lydia's. "All were struck with the stranger's air, all wondered who he could be ..." Kitty and Lydia, determined to find out, lead the way across the street and it is found that Mr. Wickham has accepted a commission in the corps: "This was exactly as it should be; for the young man wanted only regimentals to make him completely charming." The thought and the words sound not like Elizabeth's but her silly sisters', but this time she is with them. His gentlemanlike appearance, the fine countenance, good figure and very pleasing address, is followed by a happy readiness of conversation—a readiness at the same time perfectly correct—"and the whole party" are still talking together very agreeably when Darcy comes by (I, xv, 72). At that point the more perceptive Elizabeth does notice a difference, but it will be a while before she can understand what that means. At their next meeting when Wickham talks "she is very willing to hear him," and her curiosity is unexpectedly relieved by the conversation of this man who is more than ready to tell her about Darcy. She has a quick ear for the pompous style of Mr. Collins, but what does she hear in the words of Wickham?

> His father, Miss Bennet, the late Mr. Darcy, was one of the best men that ever breathed, and the truest friend I ever had; and I can never be in company with this Mr. Darcy without being grieved to the soul by a thousand tender recollections.

When a girl like Elizabeth Bennet hears that sort of language she should be trying to hide a smile, be near laughing. But this agreeable handsome man is saying what she wants to hear. She honors his feelings, "thought him handsomer than ever as he expressed them." "She could have added," this observant studier of character, "'A young man too, like *you*, whose very countenance may vouch for your being amiable.'" He speaks well, does all gracefully (I, xvi, 78, 80–81). The man was completely charming upon his entry into her life and the next time she thinks of that is at the moment when she reads the letter with the mortifying truth about him and remembers: "She could see him instantly before her, in every charm of air and address," but could remember no substantial good; she is now struck with the impropriety of what he communicated to a stranger "and wondered it had escaped her before" (II, xiii, 206–07). The last time she hears of his charm is in Lydia's language—"and what do you think of my husband? Is not he a charming man? I am sure my sisters must all envy me" (III, ix, 317), which completes the circle of the first meeting with him. As for Wickham and his several roles, he begins by playing the charming deceiver, proves to be unsuccessful as lover, and ends by marrying a fool in, to that degree, an appropriate match.

That discerning eye which gives Elizabeth such amusing power to see through character has difficulties with strangers. She may laugh at her dear Jane who is at first so uncertain in deciding the truth about Wickham and Darcy; but Jane, for her own weak reasons, does say rightly that they can't conjecture the causes or circumstances, and she will not give in: "Laugh as much as you chuse, but you will not laugh me out of my opinion." Bright Elizabeth has no difficulty seeing the truth, can't believe that Wickham should invent such a history—names, facts, everything mentioned without ceremony—her hard evidence. "Besides, there was truth in his looks." To simple Jane it is not so simple. "It is difficult indeed—it is distressing—One does not know what to think." "I beg your pardon;—one knows exactly what to think" (I, xvii, 85–86). More difficult and distressing, however, is Charlotte, her intimate friend who turns out to be strange. "The strangeness of Mr. Collins's making two offers of marriage within three days, was nothing in comparison of his being now accepted" (I, xxii, 125). "It is unaccountable! in every view it is unaccountable!" If Jane, in her ineffective way, tries to defend Charlotte, Elizabeth will have none of it. "You shall not defend her, though it is Charlotte Lucas. You shall not, for the sake of one individual, change the meaning of principle and integrity, nor endeavour to persuade yourself or me, that selfishness is prudence, and insensibility of danger, security for happiness" (II, i, 135–36). That is clear enough, but when Wickham's attentions are over and he becomes the admirer of someone else—the sudden acquisition of ten thousand pounds is "the most remarkable charm" of this young lady—Elizabeth, "less clear-sighted perhaps in his case than in Charlotte's," does not quarrel with him for his wish of independence. "Nothing, on the contrary, could be more natural ..." (II, iii, 149–50).

That stranger who gives most trouble is Darcy, another confidently superior spirit whose eye has its own problems in seeing what lies beyond his assured vision. His first remark, when he looks at her, catches her eye, withdraws his own, and speaks coldly of her, is reason enough for her to remain with no very cordial feelings towards him (I, iii, 11–12). At the point when she can't help observing how frequently his eyes are fixed on her she hardly knows how to suppose she can be an object of admiration to so great a man, but that he should look at her because he dislikes her is "still more strange." What she cannot see is that her eye has now caught his "and Darcy had never been so bewitched by any woman as he was by her." If she does not understand him it is in part because he does not understand his own mind; he really believes that but for the inferiority of her family connections he should be in some danger (I, x, 51–52). Her dislike makes her the ready dupe of Wickham's invented history: "'How strange!' cried Elizabeth. 'How abominable!'" (I, xvi, 81). Wickham's tale of injustice makes her wonder that the very pride of Darcy has not made him just, if from no better motive than that he would be too proud to be dishonest—a sharp insight of Elizabeth at her best, now lost in strangeness. Neither she nor Darcy performs very well in this area. "I should like to know how he behaves among strangers," Colonel Fitzwilliam says to her, and Elizabeth can tell him how dreadful Darcy is in his unwillingness to dance with, or even seek an introduction to, young ladies outside his own party. Darcy is by now prepared to admit he might be more forthcoming, "but I am ill qualified to recommend myself to strangers." Shall we ask him, she says to Colonel Fitzwilliam, why an intelligent and experienced man is ill qualified to recommend himself to strangers? Because he will not give himself the trouble, Fitzwilliam answers for him. Darcy's answer is that he has not the talent some possess, of conversing easily with those he has never seen before. Elizabeth, at the pianoforte, says she cannot perform as well as many women she has seen, but she has always supposed it to be her own fault, because she would not take the trouble of practicing. Darcy turns that to a compliment: "We neither of us perform to strangers" (II, viii, 174–76). They do have that in common; and what they both must find, and each will show the other, is that it takes trouble and practice to learn the art.

What is strange, as we have seen before and will see in later chapters, is in simplest terms what is outside the limits of one's ability to understand, for lack of experience or of vision. But in different tales those limits and the response to them have different meanings, and in this story they present a moral test: to stop with that deficiency of comprehension, not move to extend one's ability, is the mark of a mind either uncommonly weak or uncommonly clever. Mrs. Bennet, who sees nothing that is not beyond her, is the best example of the one and Elizabeth, who sees everything clearly, of the other. The family resemblance here is that, in their unlike ways, they both sit down with their grievances, very discontented with the ways in which other people have insisted on acting beyond their powers of comprehension, acting badly of course. Elizabeth has got to move from this and with the right moves, as the response to the perception of the strange will be a reduction or an increase of life.

She does not like Darcy's unwillingness to move in the dance, and rightly so, but she does not do very well at that liveliness herself. If he refuses her as partner she then refuses him, as she had said she would, and both of them deserve that moment. But when, at the Netherfield ball, he takes her so much by surprise in his next application for her hand, "without knowing what she did, she accepted him." She is left to fret over her own want of presence of mind with this man she says she is determined to hate. When she takes her place in the set, "They stood for some time without speaking a word." Her first dances of the evening had brought distress, with awkward and solemn Mr. Collins who is "often moving wrong without being aware of it"; but now neither she nor Mr. Darcy is capable of making the right move. The dance, as we have seen in *A Midsummer Night's Dream*, is not simply the celebration at the end when the lovers in the action fall into the right places, but it is part of the process by which they change positions in coming to find the right partners for themselves. In the present tale, where young lovers cannot easily find a way of running off to the wood, the dance is properly the best opportunity they have for private conversation, for coming to understand one another. These two must learn the language in which to talk to one another and, as the most articulate speakers and speakers of the best language in their society, at this point neither is good at this dance. Neither will break the silence, till Elizabeth, in an unpromising countermove, fancies that it would be the greater punishment to her partner to oblige him to talk. She puts him through a mock-rehearsal of the trite commonplaces of dance-conversation, which again he deserves. "Do you talk by rule then, while you are dancing?" he asks. "Sometimes. One must speak a little, you know," though for some, conversation ought to be arranged that they may have the trouble of saying as little as possible. The pace is picking up, moving from talk by rule to talk of persons present. Is she talking of her own feelings, he asks, or what she imagines to be his? Both, says she, making things more interesting by bringing them together: she has always seen a great similarity in the turn of their minds, that they are each unsocial, taciturn, unwilling to speak unless they expect to say something that will amaze the whole room. It is a deft cut, under cover of a proffered identity. He understands that it is not meant for herself (part of the irony is that she's rather closer to the whole truth than she intends); and he won't accept it for himself either, though "You think it a faithful portrait undoubtedly." "I must not decide on my own performance."

No, she should not, because this small success is going to tempt her to more dangerous performance. After another silence Darcy refers to their recent meeting in Meryton and, "unable to resist the temptation," she takes that as her opening to make him talk about Wickham. She sees that the hit goes home, "but he said not a word, and Elizabeth, though blaming herself for her own weakness, could not go on" (she is not seeing her right weakness). She has stopped the conversation and when at length he speaks of Wickham it is in constraint. She pushes the emphasis, to how Wickham is likely to suffer all his life from Darcy's treatment. "Darcy made no answer ..." They are given a short interlude, and a proper punishment, by an interruption from the foolishly well-spoken Sir William Lucas—who compliments Darcy on his very superior dancing, not often seen, except in the first circles, and adds, in a courteous after-thought, that his fair partner does not disgrace him. Sir William, with equal adroitness, offers them congratulations on what he assumes is their common pleasure in the forthcoming marriage of Jane and Bingley; and that does strike Darcy forcibly. But he will not interrupt, Sir William says, for he will not be thanked for detaining Darcy from "the bewitching converse" of that young lady, whose "bright eyes" are also upbraiding him. Such talk of bewitching converse and bright eyes could not be less to the moment. The interruption has made him forget what they were talking of, Darcy says, less than candidly. "I do not think we were speaking at all," Elizabeth replies; "Sir William could not have interrupted any two people in the room who had less to say for themselves ... and what we are to talk of next I cannot imagine." Books? he tries again. No, she's sure they have nothing in common there. Besides, she can't talk of books in a ballroom; "my head is always full of something else." It certainly is, and she is now talking "without knowing what she said, for her thoughts had wandered from the subject," as then appears by her "suddenly exclaiming." Her head is stuffed full with Wickham, which does not improve her ability to see, and her exclamation is directed at Darcy's blindness. You "never allow yourself to be blinded by prejudice?" "I hope not." She continues the cross-examination, to make out his character, but she does not get on at all, she says, and is puzzled exceedingly—which should give her pause if she means it, and give them both more time, but it was only a few pages ago that she had already known exactly what to think. He asks her not to sketch his character at present, as he has reason to fear that "the performance would reflect no credit on either," and it would not, because neither is performing creditably at present (I, xviii, 9–94). They will have to converse more of performance.

They will have to make better use of their time, the time needed to move with more credit in this dance. There is no magic here which will produce instantaneous effects, no other realm in which time and space will be suspended, for here they are marked with a careful precision. The chronology of this tale was worked out by its author and can be followed with an almanac (Chapman's Appendix, 400–07), because time is a measure of change, month by month and day by day, and Elizabeth Bennet, not yet one-and-twenty, must be changing in this daily world if she is to become a woman, capable of love and worthy of being loved, which here means capable of understanding that world and herself. She is not a clown and there is no chance that she will not change, no choice of standing still. She has the lively mind and the eyes that see and only someone so bright could go so far astray, could use that power so mistakenly; this wit must move either for the better or the worse, and if she does not move in the right direction she will corrupt, will be amusing and destructive, her father's daughter. She has come to a stopping point, when all those other people whom she has understood so well have unexpectedly refused to act as they should and disappointed her so: when Charlotte has accepted Mr. Collins; when Bingley has gone from Jane; when "The more I see of the world, the more am I dissatisfied with it" (II, i, 135). And now Wickham too has defected, to a young lady whose "most remarkable charm" was the sudden acquisition of ten thousand pounds. Of course she does know that she wasn't distractedly in love with Wickham because she doesn't feel the accepted symptoms of the deserted romantic heroine, and Kitty and Lydia take his loss more to heart than she does: "They are young in the ways of the world, and not yet open to the mortifying conviction that handsome young men must have something to live on, as well as the plain" (II, iii, 149–50). That is the witty Elizabeth we like to hear, turning the wit on herself as she has before, but there's now also something of the self-protective role of the worldly-wise disillusioned lady, which doesn't become her. She hasn't known yet what it is to love, as she sees, but then she doesn't know yet the ways of the world either, or what it is to be mortified.

She seems to be standing still, as the almanac moves on and for the first time we hear almost nothing of the days because Elizabeth is going nowhere. The next sentence and chapter begins: "With no greater events than these in the Longbourn family, and otherwise diversified by little beyond the walks to Meryton, sometimes dirty and sometimes cold, did January and February pass away." Elizabeth is looking forward to March, when she will visit Charlotte and Mr. Collins, for though she had not at first thought seriously of going there it now seems to be a greater pleasure; there will be a novelty in it, and with Jane away in London, and home as it is, "a little change was not unwelcome for its own sake" (II, iv, 151). The first stage to Hunsford is a journey of only twenty-four miles, to see Jane and the Gardiners in London, and there, as we see under the questioning of the sensible Mrs. Gardiner, the previous little note of a disillusion is sounding more like a cynicism. Mrs. Gardiner wants to hear about Wickham and his new affair, where Wickham seems to have been indelicate and the lady deficient in sense or feeling. Elizabeth keeps turning away from Mrs. Gardiner's careful distinctions, trying to blur the moral lines between money and affection—which had been so certain when she looked at Charlotte's pursuit of Mr. Collins's establishment, but are of little meaning now that she looks at Wickham's pursuit of the willing girl with ten thousand pounds. Well, have it as you choose, she says in unfair exasperation with her persistent aunt, "*He* shall be mercenary, and *she* shall be foolish." Elizabeth has had enough of men. "I am sick of them all. Thank Heaven! I am going tomorrow where I shall find a man who has not one agreeable quality, who has neither manner nor sense to recommend him. Stupid men are the only ones worth knowing, after all." Mrs. Gardiner loves her niece and will not let go. "Take care, Lizzy; that speech savours strongly of disappointment" (153–54). It does and the word is a strong one, as Elizabeth understands, the balked desire which can become spleen, a sour moroseness. Lizzy is not standing still but slipping back. She will need more than a short journey and it will have to be a journey to a better end.

She has the unexpected happiness of an invitation to join her aunt and uncle on a tour of pleasure in the summer: "We have not quite determined how far it shall carry us," says Mrs. Gardiner, "but perhaps to the Lakes." We will be interested in finding how far north this will carry Elizabeth and her need to be carried is loud in her response. "My dear, dear aunt," she rapturously cries, "what delight! what felicity! You give me fresh life and vigour. Adieu to disappointment and spleen. What are men to rocks and mountains?" So Elizabeth, unable to solve her problems at home, sees happiness in the opportunity to run off to another place, where she can leave behind all those frustrating people and find felicity, be given new life, not with men, not even Mr. Collins, but with rocks and mountains. "Oh! what hours of transport we shall spend!" We do hope not and hope that she will make better use of her hours on the journey; and we can have faith in Elizabeth from what we have seen of her and from her present insistence on what she wants it to be when she returns from the journey. "And when we *do* return, it shall not be like other travellers, without being able to give one accurate idea of any thing. We *will* know where we have gone—we *will* recollect what we have seen." It shall not be jumbled together in their imaginations and they will agree when they describe what they have seen (II, iv, 154). For Elizabeth this will not be a dream and she wants to get it all clear and get it all together, unlike other travelers. But like other runaways who want to escape into that better place she will find her journey more strange than anything she could have imagined.

At this moment of excitement she is only at the first stop in her first journey, and she is still expecting to see at the next stage a stupid man, the only kind worth knowing. Off she goes and "Every object in the next day's journey was new and interesting to Elizabeth," her spirits in a state for enjoyment and "the prospect of her northern tour ... a constant source of delight" (II, v, 155). Her time at Hunsford is both instructive and amusing as she sees and understands better the life of Charlotte at the Parsonage and is introduced to Lady Catherine and the honors of Rosings. But she also sees, and it was not an expected part of her journey, much more of Mr. Darcy. In going from Hertfordshire to Kent she is more on his ground, at the home of his aunt, with his cousin Colonel Fitzwilliam, with more and better opportunities to talk and to learn about him. Charlotte, who has a better eye for this sort of thing, watches Darcy as he looks at Elizabeth a great deal, and once or twice she suggests to Elizabeth the possibility of his being partial to her; "but Elizabeth always laughed at the idea" (II, ix, 181). She dearly loves a laugh, as she had told him, but now with his love he will astonish her beyond expression (II, xi), and from this point in her story Elizabeth's moments of laughter will be not amusing but painful; there will be more tears, and those begin by the end of this chapter. Her response to his declaration is resentment and anger, which he well deserves because he too still has a long way to go. His response to her rejection is his own anger and astonishment.

Elizabeth has been quick to read the blindness in others, in the Jane she loves for Jane's too generous feelings, in the Darcy she thinks so ill of for his ungenerous feelings, and when she receives Darcy's letter she will have her moment to define her own blindness. "Her feelings as she read were scarcely to be defined." She read in a way "which hardly left her power of comprehension" to a point "when she read with somewhat clearer attention," and her feelings become "yet more acutely painful and more difficult of definition" and the oppression of emotion makes her put the thing away hastily, protesting that "she would never look in it again." She walks on, but it will not do and "in half a minute" the letter is unfolded again "and collecting herself as well as she could, she again began the mortifying perusal ... and commanded herself so far as to examine the meaning of every sentence." It takes time and she is now down to the critical half-minutes. She does not want to see and (like Mr. Collins) "for a few moments, she flattered herself" that her wishes did not err; but she reads and re-reads line by line and every line proves more clearly what she has not been able to see before (II, xiii, 204–05).

> She grew absolutely ashamed of herself—Of neither Darcy nor Wickham could she think, without feeling that she had been blind, partial, prejudiced, absurd.... "I, who have prided myself on my discernment! ... How humiliating is this discovery!—Yet, how just a humiliation!—Had I been in love, I could not have been more wretchedly blind.... Till this moment, I never knew myself." (208)

It is the familiar moment when the young lover moves from blindness to self-knowledge (and for her the time is still not fulfilled). As we have seen it before it requires the administration of an eye-opening agency, Dian's bud in the hand of Puck or the Life Force in Nature. Jane Austen's word for that is "mortification," the just humiliation Elizabeth feels and repeats in this speech, and, as she reads on, "the terms of such mortifying yet merited reproach" which bring their sense of severe shame. But in her day-to-day world there is no designated superior power to drop the juice into the eye; Elizabeth must do it for herself, a difficult and a painful task. Happily, she has one other to help her, the man who writes the letter she must learn to read, as indeed she has been teaching him, both of them unknowingly. Both of them have been proud powers of superior discernment into the minds of, and the proper matches for, the mortals they see, but there will be none to help open their eyes except as they may be able to do it for each other. It is a process of mutual mortification.

We have seen mortification before and we will see it again, in both its trivial and its painful forms. The Devil of *Man and Superman* is mortified when Don Juan speaks a truth (p.45, ch. 2) but in the life of the Devil it is only a brief embarrassment, without effect because the Devil is a clown incapable of profiting from the truth about himself. To Hermia the law of Athens brings a literal threat of mortification if she does not depart from her love and change to another; but it is a foolish law, with the worse alternative that she may wither on the virgin thorn, and we are happy to see her simply escape from death and emerge with a better life and love. The more interesting mortification which must be faced by the lovers of *Pride and Prejudice* can be understood profitably only by characters who are capable of feeling the justice of a wound to their pride and self-esteem. It is not easy and it is part of a movement that takes time. It is here a necessary condition for the satisfactory coming together of the lovers, forcing a self-recognition that requires giving up a part of the character for which each has felt self-esteem and taking on a changed character, the end of the old and blinded self and the beginning of the renewed and more liberal life. The inception, the turning-point, and the resolution of the changing relations of Elizabeth and Darcy are marked by mortifications: the first rousing effect each has on the other; the proposal and letter; and the elopement of Lydia, the event that brings the conclusive proofs of affection. The series begins at their first encounter as Darcy sees her and withdraws his eye because she is not handsome enough to tempt him to the dance; Elizabeth could easily have forgiven *his* pride, she says, "if he had not mortified *mine*" (I, v, 20). A few pages on she becomes an object of some interest in his eyes when he finds the intelligence and beauty in hers: "To this discovery succeeded some others equally mortifying," as he is now forced to acknowledge that his critical eye has been mistaken and is now caught by her form and her manner (I, vi, 23). But neither has yet been able to benefit from this; the effect has not been strong enough, in good part because neither is in a moral position to make the other feel the effect. The occasions multiply upon Elizabeth, especially in that ball at Netherfield, in "the dances of mortification" she has, with badly timed liveliness, prepared for herself with Mr. Collins (I, xviii, 90), in the several ways in which the members of her family make her blush with shame and vexation, as though they had made an agreement to expose themselves as much as they could; and, more importantly, in the confident ways in which she has made her own unknowing contributions to this carnival of fools by her style of dancing with Mr. Darcy. All this does not come home to her until, at the eye-opening moment she reads Darcy's letter and the memory it brings of the "mortifying" family conduct at the Netherfield ball (II, xiii, 209). The proposal and letter bring, as at the start of their course, a moment of reciprocal wounded pride, but now to better effect. She has been quite right to reject him; he would not be a good husband. He has not, even in proposing, she tells him, behaved in a "gentleman-like manner" and he is startled to be told that truth, and more than startled. "You could not have made me the offer of your hand in any possible way that would have tempted me to accept it": this he must hear from the woman whose pride he mortified by saying she was not handsome enough to tempt *him*. He is astonished and he looks at her with "mingled incredulity and mortification" (I, xi, 192–93). Her accusations of his treatment of Wickham are ill founded, but, as he later says, his behavior to her merited the severest reproach. It takes time to work, as the incredulity goes but not the mortification. The recollection of what he said, his conduct, his manner, his expression, is for many months inexpressibly painful to him. Her reproof, that he had not behaved in a gentleman-like manner—the words remain with him—had been a torture, and it was some time before he was reasonable enough to allow their justice. Realizing the pride and selfishness of a lifetime is a hard lesson and he owes much to her who taught him. "By you, I was properly humbled" (III, xvi, 367–69).

His letter produces more immediately a change in her life. That fresh life and vigor she had desired so ardently from her journey will follow his effect. One of the first things she hears on her return home is Lydia's happy news that the wretched Wickham is not going to marry the young lady with the ten thousand pounds; evidently the lady has been sent safely away by worried relatives, but Lydia is certain he never cared three straws about her: "Who *could* about such a nasty little freckled thing?" "Elizabeth was shocked to think that, however incapable of such coarseness of *expression* herself, the coarseness of the *sentiment* was little other than her own breast had formerly harboured and fancied liberal!" (II, xvi, 220). It is a new moment for her, that recognition of sisterly similarity under the apparent superiority of language. That wit which dearly loved a laugh, amused at Mr. Darcy's uncommon advantage of immunity, looks different to her now. She had meant to be uncommonly clever in taking such a decided dislike to him, without any reason, she tells Jane, for it is such a spur to one's genius, "such an opening for wit ..." One may abuse a man without saying anything just, "but one cannot always be laughing at a man without now and then stumbling upon something witty" (II, xvii, 225–26). We will be seeing the effects of mortification, of different kinds, in some of the succeeding works; and we will see it again in the course of Elizabeth's life, because she has not yet come to the end of her journey. She has yet to reach Pemberley, where, in one reward of improvement she can eventually leave the mortifying society of her family (III, xviii, 384).

On her second journey, with its promised rapture of the hours of
transport in the rocks and mountains of a north without men, she does
not get quite as far as she had hoped, that longed-for place. It is a stranger
journey than she had expected and another vision. When she sees Darcy's
home ground it is she who is now the stranger. "Every disposition of the
ground was good" and the home itself she sees, with admiration of his taste,
as she compares it with the Rosings where she saw him in her first journey,
has less of splendor, and more real elegance. "'And of this place,' thought
she, 'I might have been mistress! With these rooms I might now have been
familiarly acquainted! Instead of viewing them as a stranger ...'" She sees
family portraits, "but they could have little to fix the attention of a stranger"
and she walks on in quest of the only face whose features are known to her
until at last it arrested her: "she beheld a striking resemblance of Mr. Darcy,
with such a smile over the face, as she remembered to have sometimes seen,
when he looked at her. She stood several minutes before the picture in earnest
contemplation ..." Now, with a gentler sensation towards the original than
she had ever felt, she walks out, and—this is an earned sight—"suddenly"
she sees the original. "... so abrupt was his appearance that it was impossible
to avoid his sight. Their eyes instantly met ..." It is for him too a startling
moment and each has cause for the deepest blush. But she is overpowered
again by shame and vexation, because it may seem as if she has purposely
thrown herself in his way again. "How strange must it appear to him! In what
a disgraceful light might it not strike so vain a man!" (III, i, 246, 250–52). He
is stranger than she yet knows.

She is astonished at such a change as she sees in him, that he not
merely once loved her but that he loves her still well enough to forgive all
her manner and the unjust accusations in her rejection (III, ii, 265–66). But
this is not enough and the promising indications that the course of true love
is about to reach its desired end are suddenly stopped, by Lydia's elopement.
Elizabeth and Darcy have come far in their mutual mortifications but
they have further to go, to bear the effects of their past, the old self, and
respond with the liberal conquest of the new. To Elizabeth the elopement is
"humiliation" and misery. It justifies Darcy in the two chief offenses she had
laid to his charge—his offenses against Wickham and against her family—
and it brings those two things together in such a way as to sink Elizabeth's
power over him. She believes that he has now made a self-conquest, is no
longer subject to his feelings for her, and the belief is exactly calculated to
make her understand her own wishes, that she could have loved him (III, iv,
278). After Lydia's marriage is assured, Elizabeth is heartily sorry that she
had not concealed from him her initial fears for Lydia: there was no one
whose knowledge of her sister's frailty could have "mortified her so much"

(III, viii, 311). What she does not know is that Darcy has been stronger, in a more difficult self-conquest, than she could have known. Lydia, who is incapable of understanding the meaning of her affair with Wickham, can't understand why Elizabeth doesn't share her delight and isn't curious to hear all the details of the marriage. "La! you are so strange!" But it is stranger than that. Irrepressible Lydia must tell her how it went off and, in her way, reveals to the utterly amazed Elizabeth that Mr. Darcy was at the wedding. It was exactly a scene, and exactly among people, where, as Elizabeth sees it, he had apparently least to do or temptation to go: how could a man unconnected with any of her family, comparatively speaking "a stranger to our family," be amongst them at such a time? (III, ix, 318–20). But he has seen the connection (III, x, 321–22), takes responsibility for Wickham's act. Elizabeth had thought such an exertion of goodness "too great to be probable," and painful to her in the obligation, but it is proved "beyond ... greatest extent to be true!" He has "taken on himself all the trouble and mortification" of searching out and supplicating and bribing those he had most reason to abominate, despise, avoid (326). When she finally has the opportunity she thanks him for the compassion that enabled him to "bear so many mortifications" (III, xvi, 366) and he has done it in his affection. They have both learned how to perform to strangers.

It has not been an easy course for her. When Mr. Bennet receives the last of his diverting letters from Mr. Collins, this one with the idle report, and the warning, that Elizabeth may marry Darcy, he shares the surprise with his daughter. Mr. Darcy, who never looks at any woman but to see a blemish, he says, "and who probably never looked at you in his life! It is admirable!" Elizabeth tries to join in her father's pleasantry, "but could only force one most reluctant smile. Never had his wit been directed in a manner so little agreeable to her." He won't let go of the sport. "Are you not diverted?" "Oh! yes, Pray read on." He, as always, lives "but to make sport for our neighbours, and laugh at them in our turn," and knows his favorite daughter ought share his amusement. "'Oh!' cried Elizabeth, 'I am excessively diverted. But it is so strange!'" "Yes—*that* is what makes it amusing." If it is not that for her it is because at that point she is not certain that she really understands the relations of strange and true. "It was necessary to laugh, when she would rather have cried. Her father had most cruelly mortified her," for what he has said of Darcy's indifference may be true (III, xv, 363–64).

It is only after that last deserved stroke that Elizabeth is allowed her return to laughter. The Mr. Darcy who was not to be laughed at is to be educated, by a wife who now understands better how to laugh. As they compare notes at the end he explains how he arranged Bingley's love, first interfering in the match and then assuring happiness. "Elizabeth could not help smiling at his easy manner of directing his friend." He certainly has been the superior director of the loves of foolish mortals who, in that tradition, has made a small mistake and now repairs it easily. Did he speak from his own observation, Elizabeth asks, or merely from her information about Jane? (sounding a bit like Mr. Bennet drawing out Mr. Collins). "I had narrowly observed her," he reports. And that assurance, Elizabeth supposes, carried immediate conviction to Bingley? Elizabeth sees how well Darcy still plays that role of instant power and she longs to observe that Mr. Bingley had been a most delightful friend, so easily guided, but she checks herself. "She remembered that he had yet to learn to be laught at, and it was rather too early to begin" (III, xvi, 371). Darcy, it would seem, in his aristocratic line, has been taught, like Lord Chesterfield's son perhaps, that the vulgar laugh, whereas well-bred people smile but seldom or never laugh; but we can be confident he will have a better tutor now, one who has herself earned the right. "I am happier even than Jane," Elizabeth confides to Mrs. Gardiner; "she only smiles, I laugh" (III, xviii, 383).

Note

The text for *Pride and Prejudice* is Vol. II of *The Novels of Jane Austen*, ed. R. W. Chapman, 3rd ed. (Oxford 1932), and for *Emma* Vol. IV of the same edition (1933). References are to volume, chapter and page numbers; where successive quotations in the same paragraph are from the same chapter the volume and chapter numbers are not repeated. (In reprints which number the chapters continuously Vol. II of *Pride and Prejudice* is chaps. 24–42, Vol. III is 43–61; Vol. II of *Emma* is chaps. 19–36, Vol. III is 37–55.) The chapter has drawn much upon my own book, listed below, the parts on *Emma* and *Pride and Prejudice*.

Bibliography

Babb, Howard S., *Jane Austen's Novels: The Fabric of Dialogue* (Columbus, 1962).

Brower, Reuben Arthur, *The Fields of Light: An Experiment in Critical Reading* (New York, 1951).

Butler, Marilyn, *Jane Austen and the War of Ideas* (Oxford, 1975).

Chandler, Alice, "'A Pair of Fine Eyes': Jane Austen's Treatment of Sex," *Studies in the Novel*, VII (1975), 88–103.

Duckworth, Alistair M., *The Improvement of the Estate: A Study of Jane Austen's Novels* (Baltimore, 1971).

Dussinger, John A., *In the Pride of the Moment: Encounters in Jane Austen's World* (Columbus, 1990).

Fergus, Jan, *Jane Austen and the Didactic Novel* (Totowa, N.J., 1983).

Hardy, Barbara, *A Reading of Jane Austen* (London, 1975).

Harris, Jocelyn, *Jane Austen's Art of Memory* (Cambridge, 1989).

Krieger, Murray, *The Classic Vision* (Baltimore, 1971).

Lascelles, Mary, *Jane Austen and Her Art* (Oxford, 1939).

Mansell, Darrel, *The Novels of Jane Austen: An Interpretation* (London, 1973).

Moler, Kenneth L., *Pride and Prejudice: A Study in Artistic Economy* (Boston, 1989).

Monaghan, David, *Jane Austen: Structure and Social Vision* (London, 1980).

Morgan, Susan, *In the Meantime: Character and Perception in Jane Austen's Fiction* (Chicago, 1980).

Mudrick, Marvin, *Jane Austen: Irony as Defense and Discovery* (Princeton, 1952).

Page, Norman, *The Language of Jane Austen* (Oxford, 1972).

Polhemus, Robert M., "Jane Austen's Comedy," in *The Jane Austen Companion*, ed. J. David Grey, A. Wilton Litz and Brian Southam (New York, 1986).

Sacks, Sheldon, "Golden Birds and Dying Generations," *Comparative Literature Studies*, VI (1969), 274–91.

Spacks, Patricia Meyer, "Austen's Laughter," *Women's Studies*, XV (1988), 71–85.

Tanner, Tony, *Jane Austen* (Cambridge, Mass., 1986).

Tave, Stuart M., *Some Words of Jane Austen* (Chicago, 1973).

Trickett, Rachel, "Jane Austen's Comedy and the Nineteenth Century," in *Critical Essays on Jane Austen*, ed. B. C. Southam (London, 1968).

Wright, Andrew H., *Jane Austen's Novels: A Study in Structure* (New ed., London, 1961).

CHRISTOPHER BROOKE

Pride and Prejudice

A fundamental theme of *Pride and Prejudice* is the problem of how a man and a woman get to know one another before marriage. Jane Austen solved the difficulty in her next two novels by creating hero and heroine who had known each other from the childhood of one or the other or both. In *Pride and Prejudice* it is assumed that Mr and Mrs Bennet hardly knew one another before he proposed—and he only discovered what a silly, tiresome woman she was after the event. Even Jane and Bingley fall in love very rapidly after only a few evenings together; but in their case a natural sympathy and likeness of temperament and tastes makes the prognostic happier than it might have been. But Elizabeth and Darcy have to batter their way through an almost impenetrable screen of misunderstanding and misrepresentation. Darcy's first proposal comes almost exactly halfway through the book. In the first half, the misunderstandings steadily grow. They come to a crescendo on the eve of his proposal, when she receives from Colonel Fitzwilliam confirmation that it was Darcy who had deliberately separated Bingley from Jane. In Elizabeth's eyes that was all in character, for she had already accepted from Wickham's lips his account of Darcy's heartless, cruel treatment of himself. Nor are the misunderstandings all on one side. For all that Darcy dotes on her, he sees her as an inferior creature from a world lower than his; he sees all the objections to a man of his standing marrying into a family with

From *Jane Austen: Illusion and Reality*, pp. 74–84. © 1999 by Christopher Brooke.

such vulgar connections as Mrs Bennet and her family—and so uncouth in behaviour as most of the family were, even on occasion Mr Bennet himself. Elizabeth has to clear away a fog of illusion; Mr Darcy has to learn a deeper lesson. He has to learn to respect his future wife and everything about her; to see her family as she sees them; to acknowledge that in some aspects of mind and character she is his superior—in most ways they are equals. That she is raised above her natural station by marriage to Mr Darcy of Pemberley is simply not the case: and that is for him a very puzzling, difficult, salutary lesson.

In order to see them both learning their lessons, Jane Austen had to reveal more of Mr Darcy than of any of her earlier heroes. It is obvious in a superficial sense that Jane shows us more of the female mind at work than the male: she never pursues the men into their bedrooms. But it is not true that Darcy is left remote and undeveloped, as some have asserted. First of all, she is freer with hints of his devotion than with any of her earlier or later heroes: she shows him falling in love step by step. Then she takes him to Hunsford where he stays on week after week growing ever more listless as lovers often do. But she reveals his mind most fully by the simple but powerful device of making him write a long letter of explanation of his attitude to Bingley and Jane, and of his relations with Wickham. In this letter dignity, self-reliance, arrogance, insight, intelligence and sound human feeling are displayed strangely mingled—and he invokes God's blessing on a woman who had insulted him a few hours before with all the eloquence Elizabeth and her creator could command. Elizabeth is prepared a little, and the reader a good deal more, for the encomium of the housekeeper at Pemberley a few months later. Although the latter part of the book is more and more written from Elizabeth's point of view—the suspense she must suffer in order fully to realise her change of feeling towards him dictated that it should be so—the reader is never really left in much doubt of Darcy's continuing devotion. He is Jane's first outstanding male portrait: Edward Ferrars and Colonel Brandon are lightly sketched in comparison. Of later heroes, only Mr Knightley is painted in deeper, richer colours. Mr Darcy begins with a contrasting pattern of different attributes and assumptions, and they are gradually modified under the influence of Elizabeth until he is a worthy partner for her. She changes too—less, on the surface, for from beginning to end she is the wittiest and most charming of Jane's heroines; but her judgments at the outset are sharp and superficial. Her impressions of Wickham bring nemesis and make her look deeper; and it is in the depths of personality and principle that she and Darcy are most alike. The final commendation comes from her aunt and uncle

Gardiner, of all her relations the closest to her in outlook and the most congenial as companions. Thus Mrs Gardiner: 'His behaviour to us has, in every respect, been as pleasing as when we were in Derbyshire. His understanding and opinions all please me; he wants nothing but a little more liveliness, and *that*, if he marry *prudently*, his wife may teach him.'[1]

At the superficial level the marriage of Elizabeth Bennet and Fitzwilliam Darcy united two remarkably different characters: he stiff, proud, formal, she lively, witty, playful. Nor are they alike in background or fortune. He, at 28, has been for five years master of a great estate, worth £10,000 a year; on his mother's side he is descended from the peerage. Elizabeth's father is a gentleman indeed, and she has been brought up in his comfortable house. But her father's estate is entailed to a cousin, and she has only a very modest fortune of her own. Her mother's family are in trade, or country attorneys, not, by lineage, gentlefolk; and her mother in particular is a silly, flighty, vulgar woman. Worst of all, Elizabeth's youngest sister, Lydia, by the end of the book, is married to a former protégé of Mr Darcy's father, George Wickham—a scapegrace, a gamester, always in debt; a man of surface charm, rotten at the core—who has actually tried to seduce Darcy's sister. It is a shockingly unequal marriage.

Not all of this was foreseen by Darcy when he first realised that he had fallen in love with Elizabeth; but enough to shock and horrify him.

'In vain have I struggled. It will not do. My feelings will not be repressed. You must allow me to tell you how ardently I admire and love you.'[2] The attentive reader is prepared for his declaration, not only by a series of carefully planted hints, but by a picture of a normally self-possessed, articulate man rendered hopelessly distrait and absent by being head over heels in love. Elizabeth has missed all the hints, and has had a different preparation—for several reasons she is angry with him, and instantly rejects him.

In the second half of the book (which I—unlike many readers—find the better of the two) we are shown in a variety of ways why the marriage (when it eventually comes) is not so unequal. There is social comment here, for social equality of a kind is gradually asserted; but it is Elizabeth's view of equality, or compatibility, not Jane's or ours or anyone else's, which is revealed; and at the deepest level, they are shown to be partners in a different sense—with common interests and outlook, and complementary personalities. Superficially, *Pride and Prejudice* is yet another tale of the moderately poor girl who wins a very rich husband—and that aspect of the story is emphasised, so that deeper regions may be the more fully explored. Thus Elizabeth's sister Jane, on hearing of their engagement:

'Will you tell me how long you have loved him?'

'It has been coming on so gradually, that I hardly know when it began. But I believe I must date it from my first seeing his beautiful grounds at Pemberley'

—Darcy's country house in Derbyshire.[3] To Elizabeth's celebrated jest we shall presently return.

The social comment comes closest to the surface when Darcy's aunt, Lady Catherine de Bourgh—who has been deeply incensed by a report that Elizabeth and Darcy are to marry—visits the Bennets in order to bully Elizabeth out of any such monstrous pretension.

After angry exchanges, Lady Catherine comes to the point: she intends Darcy to marry her own daughter, and it is intolerable that she should be frustrated by

'the upstart pretensions of a young woman without family, connections, or fortune. Is this to be endured! But it must not, shall not be. If you were sensible of your own good, you would not wish to quit the sphere, in which you have been brought up.'

'In marrying your nephew I should not consider myself as quitting that sphere. He is a gentleman; I am a gentleman's daughter; so far we are equal.'

Thus Elizabeth utters the classic expression of the eighteenth-century doctrine of the equality of all gentlemen.

'True. You *are* a gentleman's daughter. But who was your mother? Who are your uncles and aunts? Do not imagine me ignorant of their condition.'[4]

It is a pleasant irony in this extraordinary scene that Lady Catherine behaves with greater vulgarity than Mrs Bennet. When Darcy first declared his love for Elizabeth, she had retorted on him that the mode of his declaration 'spared me the concern which I might have felt in refusing you, had you behaved in a more gentleman like manner'.[5] Behaviour is as important as birth to any reasonable definition—in Elizabeth's eyes—of a gentleman.

Over the months which followed his first declaration, these words of hers tortured him, for—although a man of deep pride—he was also highly intelligent and brought up to believe in, and attempt to live by, good principles. He slowly learns the truths which underlie what she has said: he cannot treat his wife as an inferior; Elizabeth's conduct and character more than compensate for her less admirable relations—nor are they all beneath his notice. When they are engaged Elizabeth is still much embarrassed by the vulgar behaviour of some of her circle of friends and relatives—and looks forward 'to all the comfort and elegance of their family party at Pemberley'[6]—and it is made clear that Mrs Bennet is not invited there. 'Happy for all her maternal feelings was the day on which Mrs Bennet got rid of her two most deserving daughters.' 'Got rid' is nicely phrased. 'With what delighted pride she afterwards visited Mrs Bingley [Jane, her eldest daughter], and *talked of* Mrs Darcy, may be guessed.'[7] Elizabeth's father delighted in visiting Pemberley 'especially when he was least expected', as fits his whimsical humour.[8] Other sisters are occasional visitors, and it is a special delight to Elizabeth and Darcy when Jane and Mr Bingley settle within thirty miles of Pemberley. But their first, and most welcome visitors of all, are Elizabeth's aunt and uncle from the City—who in spite of living by trade are the most elegant of Elizabeth's relations, and who played a crucial role in bringing the Darcys together. On this note the book ends: we see that there is social comment here, but that it is Elizabeth's. Her view of society is not egalitarian in a modern sense; only gentlemen are equal—and well-bred men and women. True elegance is a matter of attitude and outlook and inner conviction. The aristocrat can be vulgar, the rich landowner can behave in ungentlemanly fashion.

The book takes its title from Darcy's pride and Elizabeth's prejudice; and so far we have dwelt on aspects of their relationship alone—and on some of the deeper, more sombre colours of the book. But Jane herself claimed to think 'the work ... rather too light and bright and sparkling'—though she revelled in it too[9]—and it is also the wittiest of her novels.

'It is a truth universally acknowledged, that a single man in possession of a good fortune, must be in want of a wife.'[10] Little as Mrs Bennet knew of the philosophies of the Enlightenment, the sentiment expresses her philosophy—and the lighter side of the book. It is about three or four marriages, not one. Mr Bingley has just come to settle near the Bennet's home, and he soon meets and falls in love with Jane Bennet. But Bingley is deeply dependent on the counsel of Darcy, his closest friend, who has seen him often in love before; and after a very promising start to the romance, Darcy and Bingley's two sisters carry him off to London and safety. The sisters, though fond of Jane, are mercilessly portrayed as heartless snobs— and yet we are left in no doubt that their father made his fortune in the north of England by trade. One of them is married, but the other, Caroline, has set her cap at Darcy—and grows jealous of Elizabeth and more hostile to the Bennets as the plot develops; till in the end she is compelled to pretend affection for Jane as her sister-in-law, and pay 'off every arrear of civility to Elizabeth' so as to be able still to visit Pemberley.[11]

Meanwhile the Bennet's cousin, the Reverend Mr Collins, has come to stay: a pompous, obsequious clergyman of grandiloquent verbosity—who physics Mr Bennet's humour delightfully, if taken in very small doses. He is the heir of the property, and comes to apologise that one day he will have to turn them all out—and to propose marriage to one of them to make amends. Jane is the eldest and most beautiful, and he plans to propose to her; but at a hint from Mrs Bennet that Jane has prospects already, he rapidly changes from Jane to Elizabeth—'and it was soon done—done while Mrs Bennet was stirring the fire'—and proposes to her.[12] When Elizabeth, who has seen enough of him to know how absurd he is, rejects him, Mrs Bennet rushes to her husband, demanding that he insist that Elizabeth change her mind.

> 'I understand that Mr Collins has made you an offer of marriage. Is it true?' [says Mr Bennet.] Elizabeth replied that it was. 'Very well—and this offer of marriage you have refused?'
>
> 'I have, sir.'
>
> 'Very well. We now come to the point. Your mother insists upon your accepting it. Is not it so, Mrs Bennet?'
>
> 'Yes, or I will never see her again.'
>
> 'An unhappy alternative is before you, Elizabeth. From this day you must be a stranger to one of your parents.—Your mother will never see you again if you do *not* marry Mr Collins, and I will never see you again if you *do*.'

—a denouement characteristic of Mr Bennet's humour, and of his treatment of his wife.[13]

But Mr Collins has been instructed by his patroness, who is no less than Lady Catherine de Bourgh, that he should marry; and marry he does. He finds Elizabeth's close friend and neighbour, Charlotte Lucas, more amenable, for Charlotte is 27 and seeks a home: her philosophy of marriage is very different from Elizabeth's.[14] So to Hunsford Rectory she departs, the wife of Mr Collins.

Much of the plot turns on the means by which Elizabeth and Mr Darcy become, first more, and then better, acquainted with one another. He had seen enough of her in her homeland to be greatly attracted. He next meets her at Hunsford, proposes and is rejected; then at Pemberley—where a new dawn breaks for them both; finally at her home, where he proposes again and successfully.

Elizabeth is induced by Mrs Collins to pay her a visit: we are shown how a sensible woman can make a reasonably comfortable home for herself in spite of having Mr Collins for husband. We are shown how one kind of clergyman behaves—especially in obsequious flattery of his patroness; we are taken to Lady Catherine's palace of Rosings, whose furnishings match her wealth and vulgar taste. Elizabeth meanwhile has been told by George Wickham—and naïvely believes him—that he has been scandalously ill-treated by Darcy. While at Hunsford, Darcy's cousin, the agreeable Colonel Fitzwilliam, inadvertently reveals to Elizabeth that Darcy has boasted to him of separating Bingley from Jane—he has not been told the names, but the circumstances of the case leave no doubt in Elizabeth's mind to whom Darcy had referred. As she nurses her wrath in the wake of this latest shock, Mr Darcy calls at the parsonage and proposes to her—and is sent on his way angry but chastened.

Next morning she meets him on the edge of the park and he gives her a long letter in which he explains his treatment of Bingley and Jane—he was genuinely convinced that Jane's feelings were cooler than Elizabeth knew them to be, and tried to save Bingley from what he imagined a passing infatuation. But he also explains his relations with Wickham—who not only received much help from him and vilified him entirely without foundation, but had also tried to seduce his young sister Georgiana. The letter is a very powerful revelation of Darcy's mind, and the fulcrum on which the story turns. It is very hard to believe that even in this extremity Darcy would have given his sister away—though he clearly suspected that Elizabeth might be in love with Wickham, and needed urgent warning; and it is hard to imagine how he could have hoped to convince her with less cogent evidence. In any case, the story naturally startles Elizabeth into a slow but steady realisation that he must be telling the truth.

After Hunsford, Elizabeth's next outing is a holiday with her uncle and aunt from the City, Mr and Mrs Gardiner. To her immense delight, the original plan had been a visit to the Lakes—but Mr Gardiner's business engagements abbreviate the tour, and Elizabeth sadly discovers that they can go no further than Derbyshire. Between Bakewell and the imaginary small town of Lambton—where Mrs Gardiner had once lived—lies Pemberley;[15] and with much hesitation—after ascertaining that Mr Darcy himself is not there—Elizabeth agrees to pay a visit to Pemberley. They are shown round the house by the elderly housekeeper, Mrs Reynolds, who tells them that Mr Darcy is a model master and landlord—greatly to the surprise of all three visitors. They then take a turn in the park under the gardener's guidance—but as they leave the house Darcy himself appears. At first both he and Elizabeth are too much surprised and embarrassed for more than a

brief encounter; but as their walk progresses, he joins them again and asks
to be introduced to the Gardiners—and though not at ease he is at his most
courteous. He has come back early, ahead of a party which will include his
sister and Bingley; and he asks to be allowed to bring Georgiana to meet her.
The very next day—when Georgiana has had hardly a moment to recover
from her journey—they come to call, and this visit and his manner reveal
to the Gardiners—what had been as far as possible from their thoughts
before—that he is in love with Elizabeth. Georgiana, aged 16 and almost
too shy to show how pleased she is to meet Elizabeth, none the less (under
her brother's instruction) invites them all to dinner at Pemberley. But before
they can come, news of a catastrophe reaches them: Lydia and Wickham
have eloped. As Elizabeth reads the letters from Jane which give this terrible
news, Darcy calls alone—it is never explained (or perhaps it is carefully not
explained) what he came for—and learns what has happened. Jane had sent
two letters, the first ill-directed and so delayed; if it had not been delayed,
Elizabeth would not have gone to Pemberley at all.

The visit to Pemberley reveals to Elizabeth—what she had hardly
imagined possible before—that Darcy has conquered her. When she later
said to Jane of her love for him 'I believe I must date it from my first seeing
his beautiful grounds at Pemberley', she spoke in jest—but she spoke the
truth.[16] The park, indeed, has symbolic value: it seems to reflect a natural
habitat. The wooded slopes of the park, the housekeeper's testimony, his
own polite reception of them—the warmth of his attentions: all this began
to change her view of him—and as she tells him of Lydia's fate, which he
will understand as no one else could, she instantly believes that it must be a
barrier between them—and that fear opens her eyes to her feeling for him.

Darcy's reaction is very different. Having gathered from Elizabeth that
the couple are thought to be in hiding in London, he makes haste to search
for them—in order to do everything he can to see them safely married,
Wickham freed from his debts and set on a possible career. In all this he
succeeds, and then calls on the Gardiners to explain what he has done—and
insist that no word passes to the Bennets that it is his doing. Mr Bennet,
after some days of fruitless search, has meanwhile returned to his sorrowing
family. They soon learn that Lydia and Wickham are to be married and Mrs
Bennet looks happily round for a home for them.

> 'Mrs Bennet, before you take any, or all of these houses, for
> your son and daughter, let us come to a right understanding.
> Into *one* house in this neighbourhood, they shall never have
> admittance. I will not encourage the imprudence of either, by
> receiving them at Longbourn.'

—And he went on to make clear that he 'would not advance a guinea' for Lydia to buy wedding clothes—even though Mrs Bennet 'could hardly comprehend' how 'his anger could be carried to such a point of inconceivable resentment, as to refuse his daughter a privilege, without which her marriage would scarcely seem valid'.[17]

But Jane and Elizabeth argue with him, and he relents—not on the clothes but the visit—and is subsequently encouraged by receiving a rebuke from Mr Collins on that account. In the course of her giddy, tumultuous chatter, Lydia reveals to Elizabeth that Darcy had been present at her wedding. Elizabeth cannot rest till she understands how this improbable, impossible circumstance, can be explained, and writes in haste to her aunt. The Gardiners are by now clearly apprised of Darcy's devotion to Elizabeth—though he has never confessed it to them; and so Mr Gardiner had accepted, however reluctantly, an arrangement which gave him all the credit which was really due to Darcy. Darcy has blamed himself for what had occurred: he had failed to apprise the world of Wickham's character. 'He called it, therefore, his duty to step forward, and endeavour to remedy an evil, which had been brought on by himself'—Thus Mrs Gardiner.

> If he *had another* motive, I am sure it would never disgrace him.... Our visitor was very obstinate. I fancy, Lizzy, that obstinacy is the real defect of his character after all. He has been accused of many faults at different times; but *this* is the true one. Nothing was to be done that he did not do himself ...

After the wedding, Mr Darcy

> dined with us the next day ... Will you be very angry with me, my dear Lizzy, if I take this opportunity of saying (what I was never bold enough to say before) how much I like him. His behaviour to us has, in every respect, been as pleasing as when we were in Derbyshire. His understanding and opinions all please me; he wants nothing but a little more liveliness, and *that*, if he marry *prudently*, his wife may teach him. I thought him very sly;—he hardly ever mentioned your name. But slyness seems the fashion. Pray forgive me, if I have been very presuming, or at least do not punish me so far, as to exclude me from P. I shall never be quite happy till I have been all round the park. A low phaeton, with a nice little pair of ponies, would be the very thing ...[18]

The denouement is not far off: Lydia's marriage speeds her sisters' on their way, little as they would have relished the thought. Mr Darcy has compelled Wickham to become Elizabeth's brother-in-law—and so his own, if his hopes may be fulfilled; and this scenario completes the humbling of his pride. He encourages Bingley to return to Jane and they are quickly engaged; he still hesitates for himself, seeking reassurance that Elizabeth's feelings are truly different from those she had expressed that evening, not many months before, in Hunsford parsonage.

The *deus*, or *dea, ex machina* takes the improbable form of Lady Catherine de Bourgh. Having failed in her attempt to secure Elizabeth's refusal to be Mrs Darcy, she calls on Darcy to disclose their conversation,

> dwelling emphatically on every expression of [Elizabeth], which, in her ladyship's apprehension, peculiarly denoted her perverseness and assurance, in the belief that such a relation must assist her endeavours to obtain that promise from her nephew, which *she* had refused to give. But, unluckily for her ladyship, its effect had been exactly contrariwise.
>
> 'It taught me to hope', said [Darcy to Elizabeth], 'as I had scarcely ever allowed myself to hope before. I knew enough of your disposition to be certain, that, had you been absolutely, irrevocably decided against me, you would have acknowledged it to Lady Catherine, frankly and openly.'
>
> Elizabeth coloured and laughed as she replied, 'Yes, you know enough of my *frankness* to believe me capable of *that*. After abusing you so abominably to your face, I could have no scruple in abusing you to all your relations.'[19]

Thus Lady Catherine's intervention brings them at last together— though before Darcy has begun to propose again, Elizabeth has set another powder trail in motion by revealing that she knows how much they owe him for Lydia's marriage. Not all the obstacles to happiness are yet removed, however. Elizabeth has not yet revealed, even to Jane, the change in her view of Mr Darcy; and she spends two uncomfortable evenings, convincing first Jane, then her father, that she loves him. She is not even sure how her mother will react, who has never ceased to refer to him as 'that disagreeable Mr Darcy'. When she tells her the news

> Its effect was most extraordinary; for on first hearing it, Mrs Bennet sat quite still, and unable to utter a syllable. Nor was it under many, many minutes, that she could comprehend what she

heard; though not in general backward to credit what was for the advantage of her family, or that came in the shape of a lover to any of them. She began at length to recover, to fidget about in her chair, get up, sit down again, wonder, and bless herself.

'Good gracious! Lord bless me! only think! dear me! Mr Darcy! Who would have thought it! And is it really true? Oh my sweetest Lizzy! how rich and how great you will be! What pin-money, what jewels, what carriages you will have! Jane's is nothing to it—nothing at all. I am so pleased—so happy. Such a charming man!—so handsome! so tall!—Oh, my dear Lizzy! pray apologise for my having disliked him so much before. I hope he will overlook it. Dear, dear Lizzy. A house in town! Everything that is charming! Three daughters married! Ten thousand a year! Oh, Lord! What will become of me, I shall go distracted.'[20]

Thus Elizabeth is able at last to answer her aunt's letter.

I would have thanked you before, my dear aunt, as I ought to have done, for your long, kind, satisfactory detail of particulars; but, to say the truth, I was too cross to write. You supposed more than really existed. But *now* suppose as much as you chuse; give a loose to your fancy, indulge your imagination in every possible flight which the subject will afford, and unless you believe me actually married, you cannot greatly err. You must write again very soon, and praise him a great deal more than you did in your last. I thank you, again and again, for not going to the Lakes. How could I be so silly as to wish it! Your idea of the ponies is delightful. We will go round the Park every day. I am the happiest creature in the world. Perhaps other people have said so before, but not one with such justice. I am happier even than Jane; she only smiles, I laugh. Mr Darcy sends you all the love in the world, that he can spare from me. You are all to come to Pemberley at Christmas.[21]

Notes

1. *PP* III, c. 10, p. 325. For Mr Darcy's age, see *PP*, pp. 200, 369.
2. *PP* II, c. 11, p. 189.
3. *PP* III, c. 17, p. 373. See pp. 81, 177.
4. *PP* III, c. 14, p. 356. See pp. 159–60.
5. *PP* II, c. 11, p. 192.
6. *PP* III, c. 18, p. 384.

7. *PP* III, c. 19, p. 385. Italics mine.

8. Ibid.

9. *Letters* L, no. 80, p. 203; C, no. 77, p. 299.

10. *PP* I, c. 1, p. 3.

11. *PP* III, c. 19, p. 387; for the origin of Mr Bingley's fortune, see *PP* I, c. 4, p. 15.

12. *PP* I, c. 15, p. 71.

13. *PP* I, c. 20, pp. 111–12.

14. See pp. 174–5. For Charlotte's age, see *PP* I, c. 22, p. 123.

15. Clearly Jane Austen conceived Pemberley as near Bakewell, and it has often been supposed that Chatsworth was the model for Pemberley. She had no first-hand knowledge of Chatsworth (so far as we know), and it seems likely that it provided only the approximate site. On the fashion for visiting the Lakes, see Moir 1964, c. 11.

16. See p. 76.

17. *PP* III, c. 8, p. 310.

18. *PP* III, c. 10, pp. 322–5. Lydia's wedding (so she tells us) took place at St Clement's church at 11 a.m. (*PP* p. 318). Since they breakfasted at 10 and had time for a carriage ride to the church after it, this cannot be St Clement Danes, well over a mile to the west through the most crowded part of the City: it must refer to St Clement Eastcheap (see Brooke and Keir 1975, pp. 123–5). Wickham lodged in the parish. The marriage evidently took place on the Monday after the banns had been called on three Sundays: they could not be married in the Gardiners' parish church since Lydia had only resided there a fortnight. (For the rules, see Cripps 1850, pp. 653–5; for the rule that marriage had to be celebrated between 8 a.m. and 12 noon, Cripps 1850, p. 676.) None the less, St Clement's is quite close to Gracechurch St., and it is curious to find that Wickham and Lydia had been in hiding not all that far from the Gardiners.

19. *PP* III, c. 16, p. 367.

20. *PP* III, c. 17, pp. 374, 378.

21. *PP* III, c. 18, pp. 382–3.

MARY JANE CURRY

"Not a Day Went by Without a Solitary Walk": Elizabeth's Pastoral World

O f all the Austen heroines, Elizabeth Bennet thinks most about that part of nature that is unbounded; where boundaries exist, she crosses them. A three mile walk from Longbourn to Netherfield "is nothing" when Jane lies ill there, and she exuberantly makes the trip, "crossing field after field at a quick pace, jumping over stiles and springing over puddles with impatient activity, and finding herself at last within view of the house, with weary ancles [sic], dirty stockings, and a face glowing with the warmth of exercise" (*Pride and Prejudice* 32). Four months later, at Rosings, Elizabeth makes her favorite walk "along the open grove which edged [the rectory] side of the park, where there was a nice sheltered path, which no one seemed to value but herself, and where she felt beyond the reach of Lady Catherine's curiosity" (169). Her freedom is curtailed as, first, Mr. Darcy joins her on several mornings (182), and second, Col. Fitzwilliam meets her, giving her the opportunity to discover his cousin's part in keeping Mr. Bingley from Jane in London (182–86). After Mr. Darcy's first proposal of marriage (189–93), he interrupts Elizabeth's solitary "ramble" when he discovers her taking a new route (to avoid him) and gives her the letter that elicits the exclamation, "'Till this moment, I never knew myself'" (195, 208).

Elizabeth's walks—solitary or in company with Mr. Darcy and the Gardiners—figure a gradual change in her. Austen places this change in the

From *Persuasions: The Jane Austen Journal* 22 (2000), pp. 175–186. © 2000 by the Jane Austen Society of North America.

context of what I argue is her proto-feminist version of the pastoral novel (Curry 1, 5). What makes *Pride and Prejudice* and the other five Austen novels incipiently feminist is the heroine's ideology of serious pastoral as a context for establishing her identity. Serious pastoral implies that country life, if enriched by intellectual and aesthetic pursuits, is better than city life; Austen's novels imply that such a country life is better for young women than city life. For her main characters, nature is a source of comfort and freedom as well as beauty.

Peter Marinelli defines serious pastoral in contrast to decorative pastoral, which is the lighter, simplistic version with stock characters (versions of the shepherd and milkmaid) and stock conflict such as two young men vying for a young woman's love (3, 6–13, 17–18). In European literature, both kinds begin with Theocritus's *Idylls* and Vergil's *Eclogues*, or *Bucolics*. Decorative pastoral is what Elizabeth Toohey discusses in her 1999 *Persuasions* paper when referring to Mrs. Elton's image of the strawberry-picking party at Donwell as presenting "the more superficial elements" of the pastoral idyll: "the shepherd's song, the rural locale, the love story" (52). Similarly, Laura Mooneyham White's "Emma and New Comedy" examines the "green world" of comic romance to establish Austen's "both enjoy[ing] and rebel[ling] from the conventions of comic romance" (131).[1] I agree, and add that Austen's treatment of decorative pastoral is only part of what serious pastoral does. In "Travelling to the Self," White's reading of Austen's open spaces as ambiguous, representing potential selfhood or loss of identity (199), interprets the psychological within a green world. My reading focuses on Austen's transforming the conventions of serious pastoral through figurative language, which operates on both the personal and the social levels.

Serious pastoral is concerned with complex problems and characters that it does not idealize, and the microcosm of serious pastoral can contain (in both senses) insidious forces. Other English novelists, of course, had already written woman-centered pastoral novels—Frances Burney, for example. The difference between their pastoral elements and Austen's is subtlety (not that Burney is not subtle in other equally important ways): Burney's Mr. Villars describes his ward Evelina as "quite a little rustic, [who] knows nothing of the world" (9). Evelina and Mr. Villars's disapproval of London social life is registered in overtly pastoral language (e.g., 13, 27–28); Evelina calls the social world's late hours "a terrible reversal of the order of nature!" (28). In contrast, Austen transforms pastoral ideology without displaying its conventional language—except, of course, when she satirizes it in such scenes as Mrs. Elton's attempt to play shepherdess at Donwell (866).

During Austen's young adulthood serious pastoral poetry was being transformed by William Wordsworth, who was only five years older than she.[2] Wordsworth, like Austen, read William Cowper, whose Book I of *The Task* expresses a typically pastoral appreciation of nature:

> For I have loved the rural walk through lanes
> Of grassy swath, close cropp'd by nibbling sheep,
> And skirted thick with intertexture firm
> Of thorny boughs; have loved the rural walk
> O'er hills, through valleys, and by river's brink,
> E'er since, a truant boy, I pass'd my bounds,
> To enjoy a ramble on the banks of Thames.

Except for the "thorny boughs," Elizabeth Bennet's "ramble" through the woods, across the valley, and over the stream at Pemberley Woods (245, 253–54) resembles Cowper's. Like his poetry and Wordsworth's, Austen's novels attribute the protagonist's self-understanding to a calming freedom produced by viewing the non-human physical world. In *Lines Composed a Few Miles Above Tintern Abbey*, Wordsworth credits his memories of nature's "beauteous forms" with his "tranquil restoration" amid the human conflict he experienced in cities (11. 23–31).

Austen's narrator tells us that Elizabeth's walks at Rosings and at Longbourn provide her the solitude to reflect on her own conflicts—encounters with Mr. Darcy (and release from those confining interiors that Charlotte Bronte so disliked). The morning after Mr. Darcy's proposal at Hunsford Parsonage, she must escape outdoors:

> She could not recover from the surprise of what had happened; it was impossible to think of any thing else, and totally indisposed for employment, she resolved soon after breakfast to indulge herself in air and exercise. She was proceeding directly to her favourite walk, when the recollection of Mr. Darcy's sometimes coming there stopped her, and instead of entering the park, she turned up the lane, which led her farther from the turnpike road. The park paling was still the boundary on one side, and she soon passed one of the gates into the ground. (195)

Pastoral in Austen's fiction is associated with boundaries—fences, gates, ha-has—those "tropes of the big novel" that Margaret Ann Doody explores (75–76). Metaphorically, the gate that separates Elizabeth from Mr. Darcy as he hands her his letter may signal her exclusion from the de Bourgh-Darcy family because of her family's faux pas as well as her relatives in trade. And it might also suggest Mr. Darcy's self-imposed imprisonment in excessive family pride. However, Austen places emphasis on Elizabeth's choice to remain outside Lady Catherine's domain and away from the place she has walked with Mr. Darcy. More importantly, Elizabeth may have just chosen, she can assume, the spinster's genteel poverty over marriage to "'the last man in the world whom [she] could ever be prevailed on to marry'" (193). Elizabeth's conflict with him is, rather than the generalized antagonism of Wordsworth's urban "din," a private clash of values: Mr. Darcy's family pride versus Elizabeth's self-worth, tied to her family. Pride in rank and wealth is anti-pastoral; judging an individual on her own merits is part of the pastoral egalitarian impulse, as we see so clearly in Shakespeare's Arden (Ettin 108). This novel asks us to respect a woman's need for freedom, both physical and social.

As Lady Catherine holds forth at Rosings, Elizabeth thinks it lucky that the great lady monopolizes the conversation with so many questions, "or with a mind so occupied, she might have forgotten where she was. Reflection must be reserved for solitary hours; whenever she was alone, she gave way to it as the greatest relief, and not a day went by without a solitary walk, in which she might indulge in all the delight of unpleasant recollections" (212). The narrator's irony here is Elizabeth's, too: she is aware that she is obsessed with the scene between Mr. Darcy and herself, and aware of her tendency to isolate herself. The solitary walk is also a way to escape the social control that Lady Catherine exemplifies in the extreme.

Another reason for lone walks is positive. Standing or moving outside park gates, Elizabeth delights in the beauty of the natural world. As for the younger Wordsworth in Tintern Abbey, for Elizabeth nature is "[a]n appetite, a feeling, and a love" (1. 80). Continuing the description of her walk just before Mr. Darcy gives her his letter, the narrative focus is upon Elizabeth's enjoyment of early spring:

After walking two or three times along that part of the lane, she was tempted, by the pleasantness of the morning, to stop at the gates and look into the park. The five weeks which she had now passed in Kent, had made a great difference in the country, and every day was adding to the verdure of the early trees. (195)

The next passage, describing her accepting the letter, seems to drop the subject of Elizabeth's enjoyment, but considered with later passages describing Pemberley Woods, we can read into the image of "verdure," above, a trope that suggests an expansion, not a breach: March greenness is birth in nature, and Mr. Darcy's letter induces the "birth" of Elizabeth's self-knowledge. His handing it to her and the letter itself are framed by passages describing Elizabeth's "wandering along the lane" (209). Here and at Pemberley Mr. Darcy's unexpected appearances are juxtaposed to Elizabeth's response to nature. Both of these appearances are surprise encounters described with overtones that are—contrary to what Charlotte Bronte, Henry James, and W.H. Auden thought about Austen—sensuous. At Pemberley the emphasis is on open topographical curves; whatever natural boundaries exist are easily crossed "by a simple bridge, in character with the general air of the scene" (253). Elizabeth's response to nature suggests a new openness to feeling, even physicality, not her customary exercise of rational thinking expressed in wit.

Introducing the estate, Austen takes a full page to describe its woods and water (a record length for her). The chapter introducing Pemberley begins with a wide prospect:

> They gradually ascended for half a mile, and then found themselves at the top of a considerable eminence, where the wood ceased, and the eye was instantly caught by Pemberley House, situated on the opposite side of a valley, into which the road with some abruptness wound. It was a large, handsome, stone building, standing well on rising ground, and backed by a ridge of woody hills;—and in front, a stream of some natural importance was swelled into greater, but without any artificial appearance. Its banks were neither formal, nor falsely adorned. Elizabeth was delighted. (245)

We do not usually think of Austen's language as poetic, but here assonance (the repetition of soft vowel sounds) reinforces one's impression of sensuous sweeping curves of hills and stream. Another layer of meaning exists in those descriptions of Elizabeth's first impressions. Following the first image of the woods and water, we read that after crossing a narrow bridge Elizabeth, barely aware of her surroundings or her companions, imagines Mr. Darcy inside his house (253). Near the end of the novel, the last walk, when Mr. Darcy proposes and Elizabeth accepts, recalls her state at Pemberley when she cannot attend to the nature before her because she is absorbed in thoughts of the man, and here the narrative attributes this state to Mr. Darcy, too, suggesting a meeting of minds: "They walked on, without knowing in what direction. There was too much to be thought, and felt, and said, for attention to any other objects" (366).

At Pemberley, her notice of the exterior returns just after the party ascends a forested slope; they reach "a descent among hanging woods, [at] the edge of the water, in one of its narrowest parts ... a spot less adorned than any they had yet visited" (253). She becomes aware of their "narrow walk amidst the rough coppice-wood which bordered [a stream]. Elizabeth longed to explore its windings" (253–54). Suggesting a wish for solitary freedom to think about Mr. Darcy rather than having to talk even to her dear aunt and uncle, her longing occurs between the first and second encounter with the new, civil Fitzwilliam Darcy, now full of "such gentleness" (252). The language suggests a merging of desires—experiencing natural beauty with forming a relationship with Mr. Darcy The grounds' natural beauty, described in all their fertility, seem a projection of his masculinity (fertility as ability to reproduce) and his imagination (fertility of mind) as well as his capacity to create himself anew for Elizabeth (fertility as ability to become a new individual).

In a passage mentioning the Lake District, widely associated in her lifetime with a male poet, Wordsworth, and the male perspective of Romanticism, Austen associates the Lakes with a woman in love with wild nature. "'What are men compared to rocks and mountains!'" Elizabeth only half-jokingly exclaims to Mrs. Gardiner when she explains their itinerary (154). When Elizabeth later learns their tour must be curtailed, she is "excessively disappointed" (239). At Pemberley in July, another terrain, the Peak District of Derbyshire (also retaining some "wildness"), becomes something other than a consolation for having to forego the Lakes because of Mr. Gardiner's business (237, 238–39). Left alone with Mr. Darcy, she and he are desperate to find a neutral topic, and they "talked of Matlock and Dovedale with great perseverance" (257). Matlock and Dovedale are reduced to safe topics when the personal cannot yet be discussed. The plot diverts Elizabeth from a solitary, Wordsworthian retreat into "rocks and mountains," and re-focuses her emotional responses on the man and his extension, the estate, where "natural beauty [is] so little counteracted by an awkward taste." A secondary focal point of the Pemberley chapters is Lambton with its happy memories of a community for Mrs. Gardiner. We shall see that the individual's relationship to the human community becomes an important part of Austen's pastoral.

Until she visits Pemberley Woods, Elizabeth metaphorically if not always literally chooses to place herself outside boundaries. White argues that "open space has potentially benign or malign significance; it may stand either for transcendence or the dissolution of selfhood" ("Traveling to the Self" 199), and Elizabeth's wit as well as her walks are attempts to avoid that dissolution. In serious pastorals, space outside man-made boundaries can also signify something larger than the individual; although the Romantic version of pastorals requires a new focus on the solitary mind, Austen's pastorals, like Shakespeare's, always conclude by bringing the central character into a new society, if not ideal at least better than the point of origin. This closure occurs in every Austen novel. Specifically, in *Pride and Prejudice* Elizabeth Bennet's marriage to Fitzwilliam Darcy creates a microcosm at Pemberley in which stewardship of people as well as land receives emphasis.

The exceptional goodness of Mr. Darcy's assistance to the poor is mentioned twice, once by the housekeeper Mrs. Reynolds (249) and once in Lambton (265). This repetition resonated with Austen's contemporaries. The novel takes place from 1811 through 1812, Chapman's Appendix notes (403, 405), and 1812 was a particularly bad year for the poor: they suffered from "low wages, high bread prices, and more enclosure of common land," historian David Spring explains (551). Roy Porter writes that enclosure had worsened the landless poor's desperate situation from the mid-eighteenth century on: farmers "improving" their lands found it cheaper to hire laborers only seasonally and these were always available from the pool of the homeless. "Such pressures were exacerbated where enclosure further reduced independence by depriving labourers of customary access to common land, which had helped them eke out a living from firing, grazing, nuts and berries, and the odd rabbit" (94). The southern counties suffered the most because there only the lowest-paying seasonal employment was available, and there were no nearby industrial towns to which the poor could migrate for work; the result was increasing expenditure by the government for charity. "By 1800, 28 per cent of the population was in receipt of poor relief," Porter notes. As Cobbett pointed out at the time, land owners had no financial incentive to help the poor since paying taxes for poor relief, though skyrocketing, was still cheaper than keeping more permanent laborers (Porter 94). Mrs. Reynolds brags that Mr. Darcy is "just as affable to the poor" as his father (249); this allusion implies that throughout this difficult period the Darcy men did not practice the kind of mercenary policy that many other landowners adopted. Elizabeth's mental response to this praise suggests her awareness that Mr. Darcy could, if he chose, act otherwise without condemnation by his peers: "As a brother, a landlord, a master, she considered how many people's happiness were in his guardianship!—How much of pleasure or pain it was in his power to bestow!—How much of good or evil must be done by him!" (250–51) In Lambton, the consensus is this: "It was acknowledged ... that he was a liberal man, and did much good among the poor" (265).

The goodness in Mr. Darcy's character, shown in these passages, marks Austen's serious pastoral as groundbreaking in the same way, at roughly the same time as Wordsworth's: both incorporate pastorals' sister form, georgics, which existed alongside each other since Vergil's composition of the *Eclogues* and *Georgics*.[3] Traditional georgic poetry is "concerned with the agricultural foundation of a great nation"; it celebrates the physical labor of farmers and hired laborers as necessary to a country's moral as well as physical well being (Griffin 866). In English poetry of the Romantic period, this georgic theme was expanded to labor of another kind: mental and emotional. Again influenced by Cowper, especially *The Task*, Wordsworth merged georgic elements with pastoral to focus on work—intellectual and spiritual as well as physical—as a means to giving one's life order and meaning. For Wordsworth, sensing the harmony of nature elicits intellectual and spiritual labor; such thought, in turn, motivates the individual to benevolent action. The epigraph of Book VIII, *The Prelude*, states: "Love of nature leads to love of man." However naive this belief may seem to us, Wordsworth expresses it with conviction here and in *Tintern Abbey* in which the memory of the Wye Valley brings

> feelings... perhaps,
> As have no slight or trivial influence
> On that best portion of a good man's life,
> His little, nameless, unremembered acts
> Of kindness and of love. (11. 30–35)

Those acts remain generalized in Wordsworth, but not in Austen. Her georgic elements, most evident in Mr. Knightley's and Mr. Martin's agricultural improvements at Donwell Abbey and Abbey Mill Farm, but also evident in Mr. Darcy's helping the poor, turn her pastoral outward toward the larger community. As Toohey says of Mr. Knightley, "Land carries a moral as well as an economic weight, and the best men [in Austen's novels] are those most rooted to the earth" (49).

Against this backdrop of benevolence and community, the conclusion focuses on people drawn into the Pemberley microcosm. Kitty divides most of her time between Pemberley and the Bingleys' new estate only thirty miles away "in a neighbouring county to Derbyshire" (S85). "Pemberley was now Georgiana's home; and the attachment of the sisters was exactly what Darcy had hoped to see. They were able to love each other, even as well as they intended" (S87). "With the Gardiners they were always on the most intimate terms. Darcy, as well as Elizabeth, really loved them; and they were both sensible of the warmest gratitude towards the persons who, by bringing her into Derbyshire, had been the means of uniting them" (388).

Pastorals also eject or neutralize antagonistic forces, and Austen's follow this pattern. Lydia and Wickham usually remain at a safe distance, overstaying their welcome with the Bingleys and taking advantage of Jane and Elizabeth's generosity, certainly (386–87). To avoid being cut off from

Pemberley entirely, Miss Bingley puts on a mask of amiability towards Elizabeth and is "fonder than ever of Georgina, [and] almost as attentive to Darcy as heretofore" (387). Lady Catherine is eventually reconciled to her nephew by Elizabeth: "after a little farther resistance on the part of his aunt, her resentment gave way, either to her affection for him, or her curiosity to see how his wife conducted herself; and she condescended to wait on them at Pemberley, in spite of that pollution which its woods had received, not merely from the presence of such a mistress, but the visits of her aunt and uncle" (388). The only charming force antagonistic to pastoral is Mr. Bennet, whose passivity as a father many readers must see as ultimately the cause of his wife's and youngest daughter's most grievous errors. He is punished by the absence of Elizabeth, for which he compensates by leaving Longbourn to see her "oftener" than he has ever left home before; he "delight[s]" in doing so "especially when he [is] least expected" (385).

Readers may leave this fictional world a bit uneasily knowing that Lady Catherine's visits and Lydia's pleas for money will continue, and that Fitzwilliam and Elizabeth Darcy will tolerate Miss Bingley. The kinds of compromises necessary to an otherwise ideal life remind us of the contingencies in real life. This fact and the appeal of nature as a refuge from conflict are two of the reasons Austen's novels enjoy such popularity today. The tangible results of our pastoral longing surround us: planned communities, tours of great estates in Britain, people renouncing careers and city life for small farms and low-stress occupations, the resurgence of interest in Austen's novels and the film versions of them, even the L.L. Bean and Eddie Bauer style. Since the sixties—with Joni Mitchell's anthem "Woodstock": "We've got to get back to the Garden"—we have confronted, and many of us have sought, a pastoral ideal, and we found our own flaws in the process. Nevertheless, we continue to find solace in whatever contact with nature we can make. At the same time, reading Austen reminds many of us that nature and the "improvement" of our minds necessary to appreciate it are luxuries available to a minority of the world's population, those luckily at the right place at the right time. The conclusion of *Pride and Prejudice* implies that chance (the Gardiners' happening to bring Elizabeth into Derbyshire at just the moment when Mr Darcy arrives a changed man) plays a role in the happy ending. The novel also implies that becoming mistress of Pemberley is Elizabeth's one good option; the alternative fate, had Mrs. Bennet's forecast proved correct, would have been homelessness—a dislocation from the natural world necessary to her identity. Who can imagine Elizabeth Bennet as a governess on someone else's estate?[4]

Notes

1. White's approach to pastorals, she notes, is influenced by Northrop Frye's 1957 classic of genre and archetypal theory *Anatomy of Criticism*, whose categories of comic mode and romance archetype articulate what my study, following Marinelli, calls "pastoral," both "serious" and "decorative."

2. On Wordsworth's contribution to pastorals, see Gill 129–30 Garber 153–55; Marinelli 4–6; and Curran 99–100. Thompson's book explores Austen's affinities with Wordsworth.

3. Dwight L. Durling argues that classical georgics influenced English poets of the last half of the eighteenth century, including Cowper, to abandon neoclassical general description in favor of more realistic detail.

4. Thanks to Sarah E. Brown for presenting my paper at the 2000 AGM in Boston; her slides from eighteenth-century prints of the Peaks, the Lakes, and from pictures of early nineteenth-century estates with features like Rosings's and Pemberley's made a true improvement.

Works Cited

Austen, Jane, *Emma*. Ed. R. W. Chapman. 3rd ed. Oxford: OUP, 1933.

———. *Pride and Prejudice* Ed. R. W. Chapman. 3rd ed., rev. London: OUP, 1965.

Burney, Frances. *Evelina, or, The History of a Young Lady's Entrance into the World* (1778). New York: W. W. Norton, 1965.

Cowper, William. *The Task, Book I. Poetical Works of William Cowper*. Ed. H. F. Cary. Vol. 2. New York: Leavitt & Allen, n.d. 2 vols. 9-180.

Curran, Stuart. *Poetic Form and British Romanticism*, New York: Oxford UP, 1986.

Curry, Mary Jane. *The Serious Pastoral in Jane Austen's Novels*. DA I-A 55/07 (1994): 9430113. Auburn University.

Doody, Margaret Ann. "A Regency Walking Dress and Other Disguises: JA and the Big Novel." *Persuasions* 16(1994): 74-77.

Durling, Dwight L. *The Georgic Tradition in English Poetry*. Port Washington, NY: Kennikat P, Inc., 1935, 1963.

Frye, Northrop. *Anatomy of Criticism*. Princeton: Princeton UP, 1957.

Ettin, Andrew V. *Literature and the Pastoral*. New Haven: Yale UP, 1984.

Garber, Frederick. "Pastoral Spaces." *Texas Studies in Literature and Language* 30 (fall 1988): 431-60.

Gill, Stephen. *William Wordsworth: A Life*. Oxford: Clarendon P, 1989.

Griffin, Dustin. "Redefining Georgic: Cowper's *Task*." *English Literary History* 57 (Winter 1990): 865-79.

Marinelli, Peter. *Pastoral London*: Methuen, 1970.

Spring, David. "Interpreters of Jane Austen's Social World: Literary Critics and Historians." *Jane Austen: New Perspectives*. Women & Lit. Series. Ed. Janet Todd. Vol. 3. New York: Holmes & Meier, Inc., 1983. 53-72.

Thompson, James. *Between Self and World: The Novels of Jane Austen*. University Park, PA.: Penn. State UP, 1988.

Toohey, Elizabeth. "*Emma* and the Countryside: Weather and a Place for a Walk." *Persuasions* 21 (1999): 44-52.

White, Laura Mooneyham. "*Emma* and New Comedy." *Persuasions* 21 (1999): 128-41.

————. "Travelling to the Self: Comic and Spatial Openness in Jane Austen's Novels." *Critical Essays on Jane Austen*. Ed. Laura Mooneyham White. New York: G. K. Hall & Co., 1998. 198-213.

Wordsworth, William. "Lines Composed a Few Miles above Tintern Abbey, on Revisiting the Banks of the Wye during a Tour, July 13, 1798." *The Complete Poetical Works of William Wordsworth*. Vol. 2. Boston: Houghton Mifflin 1911. 10 vols. 85-91.

————. *The Prelude, or Growth of a Poet's Mind. The Complete Poetical Works of William Wordsworth*. Vol. 3. Boston: Houghton Mifflin 1911. 10 vols.

JOHANNA M. SMITH

The Oppositional Reader and
Pride and Prejudice

Both Jane Austen and her contemporary women readers, one may argue, came to *Pride and Prejudice* from particular class positions and with particular ideological perceptions. This is not to say, however, that the novel or its readers uncritically accept those positions and perceptions. Using a concept of oppositional reading, we can unpack what might seem a hegemonic discourse—the novel's endorsement of class-based, masculinist and heterosexual paradigms—by attention to the ways that the text also endorses the responses of readers in conflict with that discourse. In other words, *Pride and Prejudice* offers the hegemonic paradigms but also offers opposing paradigms, thereby opening a space for the oppositional reader to weigh, argue with, counter and/or accept the possibilities of the text. Such a reading of Jane Austen can also unpack several vexed areas of the critical discourse on *Pride and Prejudice*. Is the novel radical or conservative in its class politics? Is it feminist or antifeminist in its gender politics? Is it even appropriate to ask these twentieth-century questions of an early-nineteenth-century text? I would answer yes to all these questions, in the service of nuanced oppositional readings.

In the past twenty years or so, there has been much critical reevaluation of Jane Austen's class position, as both a woman and a writer. As early as 1953, Donald Greene drew attention to both the many links between Austen's

From *A Companion to Jane Austen Studies*, edited by Laura Cooner Lambdin and Robert Thomas Lambdin, pp. 27–40. © 2000 by Laura Cooner Lambdin and Robert Thomas Lambdin.

family and the British aristocracy and Austen's consciousness of those links. More recently, critics such as Rachel M. Brownstein have critiqued Austen for "drawing snobs ... and encouraging them in snobbishness" (182), a critique that usefully reminds us that Austen's novels promulgate not some ideal of universal human values but some very specific class and gender values. The precise nature of those values, however, has continued to be debated. According to Alistair Duckworth and Warren Roberts, Darcy and his estate, Pemberley, represent the "traditional society and ethical orientation" (Duckworth 123) espoused by Edmund Burke, and Marilyn Butler concurred that Austen propounds a Burkean conservative politics. Margaret Kirkham called this position into question, first by situating Austen in the context of the radical feminists of the 1790s and then by postulating that for a woman "to become an author was, in itself, a feminist act" (33) during this period and that Austen's heroines exemplify "the first claim of Enlightenment feminism" by acting as "independent moral agents" (84, 83). Mary Poovey factored class into such a feminist analysis, demonstrating the problematics of moral agency when claimed by ladies—that is, women of the gentry rank. Ascertaining Austen's class and gender values is thus further complicated: ideological contradictions, latent in the cultural role of the Proper Lady, surface when a Proper Lady like Austen becomes a Woman Writer and when a Proper Lady heroine like Elizabeth Bennet "champion[s] the prerogatives of individual desire" (194). And these ambiguities and contradictions are symptomatic of rifts not only in Austen's novels and culture but in Austen criticism. If Mary Evans argues persuasively that Austen was "deeply critical" (2) of late-eighteenth-century capitalism, she veers away from the more radical conclusions of such an argument. In contrast, Judith Lowder Newton reaches such a conclusion when she finds *Pride and Prejudice* "devoted to ... denying the force of economics in human life" (61).

Rather than throwing up our hands in the face of such contradictions in the criticism, we can use them to analyze contradictions in the class and gender politics promulgated by *Pride and Prejudice*. To do so requires first reviewing the position of women writers in the early nineteenth century. Austen wrote *First Impressions* from 1796 to 1797, revised the manuscript from 1809 to 1810 and again in 1812, and published it as *Pride and Prejudice* in 1813. Why this gap of almost twenty years between inception and publication? Kirkham argues that Austen "felt ready to publish" (53) the manuscript in 1797 and indeed made efforts to do so; nothing came of those efforts, and "the 'Great Wollstonecraft Scandal'" (Kirkham 48) in the following year initiated an increasingly chilly climate for women writers. Although a great many women had "rushed into print" (Fergus 13) by the end of the eighteenth century, and although they had "insert[ed] into the novel" (Todd 228) the "authority" of "the woman as moralist," one effect of the Wollstonecraft scandal was to pressure women writers *into* the role of moralist. In other words, the very "ubiquity of the moral imperative for women" (Todd 229) functioned as a form of authority but also as a constraint. Indeed, as a "product of limitation" (Ferris 65) the Proper Novel might come to seem "limited and limiting," as the critical history of Austen's contemporary Maria Edgeworth suggests: Initially praised for aiding "the education and discipline of the newly literate" (Ferris 61), by 1817 Edgeworth's novels were being denigrated for precisely this didacticism.

At the end of the eighteenth century, however, the woman writer's didactic function had seemed especially crucial with the perceived split in the reading public into the (mainly male) "articulate classes" (Ferris 22) on the one hand and the much larger and more disparate group of newly literate, middle- and lower-class men and women on the other hand. The latter group raised concerns that novel reading might be "seductive and inflaming" (Ferris 40), especially to women, and this anxiety increased the pressure on the Proper Lady to write the Proper Novel. Such a novel, characterized by "realism" (Ferris 54), "social utility" and a language of "enclosure and decorum," was to fulfill the feminine cultural function of "moraliz[ing] the laboring poor" (Cole and Swartz 145). Whether by working to "suspend the subversive power of sentiment" (Watson 73), or by showing the deleterious "effects of the undisciplined or improperly disciplined imagination" (Colby 241), or by "urging the control of passion and the necessity of exertion" (Ferris 63), the Proper Novel by and for the Proper Lady was relentlessly didactic.

Of course, as Austen's own characterization of *Pride and Prejudice* suggests, the book seems "rather too light and bright and sparkling" (Chapman 2:299) to fall into the category of didactic Proper Novel. And as Kirkham points out (53–54), political and gender conservatives such as Richard Polwhele might have considered just this "'sparkle of confident intelligence'" a sign of the anti-didactic, of the author's feminist critique of masculine culture. Nevertheless, Austen was subject to many of the same pressures toward didacticism as other late-eighteenth- and early-nineteenth-century women writers, and *Pride and Prejudice* copes with these pressures in the oscillation between radical and conservative ideologies that I noted at the beginning of this essay. Hence, Austen may be seen as "at once authorizing and enacting a resistant reading of her own text" (Litvak 36).

We can get at these oscillations by looking at the problematic realism which many critics have seen in *Pride and Prejudice*. For Newton, the novel alternates between realism and a fantasy quest plot; for Poovey, the alternation is between realistic social criticism and a final "aesthetic gratification" (207); for Sarah Webster Goodwin, realism is joined to and undercut by the "possibly-real" of a feminist utopia (10). These formulations suggest that *Pride and Prejudice* is realism and/but something more, a generic mix that seems to call "realism" itself into question. For early-nineteenth-century readers, realism would have been associated with the genre of the "novel" as distinguished from that of the "romance." Where the novel was expected to represent faithfully "the ordinary train of human events, and the modern state of society" (Moir 40), the romance was defined by Austen's contemporary Walter Scott as "a fictitious narrative" of "marvelous and uncommon incidents" (qtd. in Duncan 10). Yet the distinction was not absolute, for an otherwise realistic novel of "every-day life" (Moir 42) might also incorporate the "mysterious and terrible" incidents or "powerful passion" more characteristic of the romance. And Claudia Brodsky Lacour locates *Pride and Prejudice* at a "dialectical moment" (602) of similar confusion over the nature of realism: if Austen's novel marks the point at which "literature becomes identified with the historical and the particular, the representation (or misrepresentation) of the real," it is also pervaded by the problem of realistic representation, "the difficulty of translating between abstract and representational language ... and thus of representing an abstraction, truth, in fiction" (603).

The demands of realism were complicated for women writers by cultural pressures toward didacticism. Novels like those that Jane Austen wrote might be expected to function as manuals for the proper conduct of "social and private life in the upper and upper middle classes" (Kelly 151), but they might then be condemned for "spreading false upper-class values and social expectations." More centrally for my purposes, the realistic novel offered legitimacy to women writers if they were "scrupulous about fulfilling the office of educator" (Poovey 38), so fidelity to the real might well be displaced by the didactic imperative. For instance, Beth Kowalski-Wallace sees "ideology at work" (243) in early-nineteenth-century realistic novels that legitimated a "new-style patriarchy" of "non-coercive" masculine authority by focusing reader attention on the pleasures of "domestic fulfillment." For women readers, these pleasures functioned as "compensatory gratifications, ideal rewards" (Poovey 38) for giving up other, more transgressive desires; they were the carrot at the end of the didactic stick. But realistic novels might also offer the fantasy of compensatory power, the pleasure of wielding the stick. Women are often "the legitimate agents for socializing men" (Poovey 169) in these novels; as such, they might punish insufficiently socialized men and thereby "retaliate against their legal superiors." In the novel as in the bourgeois home, of course, such power was only compensatory; in the sexual politics of fiction as of fact, women generally remained subordinate to men.

Perhaps the most significant ideological function of realistic-didactic fiction is thus its capacity to "represent an alternative form of political power [for women] without appearing to contest the distribution of power [to men] that it represented as historically given" (Armstrong, *Desire* 29).

But can we say that all women readers of realistic-didactic fiction in general, and *Pride and Prejudice* in particular, achieved—or even desired—the "compensatory gratifications" I have been discussing? Where in this scenario is the oppositional reader, the reader who resists the consolations of ideology? We can locate this reader by examining reading itself, as one of the "everyday practices, 'ways of operating' or doing things" that, Michel de Certeau argues, show us that the dominated are not necessarily "passive or docile" (xi–xii). As "users" or "consumers"—or readers—move through the "constructed, written, and functionalized" (xviii) space of their culture, they may follow not the paths laid out for them but "'indirect' or 'errant' trajectories obeying their own logic," trajectories that "trace out the ruses of other interests and desires that are neither determined nor captured by the systems in which they develop." Such trajectories also give the lie to an "ideology of consumption-as-a-receptacle" (167), an ideology in which "the efficiency of production implies the inertia of consumption." If this latter formulation is applied to writing and reading, the efficiency of authorial production implies the inertia of the reader as consumer; but if "a system of verbal or iconic signs is a reservoir of forms to which the reader must give a meaning" (169), then reading is not passive consumption but rather "the production proper to the reader." Furthermore, the reader "invents in texts something different from what they 'intended'"; "He [*sic*] combines their fragments and creates something un-known in the space organized by their capacity for allowing an indefinite plurality." In academic practice, however, "only someone like Barthes can take this liberty" (172); students tend to be "scornfully driven or cleverly coaxed back to the meaning 'accepted' by their teachers." In other words, a text may well function as a "cultural weapon" (171) in the hands of "*socially* authorized professionals and intellectuals," and the reader's autonomy as a consumer may well be relative to the "social relationships that overdetermine his [*sic*] relation to texts" (173). de Certeau calls for a "transformation" of those relationships, a "politics of reading" such that readers become truly "travellers ... poaching their way across fields they did not write" (174), moving in trajectories, indulging in "advances and retreats, tactics and games played with the text" (175). These "travellers" would be our resisting readers, and of this "politics of reading" what William Galperin says about *Emma* is equally pertinent to *Pride and Prejudice*: "Austen advocates resistance and change" (23) by "showing it" in her characters' practices and "the counterhegemonic practices of reading" she makes available. To exemplify such an oppositional reading, I want to consider Lydia Bennet and Charlotte Lucas, reading each in relation to Elizabeth Bennet as a contender for her status as heroine.

The focus of my reading is the function(s) of wit in the novel. Marilyn Butler regards Elizabeth's wit as "so seductive" (216) of the novel's predominating conservatism that *Pride and Prejudice* finally has "no clear message" (217). Similarly, Maaja Stewart argues that Elizabeth's wit is foregrounded in the novel, but that background "patterns of power" (40), which gradually render her "completely helpless," become visible in the form of Darcy's judgment; furthermore, "diametrically opposed reader responses [are] produced by the text" (59) through the contest of wit and judgment. The "unclear message" resulting from "diametrically opposed reader responses" to this contest suggests a space for the oppositional reader. Such a reader might note that it is the easily led Bingley who has "the highest opinion" (64) of Darcy's judgment, that it is Darcy's "own judgment alone" (218) that determines to detach Bingley from Jane, and that Darcy's judgment in the matter was "probabl[y]" (288) influenced by his desire to ally Bingley with his own family.

The boundary between wit and judgment is further blurred when we remember that wit is itself a form of judgment. According to Samuel Johnson's *Dictionary* of 1755, in fact, wit might be defined as "sense" or "judgment" (def. 6), and the *Oxford English Dictionary* (*OED*) lists several eighteenth-century examples of wit defined as "good judgment" (def. 6a). An early conversation between Darcy and Elizabeth displays this overlap of judgment and wit. When Elizabeth admits, "I dearly love a laugh" (102), Darcy in effect rebukes her judgment:

> "The wisest and the best of men, nay, the wisest and best of their actions, may be rendered ridiculous by a person whose first object in life is a joke."
>
> "Certainly," replied Elizabeth—"there are such people, but I hope I am not one of *them*. I hope I never ridicule what is wise or good. Follies and nonsense, whims and inconsistencies, *do* divert me, ... and I laugh at them whenever I can."

Darcy's magisterial judgment of people "whose first object in life is a joke" is presented as if it were a universal. Elizabeth's "certainly" accepts that universal, but she then distinguishes herself from "*them*" by validating her own judgment, her ability to differentiate between "what is wise or good" and the follies, nonsense, whims and inconsistencies that do deserve her ridicule. A second, implicit area of judgment here is the distinction between jokes and ridicule: joking seems to be indiscriminate, while ridicule has a carefully judged object.

Although wit is not mentioned here, it is obviously related to jokes and ridicule. The difficulty of mapping that relation, however, is suggested by the many definitions of wit in the eighteenth century. In addition to "good judgment," it might mean "quickness of fancy" (Johnson def. 2) with an accompanying "capacity of apt expression" (*OED* def. 7). Wit of this sort, according to the *OED*, is what Pope meant in the *Essay on Criticism* by "what oft was thought, but ne'er so well expressed"; stretching a point, we might say that Darcy's judgment of jokesters is witty in this sense. Still, according to the *OED*, wit is also a "talent for saying brilliant or sparkling things" (def. 7). There is no wit of that sort in the conversation between Darcy and Elizabeth, but it abounds elsewhere in this "light and bright and sparkling" novel. Elizabeth occasionally makes a remark of this sort, as when she ridicules Maria's excitement over visitors from Rosings: "I thought at least that the pigs were got into the garden, and here is nothing but Lady Catherine and her daughter!" (194). Yet Elizabeth's wit is doubly at fault here, for not only could the remark itself be seen as "bordering on the vulgar" (Johnson 76), she has made an error of judgment in taking Mrs. Jenkinson for Lady Catherine. True wit, the "apt association of thought and expression, calculated to surprise and delight by its unexpectedness" (*OED* def. 8a), thus comes to seem the exclusive prerogative of Austen narration, both her *style indirect libre*—"Mary wished to say something very sensible, but knew not how" (55)—and her third-person exposition—" The party then gathered round the fire to hear Lady Catherine determine what weather they were to have on the morrow" (201).

While these moments of wit might be categorized as jokes, they should certainly be categorized as ridicule, a point of some significance for the practice of oppositional reading. That is, since neither Mary nor Lady Catherine is "wise or good," the reader is invited to ridicule their nonsense and folly; in other words, a nonresistant appreciation of Austen's wit constitutes a judgment of Mary and Lady Catherine. As Brownstein puts it, if "we respond with approval to a snob's ruthless high standards, and to her high-handedness" (182), that response constitutes readerly "complicity with Austen's sure, exclusive Lady's tone." Such complicity in turn displays the nonresisting reader's taste, in the correct judgment of Austen's characters and the proper appreciation of Austen's wit. It thus marks such a reader as belonging to what Pierre Bourdieu calls "the aristocracy of culture" (11), for it shows her or his "elaborated taste for the most refined objects" (1). The "social hierarchy" of consumers of art, according to Bourdieu, "predisposes tastes to function as markers of 'class'" (1–2). Consumption of a novel, for instance, is "an act of deciphering, decoding, which presupposes practical or explicit mastery of a cipher or code," in other words a "cultural competence," which signifies class position. And as they exercise that competence, "social subjects ... distinguish themselves by the distinctions they make" (6), so that "taste classifies" not just the art object but the consumer of that object. I have already said that wit is a form of judgment, of making distinctions; it is thus also a form and sign of taste. I have said too that appreciating Austen's wit at the expense of her characters is a mark of complicity with the judgment implied by that wit; appreciating wit, then, is equally a form and sign of taste. If consumption of a text is "the production proper to the reader," as de Certeau claims (169), it is also the production *of* the nonresisting reader as a person of taste.

Does this mean that the resisting reader has no taste? Not necessarily, for he or she deciphers and decodes the text with a cultural competence similar to that of the accepting reader. Indeed, it might be argued that resistance attests *superior* competence: Joseph Litvak postulates a "dynamic interdependence of perversity *and* privilege" (46–47) in an "oppositional criticism" (47), which resists the normative heterosexuality of *Pride and Prejudice*'s marriage plot. An oppositional reading that resists the novel's wit might well signal a similar privilege; indeed, flaunting that privilege might place oppositional critics "in an even more privileged position to repel [distasteful] sexual and aesthetic regimes."

I want to pursue Litvak's oppositional reading of one element of these regimes in the novel, but on different trajectories. As "connoisseurs of the stupid and the vulgar" (Litvak 40) and thus as "author-surrogates," Elizabeth Bennet and her father "demonstrate the classic middle-class technique ... of making oneself look classier than the rest of the middle class" (41). Mr. Bennet does so by making witty remarks at the expense of his wife and younger daughters, Elizabeth by having "the wit to *stylize* the vulgarity" (44) of her mother and sisters and thereby captivate Darcy and marry up. Certainly this heterosexual and cross-class marriage achieved by wit both enforces and validates a particular "sexual and aesthetic regime." This happy ending can be seen as slightly more complicated, however, when it is read on a series of feminist trajectories.

We begin with Mr. Bennet. It is important to recognize that his wit is gradually called into question as it is shown to betoken a failure of judgment. When he twits Elizabeth over Darcy's supposed indifference to her, the reader joins with her in faulting "his wit" (372), in large part because his earlier witticism, about Lydia's behavior having "frightened away some of [Elizabeth's] lovers" (257), has already indicated a misjudgment not only of the nature of Elizabeth's concern but of the extent and seriousness of

Lydia's "improprieties." In other words, "Mr. Bennet goes beyond seeing the absurdity of life; he *wants* life to be absurd" (Brown 154), and "his inadequacy as a father is directly related" to this cynical wit. That inadequacy becomes ever clearer as the detachment signaled by his wit extends into self-detachment from his paternal duty to Lydia; he gives Mr. Gardiner "full powers to act in [his] name" (317) in arranging Lydia's marriage settlement, and when he learns that his proto-son-in-law Darcy in fact arranged the settlement, he rejoices in thus being "save[d] a world of trouble and economy" (385).

To go thus far on this trajectory is to perform a feminist reading of the patriarch, but it is also a Proper Lady reading of Lydia and of "sexual regimes" that traffic in women, and as such it requires another, oppositional, trajectory. Lydia fits snugly into Darcy's category of "person[s] whose first object in life is a joke" (102): her "high animal spirits" (91) emerge in such "good jokes" (248) as dressing a man in women's clothes, while running off with Wickham is another "good joke" (307) and marrying him is "very good fun" (329). At this remark "Elizabeth could bear it no longer," and the reader is invited to join her in judging her sister as "Lydia still; untamed, unabashed, wild, noisy, and fearless" (328). Certainly, to paraphrase Kingsley Amis, "to invite [Lydia] round for the evening would not be lightly undertaken" (12–13), but an oppositional reading of Elizabeth's judgment reminds us that she too "dearly love[s] a joke" (102) and that she shares her sister's "high ... spirits" (130) and capacity for "laugh[ing] heartily" (208). More important, Elizabeth's (mis)judgments of Wickham replicate Lydia's: as Elizabeth herself admits, "We all were ... ready enough to admire him" (302) initially, and when Lydia opines that Wickham "never cared three straws about [Miss King]" (247), Elizabeth recognizes that "however incapable of such coarseness of *expression* herself, the coarseness of the *sentiment*" is a mirror of her own. What finally distinguishes Elizabeth from Lydia, in other words, is taste—eschewing "coarseness of expression" and learning to eschew "coarseness of sentiment." Elizabeth's concluding judgment of Lydia might be called a Proper Lady distaste: although she is apparently party to the machinations whereby Kitty is "carefully kept" (393) from Lydia, she does allow Lydia an occasional visit to Pemberley (395). This tolerance is in sharp contrast to Mr. Collins's view that the proper response to Lydia and Wickham's sin would be "never to admit them in your sight" (372), and to Lady Catherine de Bourgh's view that "the shades of Pemberley" (367) would be "polluted" by the presence of Lydia's sister. Between Mr. Bennet's culpable indifference on the one hand, and Mr. Collins's and Lady Catherine's ferocity on the other, stands Elizabeth's tolerant distaste.

I have already noted that the novel invites readers to ridicule Lady Catherine, and following that trajectory provides another take on the Proper

Lady. If Lady Catherine did not exist, it would be necessary to invent her, for improper class pride must be offloaded from Darcy onto her. (In much the same way, Bingley's "easy, unaffected manners" [58] are brought into high relief by his sisters' belief that even though the family fortune was acquired through trade, "associating with people of rank" nonetheless "entitled [them] to think well of themselves, and meanly of others" [63].) Darcy's early class pride—his considering himself "above his company" (58), his stuffy insistence on maintaining "a family library in such days as these" (84), his impossibly exaggerated notion of a "really accomplished" lady (85) and his censures of Elizabeth's "objectionable" relations (228) become as nothing to Lady Catherine's "self-importance" (197), her disciplining of cottagers "disposed to be quarrelsome, discontented or too poor" (203), the "impertinence" (198) of her questions about Elizabeth's accomplishments and her fear of Pemberley's pollution. The reformation of Darcy's manners is distinguished from the continued class arrogance of his aunt, a distinction brought home in the confrontation between Lady Catherine and Elizabeth. Where Darcy has been "properly humbled" (378) by Elizabeth's reproofs of his ungentlemanly behavior, Lady Catherine bridles when Elizabeth directs "such language as this" at herself (364).

That confrontation serves another function as well, by clarifying some class distinctions between Lady Catherine and Proper Lady Elizabeth. This is a complicated issue; although I have focused on and will return to Lady Catherine's overestimation of her class status, another and more oppositional reading is possible. From this point of view, despite her title, Lady Catherine sometimes functions as one of Austen's "marginal women" (Fraiman 168) who "voice anger and defiance that split open ostensibly decorous texts." If we attend to the question of entail in the novel, we can fold Mrs. Bennet into such an oppositional reading as well, for Lady Catherine's "I see no occasion for entailing estates from the female line" (198) is not so different from Mrs. Bennet's cry to her husband that "it is the hardest thing in the world, that your estate should be entailed away from your own children" (106). That is, we are certainly invited to dismiss Mrs. Bennet as "a woman of mean understanding [and] little information" (53) and to disregard Lady Catherine's "mere stateliness of money and rank" (196), but their shared concern with the entailing of property away from women reminds us of the Proper Lady's economic disadvantages. Yet we should also remember that the disposal of real estate is a problem peculiar to ladies; in other words, property is a sign of class status. This returns us to the confrontation between Lady Catherine and Elizabeth and the class distinctions it enables. Lady Catherine's disparaging remark about the Bennet "park" (362) reminds the reader of her class arrogance but also of the Bennets' status as landed gentry; her similarly disparaging remark about Elizabeth's class "sphere" (365) allows Elizabeth to state that as "a gentleman's daughter" (368), she is "equal" to Darcy, whereby she displays a proper class consciousness. In what is arguably her strongest speech of this sort, Elizabeth then states her "resolve to act in that manner, which will, in my own opinion, constitute my happiness, without reference to *you*" and without "one moment's concern" (367) for Lady Catherine's objections. With this insistence on "her own opinion," Elizabeth signals the shift postulated by Michel Foucault away from "deployments of alliance" or property in marriage arrangements and toward "deployments of sexuality" or individual desire. Yet she also signals that she deserves to marry up, in two ways. Where Lydia's deployments of sexuality led to seduction and were thus "antithetical to the social order" (Allen 438), Elizabeth's are directed toward marriage and thus affirm the social order. And if Elizabeth's desire does destabilize the class order figured by Lady Catherine, her resistance to that improper class pride demonstrates her proper class consciousness and distinguishes it from the toadying of her cousin Mr. Collins. Indeed, insofar as Elizabeth's behavior to Lady Catherine is more admirable than his, we might see it as another instance of Austen's Enlightenment feminism—her belief that women can act as moral agents without the aid of "such moral teachers as Mr. Collins" (Kirkham 84).

But "what becomes of the moral" (389), as Elizabeth asks in a slightly different context, if we turn from her quarrel with Lady Catherine to her romance with Pemberley? When Elizabeth dates her love for Darcy "from my first seeing his beautiful grounds at Pemberley" (382) and Jane entreats her to "be serious," the reader is invited to dismiss her statement as a joke. But an earlier remark—"she felt, that to be mistress of Pemberley might be something!" (267)—is harder to read: it too might be a joke, but the *style indirect libre* makes the tone uncertain, and this appreciation of Darcy's estate is also "admiration of his taste" (268), an admiration that the reader is invited to share. Similarly, when Darcy's housekeeper praises his conduct as a landlord and master, are we to agree with Mr. Gardiner that this is "excessive commendation" (270) arising from "family prejudice"? Or are we to agree with the opposite view—seemingly Elizabeth's, but stated in *style indirect libre* and hence not clearly so—that "what praise is more valuable than the praise of an intelligent servant?" (272). And what are we to think of the novel's prepenultimate paragraph, which underlines Elizabeth's position as mistress of Pemberley by stating that Darcy reconciled with Lady Catherine at "Elizabeth's persuasion" (395)? That is, if both Lydia and Lady Catherine now visit Pemberley, then the "multiplexity of relationships" (Deresiewicz 530) that have formed around Elizabeth's marriage functions as "something of an imagined community." But *imagined* is the key word, for this community is what Poovey calls an "aesthetic solution" (206) that "pushes aside" the novel's earlier "social realism and criticism."

An oppositional reading of this aesthetic solution would resist its closure, its happy ending in marriages. Such a reading would point to the fact that if the novel has earlier criticized Mr. Bennet's paternal failings, it concludes with a Lévi-Straussian exchange of women that functions to legitimate male homosocial power relations (Fraiman 173). Such a reading would also interrogate "the comfort and elegance of [the] family party at Pemberley" (392), not only by "investigat[ing] the contradictory, disparate elements" (Newman 195) from which this imagined community is made but also by noting the elements from which it is *not* made. Mr. Collins and Charlotte Lucas Collins do not figure in the imagined community of Pemberley, and I want to conclude with this exclusion, because it returns us to the issues of wit and ridicule, taste and distinction that are integral to an oppositional reading of *Pride and Prejudice*.

Mr. Collins is the butt of relentless ridicule in the novel, but at first blush one would not associate Charlotte with wit or, given her marriage to Collins, with taste. Yet her view of marriage suggests elements of both. If we postulate that Austen "wrote her novels anticipating that they would be read aloud" (Michaelson 65) and if we try to *hear* Charlotte's conversation with Elizabeth about marriage, it seems a piece of performative wit. To Charlotte,

> "Happiness in marriage is entirely a matter of chance. If the dispositions of the parties are ever so well known to each other, or ever so similar before-hand, it does not advance their felicity in the least. They always continue to grow sufficiently unlike afterwards to have their share of vexation; and it is better to know as little as possible of the defects of the person with whom you are to pass your life."
>
> "You make me laugh, Charlotte" [replies Elizabeth]; "but ... you know it is not sound, and that you would never act in this way yourself." (69–70)

Elizabeth's "you make me laugh" seems a cue to auditors—and readers—that Charlotte's argument is a tour de force of wit. It displays her "capacity for apt expression" (*OED* def. 7), and it is also witty in the sophistic sense of "'making the worse argument seem the better'" (qtd. in de Certeau 38). Certainly we already suspect (from Chapter 1) what we are later told explicitly (in Chapter 42): that the Bennets married on the principle Charlotte seems to espouse and thus that it *is* "the worse argument." And while Elizabeth's belief that Charlotte "would never act in this way" seems a dramatic irony, it is in fact correct, for Charlotte marries Collins knowing full well that he "was neither sensible nor agreeable" (163). She has also judged his "character, connections, and situation in life" (165) and thus has some grounds for being "convinced that my chance of happiness with him, is as fair" (166) as could be expected. We might add that her judgment in other areas of courtship proves correct. Her warning that "it is sometimes a disadvantage [for a woman] to be so very guarded" (68), for instance, is borne out by Darcy's failure to perceive in Jane "any symptom of peculiar regard" (228) for Bingley; while this failure may or may not be a misjudgment on Darcy's part, it certainly signals Charlotte's percipient recognition of "the uncomfortable limits of sexual signals" (Armstrong, "Politics" 172) available to a marriageable Proper Lady. Finally, the fact that Charlotte has weighed her own options and chosen marriage as her "pleasantest preservative from want" (163) suggests at least a degree of taste; although Mr. Collins is no prize, still we might say that Charlotte has sufficient cultural competence to make distinctions among "preservatives from want."

If Charlotte displays wit in both the "apt expression" and "good judgment" senses, Elizabeth's judgment of her friend's choice is called into question. Initially we are invited to agree with Elizabeth that Charlotte's match is "unsuitable" (166), that she has "sacrificed every better feeling to worldly advantage" and that she cannot be "tolerably happy." But we are then invited to agree with Jane that Elizabeth's language is "too strong" (174) when she accuses Charlotte of "selfishness" and "insensibility," and what we learn of Charlotte's marriage indicates that she *is* "tolerably happy." Most telling, when Elizabeth forgives Wickham for pursuing precisely the same kind of prudential marriage as Charlotte's, the hint that she was "less clear-sighted perhaps in his case" (186) undermines her harsh judgment of Charlotte. Of course, it is true that Elizabeth's marriage is a far happier ending than Charlotte's and that she earns that ending by correcting her tendency toward such faulty judgments. But it is also true that there is something smug and smothering about the "family party at Pemberley" (392), and that Austen authorizes the happy ending of *Pride and Prejudice* but also the oppositional readings I have been pursuing.

Works Cited

Allen, Dennis W. "No Love for Lydia: The Fate of Desire in *Pride and Prejudice.*" *Texas Studies in Literature and Language* 27.4 (Winter 1985): 425–43.

Amis, Kingsley. "What Became of Jane Austen?" In *What Became of Jane Austen? and Other Questions*. London: Panther-Granada, 1970. 11–15.

Armstrong, Isobel. "Politics, Pride, Prejudice and the Picturesque." In Clark, Robert, ed. *New Casebooks: "Sense and Sensibility" and "Pride and Prejudice."* New York: St. Martin's Press, 1994. 159–79.

Armstrong, Nancy. *Desire and Domestic Fiction: A Political History of the Novel.* New York: Oxford University Press, 1987.

Austen, Jane. *Pride and Prejudice.* 1813. London: Penguin, 1987.

Bourdieu, Pierre. *Distinction: A Social Critique of the Judgement of Taste.* 1984. Trans. Richard Nice. London: Routledge, 1989.

Brown, Julia Prewitt. "Necessary Conjunctions." In Clark, Robert, ed. *New Casebooks: "Sense and Sensibility" and "Pride and Prejudice."* New York: St. Martin's Press, 1994. 145–58.

Brownstein, Rachel M. "Irony and Authority." In Clark, Robert, ed. *New Casebooks: "Sense and Sensibility" and "Pride and Prejudice."* New York: St. Martin's Press, 1994. 180–92.

Butler, Marilyn. *Jane Austen and the War of Ideas.* Oxford: Clarendon, 1975.

Chapman, Robert W., ed. *Jane Austen's Letters to Her Sister Cassandra and Others.* 2 vols. Oxford: Clarendon, 1932.

Clark, Robert, ed. *New Casebooks: "Sense and Sensibility" and "Pride and Prejudice."* New York: St. Martin's Press, 1994.

Colby, Vineta. *Yesterday's Woman: Domestic Realism in the English Novel.* Princeton: Princeton University Press, 1974.

Cole, Lucinda and Richard Swartz. "'Why Should I Wish for Words?' Literacy, Articulation, and the Borders of Literary Culture." *At the Limits of Romanticism: Essays in Cultural, Feminist, and Materialist Criticism.* Ed. Mary A. Favret and Nicola J. Watson. Bloomington: Indiana University Press, 1994. 143–70.

Copeland, Edward, and Juliet McMaster, eds. *The Cambridge Companion to Jane Austen.* Cambridge: Cambridge University Press, 1997.

de Certeau, Michel. *The Practice of Everyday Life.* Trans. Steven Rendall. Berkeley: University of California Press, 1984.

Deresiewicz, William. *Community and Cognition in Pride and Prejudice." ELH* 64.2 (Summer 1997): 503–35.

Duckworth, Alastair M. *The Improvement of the Estate: A Study of Jane Austen's Novels.* Baltimore: Johns Hopkins University Press, 1971.

Duncan, Ian. *Modern Romance and Transformations of the Novel: The Gothic, Scott, Dickens.* Cambridge: Cambridge University Press, 1992.

Evans, Mary. *Jane Austen and the State.* London: Tavistock, 1987.

Fergus, Jan. "The Professional Woman Writer." In Edward Copeland and Juliet McMaster, eds. *The Cambridge Companion to Jane Austen.* Cambridge: Cambridge University Press, 1997. 12–31.

Ferris, Ina. *The Achievement of Literary Authority: Gender, History, and the Waverley Novels.* Ithaca, NY: Cornell University Press, 1991.

Foucault, Michel. *The History of Sexuality. Volume 1: An Introduction.* Trans. Robert Hurley. New York: Vintage, 1977.

Fraiman, Susan. "The Humiliation of Elizabeth Bennet." In *Refiguring the Father: New Feminist Readings of Patriarchy.* Ed. Patricia Yaeger and Beth Kowalski-Wallace. Carbondale: Southern Illinois University Press, 1989. 168–87.

Galperin, William. "The Picturesque, the Real, and the Consumption of Jane Austen." *Wordsworth Circle* 28.1 (Winter 1997): 19–27.

Goodwin, Sarah Webster. "Knowing Better: Feminism and Utopian Discourse in *Pride and Prejudice*, *Villette*, and 'Babette's Feast.'" In *Feminism, Utopia, and Narrative*. Ed. Libby Falk Jones and Goodwin. Knoxville: University of Tennessee Press, 1990. 1–20.

Greene, Donald. "Jane Austen and the Peerage." *PMLA* 68 (1953): 1017–31.

Johnson, Claudia L. *Jane Austen: Women, Politics, and the Novel*. Chicago: University of Chicago Press, 1988.

Kelly, Gary. "Religion and Politics." In Edward Copeland and Juliet McMaster, eds. *The Cambridge Companion to Jane Austen*. Cambridge: Cambridge University Press, 1997. 149–69.

Kirkham, Margaret. *Jane Austen, Feminism and Fiction*. 1983. New York: Methuen, 1986.

Kowalski-Wallace, Beth. "Home Economics: Domestic Ideology in Maria Edgeworth's *Belinda*." *Eighteenth Century: Theory and Interpretation* 29.3 (Fall 1988): 242–62.

Lacour, Claudia Brodsky. "Austen's *Pride and Prejudice* and Hegel's 'Truth in Art': Concept, Reference, and History." *ELH* 59.3 (Fall 1992): 597–623.

Litvak, Joseph. "Delicacy and Disgust, Mourning and Melancholia, Privilege and Perversity." *Pride and Prejudice*. *Qui Parle* 6.1 (1992): 35–51.

Michaelson, Patricia Howell. "Reading *Pride and Prejudice*." *Eighteenth-Century Fiction* 3.1 (October 1990): 65–76.

Moir, George. "Modern Romance and Novel." 1842. In *Victorian Criticism of the Novel*. Ed. Edwin M. Eigner and George J. Worth. Cambridge: Cambridge University Press, 1985.

Newman, Karen. "Can This Marriage Be Saved: Jane Austen Makes Sense of an Ending." In Robert Clark, ed. *New Casebooks: "Sense and Sensibility" and "Pride and Prejudice."* New York: St. Martin's Press. 193–212.

Newton, Judith Lowder. *Women, Power, and Subversion: Social Strategies in British Fiction, 1778–1860* (1981). London: Methuen, 1985.

Poovey, Mary. *The Proper Lady and the Woman Writer: Ideology as Style in the Works of Mary Wollstonecraft, Mary Shelley, and Jane Austen*. Chicago: University of Chicago Press, 1984.

Roberts, Warren. *Jane Austen and the French Revolution*. New York: St. Martin's Press, 1979.

Stewart, Maaja A. *Domestic Realities and Imperial Fictions: Jane Austen's Novels in Eighteenth-Century Contexts*. Athens: University of Georgia Press, 1993.

Todd, Janet. *The Sign of Angellica: Women, Writing, and Fiction, 1660–1800*. New York: Columbia University Press, 1989.

Watson, Nicola J. *Revolution and the Form of the British Novel, 1790–1825: Intercepted Letters, Interrupted Seductions*. Oxford: Clarendon, 1994.

JOE BRAY

The Source of "Dramatized Consciousness": Richardson, Austen, and Stylistic Influence

To his observation that Henry James was, like George Eliot, "a great admirer of Jane Austen," F. R. Leavis adds the following footnote: "He can't have failed to note with interest that *Emma* fulfills, by anticipation, a prescription of his own: everything is presented through Emma's dramatized consciousness, and the essential effects depend on that" (10n). Perhaps he has in mind passages in *Emma* such as the following:

> "Have you any idea of Mr. Knightley's returning your affection?"

> "Yes," replied Harriet modestly, but not fearfully—"I must say that I have."

> Emma's eyes were instantly withdrawn: and she sat silently meditating, in a fixed attitude, for a few minutes. A few minutes were sufficient for making her acquainted with her own heart. A mind like her's, once opening to suspicion, made rapid progress. She touched—she admitted—she acknowledged the whole truth. Why was it so much worse that Harriet should be in love with Mr. Knightley, than with Frank Churchill? Why was the evil so

From *Style* 35, no. 1 (Spring 2001), pp. 18–33. © 2001 *Style*.

> dreadfully increased by Harriet's having some hope of a return?
> It darted through her, with the speed of an arrow, that Mr.
> Knightley must marry no one but herself! (335)[1]

Here Harriet's supposedly reciprocated feelings for Knightley force Emma
to acknowledge the truth of her own heart. "A few minutes" of reflection
are enough for revelation to be reached. Notice that the trajectory by which
Emma arrives at the truth, from touching, to admitting, to acknowledging,
is first described indirectly, from the vantage-point of an external narrator,
and then presented more directly, as the narrative enters into her mind. It is
Emma who asks herself "Why was it so much worse that Harriet should be
in love with Mr. Knightley, than with Frank Churchill?" and "Why was the
evil so dreadfully increased by Harriet's having some hope of a return?" Her
consciousness could be said to be "dramatized" here if by this is understood
the narrative's attempt to re-enact, rather than describe externally, the
character's actual thought-processes. From "Why was it so much worse"
onwards the reader is granted intimate access to Emma's thoughts and
anxieties, leading up to her final moment of anagnorisis. Notice, though, that
the narrator's perspective is partly retained through the use of the past tense
and the third person; Emma's thoughts would have been "Why is it so much
worse [...]?" and "Mr. Knightley must marry no one but me!"

Though it is going too far to claim that "everything" in the novel
is presented in this way, there are certainly many other instances of the
narrative slipping into Emma's consciousness. Take her first encounter with
Mr. Martin as she and Harriet bump into him on the Donwell road:

> Emma was not sorry to have such an opportunity of survey; and
> walking a few yards forward, while they talked together, soon
> her made her quick eye sufficiently acquainted with Mr. Robert
> Martin. His appearance was very neat, and he looked like a
> sensible young man, but his person had no other advantage; and
> when he came to be contrasted with gentlemen, she thought he
> must lose all the ground he had gained in Harriet's inclination.
> Harriet was not insensible of manner; she had voluntarily noticed
> her father's gentleness with admiration as well as wonder. Mr.
> Martin looked as if he did not know what manner was. (28)

Emma's first impression of Mr. Martin is heavily influenced by her prejudices
against his social background and her plans for Harriet. In her mind he is
simply an obstacle to Harriet's elevated future, and she is already rehearsing
the grounds on which he will be supplanted. The final two sentences must,

from the context, come from Emma's perspective rather than the narrator's. "She thought" is a strong hint that representation of her consciousness will follow, and "her father," referring to Mr. Woodhouse, a clue that her perspective predominates. With "Mr. Martin looked as if he did not know what manner was," the narrative must be inside Emma's mind, even though no linguistic signals have explicitly marked the point of entry, and again the past tense remains as an indirect feature. A practiced Austen reader would certainly recognize the shift in perspective, knowing that none of her narrators would be likely to make such a definitive, negative judgment against a character who has only just been introduced. Rather than being marked formally then, the predominance of the character's consciousness here is dependent on what Fludernik calls "the *content* and the *context* of a passage" (*Fictions* 198).[2]

Such slippage inside a character's consciousness has been frequently detected in Austen's novels. Lascelles, for example, argues that between *Sense and Sensibility* and *Persuasion* Austen "has learnt to say what she has to say through her books, above all through the medium of her characters' consciousness" (93). She charts Austen's gradual mastery of the "technique for using the consciousness of her characters as a means of communication with the reader" (194). More recent criticism has also highlighted this technique: Gard, for example, identifies both Austen and Flaubert as "great innovators" in "the rendering of the action through the consciousness of the characters" (148). The style, which, in Lodge's words, "allows the novelist to give the reader intimate access to a character's thoughts" (126), has attracted a wide variety of names, including most commonly "free indirect style," which is the closest translation of the French term first used by Bally in 1912, "style indirect libre."[3] For Hough, "free indirect style" is a concentration of what he calls "colored narrative," by which he means "narrative or reflection or observation more or less deeply colored by a particular character's point of view" (204). He confirms the evidence of the first example above by noting that in *Emma* "passages of colored narrative [...] characteristically occur in scenes of undeception, of anagnorisis, where things are at last recognized for what they are" (213).

The examples from *Emma* suggest that free indirect style typically involves a combination of language "colored by a particular character's point of view" with the third person and past tense associated with indirect report, or the narrator's perspective. Leech and Short divide the style into "free indirect speech," in which a character's spoken words are represented, and "free indirect thought," which is concerned only with his or her consciousness, claiming that the two share "formal differentia." Their "characteristic features in the novel" are "almost always the presence of third-person pronouns and past tense, which correspond with the form of narrative report and indicate indirectness, along with a number of features both positive and negative indicating freeness" (325). The combination of features associated with the narrator with those associated with the character in free indirect style has led some critics to claim that, in Pascal's words, "we hear in 'style indirect libre' a dual voice, which, through vocabulary, sentence structure, and intonation subtly fuses the two voices of the character and the narrator" (26).[4] According to Pascal, this "dual voice" is capable of generating a variety of effects: "The duality of narrator and character [...] may be heard as a tone of irony, or sympathy, of negation or approval, underlying the statement of the character" (17). In Austen's novels, and *Emma* in particular, the mixture of narrator's and character's perspectives frequently achieves tones of irony, as, in Lodge's words, "the authorial narrator mediates virtually all the action through the consciousness of an unreliable focalizing character" (128). In the above examples, the presence of the narrator's voice undercuts Emma's realization of her love for Knightley and her assessment of Mr. Martin, suggesting that the first is overdue and the second too sudden and prejudiced. It may dart through Emma, "with the speed of an arrow," that "Mr. Knightley must marry no one but herself," yet her feelings have long been clear to the discerning reader, for whom the wonder is that she has hidden them from herself for so long. The reader can also recognize that her "quick eye" is too quick to judge that Mr. Martin's "appearance was very neat, and he looked like a sensible young man, but his person had no other advantage," and that he "looked as if he did not know what manner was." In both cases, the mingling of the narrator's voice with the character's consciousness allows the possibility of an alternative, ironic, perspective on her thoughts.

There has been a critical consensus regarding with whom this style, described by Doody as "of the highest importance in the history of the novel" (287), originates. Gard describes "that flickering and subtle immediacy in representation of consciousness" as "one of Jane Austen's great gifts to the English novel" (56), and Lodge too claims that she "was the first English novelist" to use "free indirect speech" "extensively" (126). Other critics of the style agree; Pascal's view is that "when it first appears as a prominent and continuous feature in a novel, in Goethe and Jane Austen, it is already used with the greatest skill and propriety" (34). It is not my intention here to question this fact, but rather to seek a possible explanation for it. It is indeed the case that no writer in English employs free indirect style "extensively" and "continuously" before Austen. Yet, in order to emphasize her innovativeness, critics have usually been content to leave it at this. It is not denying Austen her creativity to question the belief that this vital stylistic technique arose spontaneously, and to look for immediate eighteenth-century sources of her assured probing into the consciousness of her characters. All accounts of free indirect style that open, abruptly, at the beginning of the nineteenth century need to consider Bakhtin's view that "New forms of artistic vision take shape slowly, over centuries; a single epoch only creates the optimal conditions for the final maturation and realization of a new form" (30). My concern is to establish what Bakhtin calls the "genre sources" or "genre contacts" of the dramatized consciousness that is such a pervasive feature of Austen's novels. As he writes: "The fuller and more concrete our knowledge of an artist's *genre contacts*, the more profound will be our penetration into the characteristics of his form and the corrector our understanding of the interrelationships of tradition and innovation within that form" (131).

This is not to say that no attention has been paid to pre-nineteenth-century examples of free indirect style. Several isolated instances have been found; for example in Fanny Burney's novels by Doody. Some seventeenth-century examples have been unearthed too; in *Grace Abounding* by Adamson and in Aphra Behn by both Fludernik ("Linguistic Signals") and Wright. Most of these studies are concerned with free indirect speech, rather than free indirect thought, my concern here. Furthermore, though these analyses do produce some clear examples, what they all lack is an attempt to link their findings with later incarnations of free indirect style in Austen or elsewhere. Thus, as Pascal complains, there is no "continuous tradition of its use and transmission as a literary technique" (34). No one has established an immediate "genre source" for the dramatized consciousness in Austen's novels, traced a continuity with earlier writing, and shown exactly how the style might have developed.

These gaps may result from the fact that one particular genre has hardly been examined at all in this connection. Those searching for the roots of dramatized consciousness have very rarely paid any attention to the eighteenth-century epistolary novel, perhaps because of an assumption that the style cannot occur in the first person at all.[5] Yet first-person narrators can dramatize their own consciousness when recalling their own past thoughts. As Cohn notes, "autobiographical narrators also have inner lives (their own past inner lives) to communicate," and "*retro*spection into a consciousness, though less 'magical,' is no less important a component of first-person novels than *in*spection of a consciousness is in third-person novels" (*Transparent Minds* 14). As a complement to her third-person "narrated monologue," Cohn proposes a first-person "self-narrated monologue," claiming that "The relationship of the narrating self to the experiencing self in these self-narrated monologues corresponds exactly to the relationship of a narrator to his character in a figural third-person novel: the narrator momentarily identifies with his past self, giving up his temporally distanced vantage point and cognitive privilege for his past time-bound bewilderments and vacillations" (167). As I will demonstrate in the rest of this essay, this ability of first-person narrators to identify with, or dramatize, their own past selves has important consequences for the history of free indirect style. The "duality of narrator and character" that generates the style's key meanings, including irony, may have part of its origins in a very different kind of duality. In the first-person form of free indirect style the two, subtly fused, voices belong not to ironically mismatched perspectives of narrator and character, but to temporally conflicting selves of the same character.

For examples of "*retro*spections into a consciousness" that bear directly on "the dramatization of consciousness" in Austen I will turn to Richardson's third epistolary novel, *The History of Sir Charles Grandison* (1753–54). This choice is not arbitrary; Austen's familiarity with *Grandison* has been a critical commonplace ever since Henry Austen's "Biographical Notice" of his sister written shortly after her death in 1817. It is the only novel to be picked out by name in his discussion of his sister's reading: "Richardson's power of creating, and preserving the consistency of his characters, as particularly exemplified in 'Sir Charles Grandison,' gratified the natural discrimination of her mind, whilst her taste secured her from the errors of his prolix style and tedious narrative" (6–7). Further testimony to her fondness for the novel comes from her nephew James Edward Austen-Leigh, who in his memoir of his aunt writes that "Her knowledge of Richardson's works was such as no one is likely again to acquire, now that the multitude and the merits of our light literature have called off the attention of readers from that great master. Every circumstance narrated in Sir Charles Grandison [...] was familiar to her" (109–10).

The influence of *Grandison* is often signalled explicitly in Austen's writing. Her short play *Sir Charles Grandison* is shot through with detailed satirical references to specific incidents in the novel,[6] and it is also the target of frequent allusions, both oblique and direct, in the rest of her juvenilia.[7] Critics have often commented on what Barker (13) calls the "pervasive" influence of *Grandison* on her mature writing, though this influence has usually been described in broad generalizations rather than specified precisely.[8] Some tangible connections have been drawn by Harris, who demonstrates the novel's "prevalent" influence on *Sense and Sensibility* by identifying "three themes common to both novels": marriage to a rake, "marriages of persons of unequal years" and "the superiority of prudent second attachments over romantic first ones." Her discussion of its influence on *Pride and Prejudice* centers more on character; she believes that "Darcy's character derives from Richardson's hero" (110), and that "Harriet

Byron's frankness, her fault-finding in her suitor, her studying of character, and her humbled repentance of her satiric tongue are what make Elizabeth interesting" (102). Another comparison between the novels is offered by Fergus, for whom "The most significant connection between *Pride and Prejudice* and *Grandison* lies in their common concern with the accuracy and persistence of first impressions" (74).

Yet I believe that attention to themes and character does not fully bring out the importance of Richardson's third novel for Austen. A stylistic perspective can give more concrete substance to the novel's "pervasive" influence. I agree with Neumann that *Grandison*'s "influence on the eighteenth- and nineteenth-century novel—including its contribution to FID [free indirect discourse]'s subsequent widespread use—is greater than its current readership reflects" (134). In particular, the roots of the dramatized consciousness handled so skillfully by Austen in the third person can be traced back to the first-person narratives of Harriet Byron, Richardson's most reflective, retrospecting heroine,[9] as her conflation of past and present selves leads into the "dual voice" of narrator and character in Austen. The representation of consciousness no doubt underwent many developments and transformations between Richardson and Austen, and positing a straight line of influence is too easy. Yet in claiming *Grandison* as one possible source for the mastery of Austen's mature free indirect style, I am taking a first step toward establishing a "continuous tradition of the use and transmission" of the technique that, according to Flavin, "result[s] in a greater psychological depth of character" (137).

A step toward locating free indirect style in *Grandison* has been taken by Neumann, in support of a claim that "free indirect discourse is already widespread in eighteenth-century fiction" (113). Like most of the other treatments of pre-nineteenth-century free indirect style mentioned above, Neumann deals only with free indirect speech, "out of which, I hypothesize, free indirect thought evolved" (114). She shows how characters in the novel frequently quote each others' and their own words in their letters, often without explicit attribution, and argues that this technique reflects not only "the novel's instruction in how to assess characters" (126), but also "how contemporary readers could, or did, quote and discuss their own conversations and reading" (127). Though the way that *Grandison*'s letter-writers recall their own "past time-bound bewilderments and vacillations" is not Neumann's concern, her discussion of the features of free indirect speech in the novel does have implications for the formally similar free indirect thought. Her confirmation that "free indirect discourse is indeed 'double-voiced'" (113) in *Grandison* is especially relevant to my purposes. She notes that italics are a common means of identifying which words are being quoted, and concludes that "FID [Free indirect discourse] with italics in eighteenth-century fiction supports the 'double-voice' theory by modelling how the subjective and evaluative expressions of one character can interweave with those of another" (116). Crucially for her this phenomenon "demonstrates incontrovertibly that the double-voice theory of reported discourse does not depend on a narrator for its second voice" (118).

This finding is supported when examples of free indirect thought in the novel are considered. *Grandison*'s heroine and main letter-writer, Harriet Byron, frequently recalls her "past time-bound bewilderments and vacillations," identifying with her "past self." In volume VI she recounts how she was repeatedly pressed by Sir Charles, following their engagement, to name an early day for their wedding. He proposes a fortnight hence, she a month, to which he insists that he be allowed to return in a fortnight to take up residence with her:

> My heart *wanted*, I thought, to oblige him; but to allow him to return sooner, as he was to take up his abode with us, what was that, but, in effect, complying with his first proposal? (6: 197)[10]

Here Harriet remembers a conflict between her heart and her sense of what was right. Unable to come to a resolution, she only chides Sir Charles for being too "urgent" and asks permission to retire and consider it further. As Harriet recalls her vacillation and inner debate, she attempts to re-enact her actual thought-processes at the time, to dramatize her past consciousness. While the italicization of '*wanted*' hints at the strength of her heart's desire, the return of her moral propriety after the pivotal semicolon is signalled by the two adversative "buts." Her argument for resisting an early date is encased in a reasoned, intricate syntax and more formal vocabulary: "abode," "complying." Though this side of the debate is more developed and carries more rhetorical weight, the final question mark indicates in Harriet's present narration her past vacillating and deferral of a final decision.

Harriet's present description here in her letter to Lucy thus becomes tinged with past feeling, as her remembered thoughts are dramatically re-enacted in her narrative. The reliving of past debate and emotion is in fact a constant feature of Harriet's first-person narration in *Grandison*, often with the result that her past and present selves, like the voices of narrator and character in *Emma*, are conflated and hard to distinguish. Both Richardson's and Austen's varieties of free indirect style offer evidence in support of Couturier's view that its "two selves" are so complexly intertwined that "ultimately, the reader can never separate completely the one from the other" (27). In one letter in volume 3 Harriet makes this intertwining explicit, suggesting that her past emotion even becomes greater as she re-experiences it in the present: "I am not generally so much affected at the moment when any-thing unhappy befalls me, as I am upon reflexion, when I extend, compare, and weigh consequences" (3: 173). Such extending, comparing, and weighing runs through her letters, as her feelings for Sir Charles are recalled in reflective, often emotive, detail. In another letter to Lucy she exclaims "what a *rememberer*, if I may make a word, is the heart!—Not a circumstance escapes it" (4: 60).

Whilst the "duality of narrator and character" frequently creates an ironic tone in Austen's third-person form of free indirect style, the conflation of past and present selves in *Grandison*'s first-person letters draws attention to the difficulties of letter-writing itself. Richardson's third novel, like his second, focuses, in Keymer's words, "first and foremost on the experience of *writing*" (xvi). Harriet often finds her heart's memories hard to describe. In volume 6 she tells Sir Charles's sister of her mixed emotions when it finally became clear that he had disentangled himself from Clementina and was free to marry her:

> I felt such a variety of sensibilities in my heart, as I never felt before, sensibilities mixed with wonder; and I was sometimes ready to doubt whether I were not in a reverie; whether indeed I was in this world, or another; whether I was Harriet Byron—I know not how to describe what I felt in my now fluttering, now rejoicing, now dejected heart. (4: 26)

Here Harriet finds it difficult to isolate her past, confused emotions and recount them clearly to Lady Grandison. Her "past time-bound bewilderments and vacillations" are represented directly, as she recalls doubting "whether I were not in a reverie; whether indeed I was in this world, or another; whether I was Harriet Byron." This triple vacillating is mirrored in her description of her "now fluttering, now rejoicing, now dejected" heart. The repetition of "now" helps to recreate in Harriet's present writing her past conflict of emotions, while the dashes in this passage add to the sense of fragmented and inchoate bewilderment she is attempting to convey. Harriet's consciousness is again dramatized, as she recreates in her stumbling letter to Lucy the confusion of her actual thought-processes at the time, again conflating, or subtly fusing, her past and present selves.

Harriet's first-person retrospection thus invites parallels with the way Austen's third-person narrative reveals, or "inspects," Emma's thoughts. Compare Emma's piercing moment of anagnorisis: "It darted through her, with the speed of an arrow, that Mr. Knightley must marry no one but herself!" with Harriet's reflections on Sir Charles's "glorious benevolence" and "enlarged sentiments" as demonstrated in one particular conversation with her grandmother in volume 6:

> What a happy, thrice happy woman, thought I, several times, must she be, who shall be considered as a partaker of his goodness! Who shall be blest not only *in* him, but *for* him; and be his, and he hers, to all eternity! (205)

There are clear similarities between Harriet's recognition of the blessings of marrying Sir Charles and Emma's realization that she "must" marry Knightley. The self-revelations of both heroines are shown directly at these pivotal moments, as their thoughts enter, without explicit attribution, into the narrative. The darting exclamation mark that dramatizes Emma's sudden self-recognition is matched by the two exclamation marks indicating Harriet's excess of emotion. The impression of thoughts rushing through Harriet's consciousness is also recreated by the lack of main verb in her second exclamation, which is, like "who shall be considered as a partaker of his goodness," a relative clause dependant on "she." Yet, as a result of their very different personalities, there are also contrasts in the ways their two consciences are represented at these moments of crisis. In contrast to Emma's sudden, painful admission of "the whole truth," Harriet's recollection of her past, excited thoughts is carefully and rhetorically structured. Her second exclamation in this example is divided by the semicolon into two halves, the first of which includes a subtle contrast marked emphatically by italicization, and the second of which reverses the idea of the understood "she" being "his": "and he hers." While Emma's self-centeredness is apparent in her conclusion that "Mr. Knightley must marry no one but herself!," Harriet characteristically remembers thinking not of herself but of the "thrice happy woman" who will marry Sir Charles, thus distancing herself from this prospect by the use of the third person. Furthermore, in contrast to Emma's instantaneous self-recognition, Harriet's thoughts on the joys of the "thrice happy woman" are repeated "several times," in line with her more reflective, less spontaneous nature. Yet despite these differences in their thought-processes, there are clear points of connection between Harriet's entry into her past self and the third-person narrator's dramatization of Emma's consciousness.

A final comparison can clarify. In volume 5, Lady Grandison sends Harriet a number of her brother's letters to Dr. Bartlett that reveal his traumatic dealings with Lady Clementina and her family. Harriet's reply thanks her for the letters and recalls her inner struggles as she read them:

Were I to tell you what I thought, what were my emotions, as I
read now his generous pity for the Count of Belvedere—Now
his affectionate and respectful address to the noble Lady—Her
agitations of mind, previous to the delivery of her paper to him—
That paper, the contents so greatly surpassing all that I had read
of woman! Yet so much of a piece with the conduct she shewed,
when the struggle between her Religion and her Love, cost her
her reason. His delicacy, yet equal steadiness, in his religion.—In
short, the whole of his conduct and hers, in the various lights in
which they appeared in the different conversations with her, with
her family—Were I to tell you, I say, what I thought, and what
were my emotions, as I read, a volume would not be sufficient;
nor know I what measure would contain my tears. (5: 204–05)

Again there is ambiguity between past and present selves here as Harriet's
past agitation is recaptured in the fragmentary nature of her first-person
narrative. She dramatizes another remembered conflict, this time between
her feelings for Sir Charles and her admiration of Lady Clementina, her
potential rival for his love. Her emotions as she read are re-enacted, as
she recalls being affected by his noble qualities in turn: "now his generous
pity for the Count of Belvedere—Now his affectionate and respectful
address to the noble Lady." Harriet's repetition of "now," bringing to mind
her memory of "my now fluttering, now rejoicing, now dejected heart,"
again recreates past transitions and abruptions of thought in her present
writing. The punctuation assists in the dramatization, as the exclamation
mark and dashes in this passage help to suggest the fevered and disordered
state of Harriet's mind both at the time and in the present. The confused
grammatical structure adds to this impression; after "as I read now his
generous pity," the narrative jumps to other objects of her reading, each
connected to other only by dashes, until mention of Lady Clementina's
paper leads Harriet into two parenthetical asides, the first an exclamation
on the paper itself, the second a general comment on Lady Clementina's
virtuous conduct. Both of these interruptions lack a main verb, as does
the next segment between full stops: "His delicacy, yet equal steadiness,
in his religion," which is another object governed by the initial "I read
now." Harriet then attempts to summarize all of her jumbled thoughts "In
short," before repeating the opening of the first sentence and, after much
circuitous diversion, finally arriving at its main clause: "Were I to tell you, I
say, what I thought, and what were my emotions, as I read, a volume would
not be sufficient." The incoherence and muddle of the syntax dramatizes
Harriet's consciousness both as she read the letters and as she attempts to

recount her emotions, again drawing attention to the difficulties of writing the heart.

Compare Elizabeth's reaction to the letter from her aunt near the end of *Pride and Prejudice* that sets out the part Darcy played in her sister's marriage:

> The contents of this letter threw Elizabeth into a flutter of spirits, in which it was difficult to determine whether pleasure or pain bore the greatest share. The vague and unsettled suspicions which uncertainty had produced of what Mr. Darcy might have been doing to forward her sister's match, which she had feared to encourage, as an exertion of goodness too great to be probable, and at the same time dreaded to be just, from the pain of obligation, were proved beyond their greatest extent to be true! (262)

Though Elizabeth's "flutter of spirits" certainly seems less agitated than Harriet's inner struggle, there are clear similarities between the third-person narrator's inspection of Elizabeth's consciousness and Harriet's retrospection of her own. Like Harriet, Elizabeth is thrown into confusion by reading about the good conduct of the man with whom she is gradually realizing she is in love. She too is torn between emotions, pleasure at Darcy's intervention and pain for the embarrassment and obligation she and her family now owe him. This inner conflict, though less anguished than Harriet's, is also dramatized. The "flutter" in her mind is matched in the narrative by the convoluted, complex sentence that begins "The vague and unsettled suspicions," a sentence that is "vague and unsettled" itself. It wanders into two long relative clauses, the first of which has "uncertainty" as its subject and is governed by a conditional verb, the second of which has two qualifying phrases ("as an exertion of goodness too great to be probable," "from the pain of obligation"), before finally arriving at its main, passive verb: "were proved." By this point the narrative has slipped unobtrusively into Elizabeth's consciousness, as "the *content* and the *context*" of this sentence suggest her perspective. Though the narrator's "voice" is retained through the third person and past tense, some subtle dramatization of Elizabeth's emotion is achieved. Her "flutter," by turns excited and painful, is partly captured by the hyperbole of "beyond their greatest extent" and the final exclamation mark. Recall Harriet's "That paper, the contents so greatly surpassing all that I had read of woman!"

According to Tanner, "James learned as much from Jane Austen as Jane Austen did from Richardson. Which is to say, a great deal" (9). Included in both "great deals," I believe, is a vital stylistic technique. In his Preface to the New York Edition of *Roderick Hudson*, his first novel to be published in book form, James writes: "The center of interest throughout *Roderick* is in Rowland Mallet's consciousness, and the drama is the very drama of that consciousness" (460). As has frequently been noted, the "drama" with which James represents the thoughts of all his other central characters owes much to Austen's dramatization of consciousness such as Emma Woodhouse's and Elizabeth Bennet's. What has been less well-observed though, and is of perhaps equal importance in the development of the novel, is the fact that it was from Richardson, amongst others, that Austen learnt how to dramatize consciousness in this way. Harriet Byron's representation of her past and present selves and their interaction has significant, as yet unappreciated consequences for the nineteenth- and twentieth-century English novel. She is connected to descendants such as Elizabeth Bennet by more than just "frankness" and "fault-finding in her suitor," for the ways in which their consciousness are dramatized, in the first person in Harriet's case and in the third in Elizabeth's, suggest a stylistic link between them. Richardson's attempt to allow intimate access to Harriet's mind, to re-enact in her narrative the twists and turns of her past thought-processes grants a new perspective on the apparently spontaneous origins of the style that is so central to the achievement of Austen's art. Identifying the epistolary novel, and the neglected *Grandison* in particular, as one "genre source" for the dramatized consciousness that pervades the later history of the third-person novel, helps both to clarify the balance of "tradition and innovation" in Austen's novels and to specify just what she learnt from her "great master."

Notes

1. The recent Penguin Edition of Austen's novels (Textual Adviser: Claire Lamont) has highlighted discrepancies in R. W. Chapman's Clarendon edition of 1923, which has been the standard text since its publication. It has been shown not only that Chapman took the second editions of *Sense and Sensibility* and *Mansfield Park* as his copy-texts, but also that he made some silent corrections to Austen's punctuation and grammar. The new Penguin Edition returns to the first editions of all the novels and edits them afresh (for a full justification see Lamont's introduction to each of the new editions). To support this policy, I quote from the new Penguin Editions of both *Emma* and *Pride and Prejudice*.

2. This is not to say that in other instances there may not be clear linguistic markers of this style. In the considerable debate that has sprung up around the question of how formally this technique should be described, I favor a middle ground of the kind taken up by Bronzwaer: "In many cases, such passages show a certain predilection for certain stylistic phenomena that do not in themselves add up to a set of linguistic markers of free indirect style. In other cases, dependence on the context may be the only pointer to free indirect style" (50).

3. Some of the other names used for the style include (in chronological order): "erlebte Rede" (Lorck, 1921), "represented speech" (Jespersen, 1924), "narrated monologue" (Cohn, 1966), "quasi-direct discourse" (Volosinov, 1973), "represented speech and thought" (Banfield, 1978), "free indirect discourse" (McHale, 1978) and "empathetic narrative" (Adamson, 1994). Each implies a slightly different take on the style's function, as Cohn acknowledges: "But if these critical topoi allow one to recognize an identical thing under different names, the names themselves are symptomatic of different attitudes towards the thing" ("Narrated Monologue" 171).

4. Some critics have taken this even further; Flavin for example argues that in some passages in *Mansfield Park* Austen layers "three voices" (139) as the effect of speech on a character's consciousness is presented, via the narrator. Flavin even claims intriguingly (though without providing evidence) that "in Austen's last novel, *Persuasion*, even greater complexity is achieved as four voices are layered" (139).

5. Chief among those who have argued that the style cannot occur in the first person is Hamburger: "the narrated monologue and even straight monologue—in short, the formation of third-person subjectivity—cannot occur in the first-person novel" (316). Others, while not denying that the style can have a first-person form limit it to the third person in their definitions (see, for example, Chatman [201] and Ehrlich [5]), while others unnecessarily restrict their discussion to third-person examples (see, for example, Doody's neglect of *Evelina*).

6. These are discussed by Southam in his Introduction to his 1980 edition of the work. He perceptively describes this "miniature play" as a "*reductio ad absurdum*," a pin-prick to deflate *Grandison*'s epic proportions and the elaboration and leisureliness of its procedure (21).

7. Examples of direct reference: in "Evelina" (*Volume the Third*) Maria is given an opportunity "of shining in that favorite character of Sir Charles Grandison's, a nurse" (186), and in "Jack and Alice" (*Volume the First*) Lady Williams "like the great Sir Charles Grandison scorned to deny herself when at Home" (15). Other, more subtle, allusions are detected by Harris in her appendix "*Sir Charles Grandison* in the juvenilia."

8. See for example Southam (3), Jack (177), McKillop (213), and Honan (172).

9. Compared with Harriet, both Pamela and Clarissa tend to concentrate more in their letters on their present responses and reactions, favoring the style described by Richardson in a letter of 1756 to Lady Bradshaigh as "this way of writing, to the moment" (Forster Collection, vol. 11, f. 80). The Preface to the first edition of *Clarissa* acknowledges that it abounds "with what may be called *instantaneous* Descriptions and Reflections" (1: v). Take for example Clarissa's last letter from Harlowe Place: "It would be hard, if I, who have held it out so sturdily to my father and uncles, should not—But he is at the garden-door—[...] I was mistaken!—How may noises *un*-like, be made *like* what one fears!—Why flutters the fool so!" (2: 305).

10. The study of Richardson's novels is complicated by his obsessive desire to keep revising all of them; as Eaves and Kimpel observe, "Richardson, who read little else, read his own works constantly and seldom read them without changing something" (91). In all there are five editions of *Grandison* in which he is known to have had a hand; here reasons of space unfortunately prevent a thorough comparison of editions, and thus I stick to citing the first, of 1753–54. Though no manuscript evidence is available to help determine to what extent Richardson's intentions regarding the textual detail of the novel were met, his role as his own printer, supervising each of his novels through his own presses, suggests that he had the final responsibility for both "substantives" and "accidentals."

Works Cited

Adamson, Sylvia. "From Empathetic Deixis to Empathetic Narrative: Stylisation and (De) Subjectivisation as Processes of Language Change." *Transactions of the Philological Society* 92.1 (1994): 55–88.

Austen, Henry. "Biographical Notice of the Author." Jane Austen, *Northanger Abbey*. 1818. Edited with an introduction by Marilyn Butler. London: Penguin, 1995. 3–7.

Austen, Jane. *The Novels of Jane Austen: Volume VI: Minor Works*. Ed. R. W. Chapman. Oxford: Oxford UP, 1954.

———. *Pride and Prejudice*. 1813. Ed. with an introduction by Vivian Jones. London: Penguin, 1996.

———. *Emma*. 1816. Ed. with an introduction by Fiona Stafford. London: Penguin, 1996.

———. *Sir Charles Grandison*. Ed. Brian Southam. Oxford: Clarendon, 1980.

Austen-Leigh, James Edward. *A Memoir of Jane Austen*. London, 1870.

Bakhtin, Mikhail. *Problems of Dostoevsky's Poetics*. Trans. R. W. Rotsel. Minneapolis: U. of Minnesota P; Ardis, 1973.

Bally, Charles. "Le Style Indirect Libre en Français Moderne I." *Germanische-Romanische Monatsschrift* 4 (1912): 549–56.

———. "Le Style Indirect Libre en Français Moderne II." *Germanische-Romanische Monatsschrift* 4 (1912): 597–606.

Banfield, Anne. "The Formal Coherence of Represented Speech and Thought." *PTL: A Journal for Descriptive Poetics and Theory of Literature* 3 (1978): 289–314.

Barker, Gerard. *Grandison's Heirs: The Paragon's Progress in the Late Eighteenth-Century English Novel*. Newark: U of Delaware P; London: Associated UP, 1985.

Bronzwaer, W. J. M. *Tense in the Novel: An Investigation of Some Potentialities of Linguistic Criticism*. Groningen: Wolters Noordhoff, 1970.

Chatman, Seymour. *Story and Discourse: Narrative Structure in Fiction and Film*. London: Cornell UP, 1978.

Cohn, Dorrit. "Narrated Monologue: Definition of a Fictional Style." *Comparative Literature* 18.2 (1966): 97–112.

———. *Transparent Minds: Narrative Modes for Presenting Consciousness in Fiction*. Princeton: Princeton UP, 1978.

Couturier, Maurice. "Free Indirect Style and Interior Monologue Revisited." *Cycnos: Les Sujets de la Lettre* 3 (1986): 17–31.

Doody, Margaret. "George Eliot and the Eighteenth-Century Novel." *Nineteenth-Century Fiction* 35.3 (1980): 260–91.

Eaves, T. C. D., and Ben D. Kimpel. *Samuel Richardson: A Biography*. Oxford: Clarendon, 1971.

Ehrlich, Susan. *Point of View: A Linguistic Analysis of Literary Style*. London: Routledge, 1990.

Fergus, Jan. *Jane Austen and the Didactic Novel*. London: Macmillan, 1983.

Flavin, Louise. "*Mansfield Park*: Free Indirect Discourse and the Psychological Novel." *Studies in the Novel* 19.2 (1987): 137–59.

Fludernik, Monika, *The Fictions of Language and the Languages of Fiction: The Linguistic Representation of Speech and Consciousness*. London: Routledge, 1993.

———. "Linguistic Signals and Interpretative Strategies: Linguistic Models in Performance, with Special Reference to Free Indirect Discourse." *Language and Literature* 5.2 (1996): 93–113.

Gard, Roger. *Jane Austen's Novels: The Art of Clarity*. London: Yale UP, 1992.

Hamburger, Käte. *The Logic of Literature*. 1957. 2nd rev. ed. Trans. M. J. Rose. London: Indiana UP, 1973.

Harris, Jocelyn. *Jane Austen's Art of Memory*. Cambridge: Cambridge UP, 1989.

Honan, Park. "Richardson's Influence on Jane Austen (Some Notes on the Biographical and Critical Problems of an 'Influence')." *Samuel Richardson: Passion and Prudence.* Ed. V. G. Myer. London: Vision and Barnes & Noble, 1986. 165–77.

Hough, Graham. "Narrative and Dialogue in Jane Austen." *Critical Quarterly* 12.3 (1970): 201–29.

Jack, Ian. "The Epistolary Element in Jane Austen." *English Studies Today* 2nd ser. (1961): 173–86.

James, Henry. "Preface to *Roderick Hudson*." *The Critical Muse: Selected Literary Criticism.* Ed. with an introduction by Roger Gard. London: Penguin, 1987. 450–63.

Jenkins, Elizabeth. *Jane Austen: A Biography*. London: Victor Gollancz, 1938.

Jespersen, Otto. *The Philosophy of Grammar*. London: Allen & Unwin, 1924.

Keymer, Thomas. *Richardson's* Clarissa *and the Eighteenth-Century Reader*. Cambridge: Cambridge UP, 1992.

Lascelles, Mary. *Jane Austen and Her Art*. London: Oxford UP, 1939.

Leavis, F. R. *The Great Tradition*. London: Chatto & Windus, 1948.

Leech, Geoffrey, and Michael Short. *Style in Fiction: A Linguistic Introduction to English Fictional Prose*. London: Longman, 1981.

Lodge, David. "Composition, Distribution, Arrangement: Form and Structure in Jane Austen's Novels." *After Bakhtin: Essays on Fiction and Criticism*. London: Routledge, 1990. 116–28.

Lorck, E. *Die 'erlebte Rede.' Eine sprachliche Untersuchung*. Heidelberg: Carl Winter, 1921.

McHale, Brian. "Free Indirect Discourse: A Survey of Recent Accounts." *PTL* 3 (1978): 249–87.

McKillop, Alan. *Samuel Richardson: Printer and Novelist*. Chapel Hill: U of North Carolina P, 1936.

Neumann, Anne. "Free Indirect Discourse in the Eighteenth-Century English Novel: Speakable or Unspeakable? The Example of *Sir Charles Grandison*." *Language, Text and Context: Essays in Stylistics*. Ed. Michael Toolan. London: Routledge, 1992. 113–35.

Pascal, Roy. *The Dual Voice*. Manchester: Manchester UP, 1977.

Richardson, Samuel. *Clarissa: or, The History of a Young Lady*. 1st ed. 7 vols. London, 1747–48.

———. *The History of Sir Charles Grandison*. 1st ed. 7 vols. London, 1753–54.

———. *Forster Collection* (correspondence). London: Victoria and Albert Museum.

Southam, Brian. Introduction. *Sir Charles Grandison*. By Jane Austen. Oxford: Clarendon, 1980. 1–34.

Tanner, Tony. *Jane Austen*. London: Macmillan, 1986.

Volosinov, V. N. *Marxism and the Philosophy of Language*. Trans. L. Matejka, and I. R. Titunik. London: Seminar, 1973.

Wright, Susan. "The Subject, The Speaker and Experiential Syntax." *Subjecthood and Subjectivity: The Status of the Subject in Linguistic Theory*. Ed. M. Yaguello. Paris: Ophreys, 1994. 149–69.

ALEX WOLOCH

The Double Meaning of Character

*P**ride and Prejudice* does sometimes seem to stratify itself into two distinct
levels. It is as though the text encourages us to take in the increasingly
intense relationship between Elizabeth and Darcy on one register, while
apprehending the many memorable minor characters on another. However,
analysis of the novel needs to highlight the dialectical links between these two
narrative registers, to bring out the textual logic that makes them coalesce
into a unified whole. We can see an early example of these two descriptive
modes in the first moment of detailed characterization in the novel, the
depiction of Mr. and Mrs. Bennet that ends chapter 1. This opening chapter
consists mainly of quoted dialogue between Mr. and Mrs. Bennet; after the
first two sentences the narrator rarely intrudes (except to present indirect
quotations or an occasional light-hearted comment). In the chapter's last
paragraph, however, the narrator shifts into a quite different tone, offering a
summary judgment of the characters who have been talking:

> Mr. Bennet was so odd a mixture of quick parts, sarcastic humour,
> reserve, and caprice, that the experience of three and twenty years
> had been insufficient to make his wife understand his character.
> *Her* mind was less difficult to develope. She was a woman of mean
> understanding, little information, and uncertain temper. When

From *The One vs. the Many: Minor Characters and the Space of the Protagonist in the Novel*, pp. 50–
56. © 2003 by Princeton University Press.

she was discontented she fancied herself nervous. The business of
her life was to get her daughters married; its solace was visiting
and news. (5)

Juxtaposed against the clipped conversation, this description announces the
omniscient narrator's analytic seriousness, showing us that the novel will not
be concerned simply with presenting surface appearances but will scrutinize
its characters' essential qualities. To read such a complex, intimate appraisal
of a character so early in a novel is jarring—the reader is forced to pause
and try to figure out what it means to describe a human being as "a mixture
of quick parts, sarcastic humour, reserve and caprice." This pause can be
explained technically and analyzed on a formal level: phonetically, through
the lack of assonance and the polysyllabic words; syntactically, through the
heavy presence of abstract nouns; and semantically, through the simultaneous
deployment of both contradictions ("quick parts"/"reserve") and synonyms
("sarcastic humour"/"caprice"). But we also have to slow down because of
what the language is describing, because of the startling way in which the
narrator presents a human being, encapsulating such a complicated person
in only ten words when "three and twenty years" is insufficient to reveal his
"character" to his wife. The formal qualities of the sentence are a reflection
of the narrator's insistence on accurately presenting the inner nature of Mr.
Bennet's character.

This is an uncommon and original understanding of how to align a
work of literature with an individual life—of how a sense of the human can
be refracted through a literary text. As Raymond Williams writes:

In most drama and fiction the characters are already pre-formed,
as functions of certain kinds of situation and action. "Creation"
of characters is then in effect a kind of tagging: name, sex,
occupation, physical type. In many important plays and novels,
within certain class modes, the tagging is still evident, at least
for "minor characters," according to social conventions of
distribution of significance (the characterization of servants, for
example). Even in more substantial characterization, the process
is often the activation of a known model.... The detailed and
substantial *performance of a known model* of "people like this,
relations like this," is in fact the real achievement of most serious
novels and plays. Yet there is evidently also a mode beyond
reproductive performance. There can be new formations of
"character" and "relationship," and these are normally marked by
the introduction of different essential notations and conventions,

extending beyond these specific elements to a total composition. Many of these new articulations and formations become, in their turn, models. But while they are being formed they are creative in the emergent sense. (*Marxism and Literature*, 208–9)

The description of Mr. Bennet is arguably part of a "new formation of character" in Austen, which is more psychological and analytic than that of previous British fiction. This new mode of characterization emerges in relation to Austen's strikingly original voice, perhaps the most notable use of omniscient narrative in the British novel since Henry Fielding, whose own omniscience is in quite a different mode. And part of the originality in Austen's omniscient, impersonal narrative is precisely what we see in this passage: the authority it gives her to probe the psychological workings of her characters.

Besides grounding stylistic or formal originality in the realm of characterization, Williams stresses that both "minor characters" and more rounded characters are subsumed under this creative model—that a signal method of narrative will somehow be directed toward both "character" *and* "relationship." How a novel finds new forms of representing individuals is connected, in other words, to how a novel "*distributes*" significance across a group of characters implicated within a single narrative. Austen's new style of omniscience also, crucially, intensifies this narrative relationship between characters, who are juxtaposed and concatenated within a closed and intricately organized discursive structure. What is so interesting about the closing paragraph of chapter 1 is not merely that Austen's intriguing description of Mr. Bennet absorbs us, but, also, that we are immediately forced to shift our attention elsewhere. While we expect the concise appraisal of Mr. Bennet's odd character to be elaborated, we are instead directed toward Mrs. Bennet's qualitatively different character. The shift is accomplished through the heavily emphasized "*her*": a use of italics that occurs throughout the novel to foreground a particular character. The narrator again unfurls her nuanced psychological vocabulary, but now a single characteristic emerges in different terms—"mean," "little," "uncertain." It is as though the language of precision—confronted with Mrs. Bennet's shallow mind—is drained of its own specificity.

We can already see a central tendency of the narrator: to closely link the description of an "intricate" mind with a counterpoised description of a "simple" one. Of course, it makes sense that descriptions of a husband and wife are placed side by side, but this overt motivation for the sentence does not fully explain the logic of the juxtaposition. The sentence places complexity and superficiality together in a way that will be repeated throughout the novel. Besides the two different characters who are linked by marriage, the paragraph suggests two linked modes of existence—and two registers of description that reflect these modes. And the abrupt shift from Mr. Bennet's depth to Mrs. Bennet's shallowness implies some kind of interconnection, some logic of "relationship," which governs both these modes of existence, and out of which they both emerge.

The achievement of Austen's narrative is to densely correlate two kinds of comparison—so that the abstract comparison between different personal qualities, or the discrimination of interior consciousness and personality, is grounded in the more concrete juxtaposition of different characters, or individuals, within a social field. "In understanding Darcy was the superior. Bingley was by no means deficient, but Darcy was clever" (16). These two short sentences are a very condensed example of a process that repeats itself over and over again in *Pride and Prejudice*. The passage establishes two kinds of comparison: the social distinction between two persons and the more conceptual, abstract distinction between two kinds of intelligence. This second relation—between "understanding" and "cleverness"—does not distinguish Darcy and Bingley per se but rather illustrates more general gradations of human consciousness through Darcy and Bingley. But the nuanced distinction between "understanding" and "cleverness," which concerns the interior realm of human character, is built in-and-through a social comparison that is necessarily exterior. The early juxtaposition of Mr. and Mrs. Bennet, set off at the end of chapter 1, is the novel's first major example of this process, as the interior comparison of different characteristics gets entangled with the exterior juxtaposition of different characters.

All of Austen's novels—and not least of all *Pride and Prejudice*—are full of these double comparisons: where an abstract elaboration is purchased through a social distinction. Here are two more examples, one subtly juxtaposing Elizabeth and Jane, and the other more harshly juxtaposing Mr. Darcy and Mr. Hurst.

> Elizabeth listened in silence, but was not convinced; their behavior at the assembly had not been calculated to please in general; and with more quickness of observation and less pliancy of temper than her sister, and with a judgment too unassailed by any attention to herself, she was very little disposed to approve them. (15)

> Mr. Darcy said very little, and Mr. Hurst nothing at all. The former was divided between admiration of the brilliancy which exercise had given to her complexion, and doubt as to the

occasion's justifying her coming so far alone. The latter was thinking only of his breakfast. (33)

In the first example we see the rich psychological distinction between "observation" and "temper" (a distinction that bears on the very crux of epistemology) getting constructed only in-and-through a social comparison. In the second example these two types of discrimination have been temporally separated, so that the psychological juxtaposition of "admiration" and "doubt" precedes the harsh social comparison between Mr. Darcy and Mr. Hurst. But the motivation of this second comparison, the reason that the narrative suddenly turns to Hurst, lies in the processes of the first comparison: it is an extension and an elaboration of Darcy's depth of character to compare his divided consciousness with Hurst's. And it is precisely in this moment, when the interior is being separated from the social, that we see a truly flattened character. Flatness and asymmetry enter into the novel through this dissociation; they are a residue of the denied relationship between thought and social being.

   This dissociation of the two types of comparison helps account for the passages' different tones: the irony that is so clearly emphasized in the second passage is almost imperceptible in the first. This is due to the positions of Hurst and Jane within the asymmetrical character-structure of the narrative as a whole. Hurst is a quintessentially reduced and flattened caricature, while Jane is the character who more than any other seems to gloss over the very fact of asymmetry: the one sister who is not harshly juxtaposed with Elizabeth, who does not experience a radically different fate, and who might be minor but certainly does not suffer from this minorness. Remembering this difference, we can begin to see more clearly the similarity between the two passages. It makes sense that the social distinction which facilitates the first comparison (between "observation" and "temper") is hidden in a subordinate clause, while the second comparison (between Darcy's "admiration" and "doubt") is emphasized through a clipped second sentence and in the mode of comic juxtaposition. It is as though Mr. Hurst is *so* different from Mr. Darcy that he cannot even be assimilated into the same grammatical structure.[6]

   All of these examples illustrate two different conceptions of character that coexist in Jane Austen: character as social being (a person *is* a character) and character as inner quality (a person *has* a character). The narrative structure that mediates between them is precisely asymmetry. Austen famously transforms the novel into a genre that abstracts, elucidates, and diagnoses human characteristics: facilitating contrasts between inner qualities like "observation" and "temper." This is most apparent in the well-known contrast of abstract nouns in the twin titles *Pride and Prejudice* and *Sense and Sensibility*. These two titles show how important such juxtapositions are. They alert us to a process of psychological analysis—built on the abstraction and dialectical comparison of characteristics—that runs throughout the novels, so that similar contrasts are continually rippling across and animating the text. These two titles suggest that the rich and complex texture of human interiority should be the subject of literature; and that the activity of the novelist revolves around discriminating between (and thus elucidating) different modes of thinking and feeling.

Characters, in this light, quickly become transformed into characteristics: the social relation of *individuals* rendered as the dialectical relationship between discrepant interior states. When Marianne criticizes Edward early in *Sense and Sensibility*, she says: "He admires as a lover, not as a connoisseur. To satisfy me, those characters must be united" (17). The specific point that Marianne is making is not nearly as important as the structure of feeling that she is enacting: the sense that human character can be neatly analyzed, categorized, divided—and that the ideal character will be some sort of synthesis, or nuanced modulation, rather than an exaggeration of one particular trait. Austen's novels hinge on transforming secondary characters—fictional human beings like Edward—into the repository of character—the internal and abstracted qualities of being human. The dual use of "character" thus lies at the heart of the birelational process we have been looking at, where the nuanced adumbration of inner qualities emerges only through the social juxtaposition of different people. This dichotomy is summed up in a crucial conversation among Bingley, Elizabeth, and Darcy:

> "I did not know before," continued Bingley immediately, "that you were a studier of character. It must be an amusing study."
>
> "Yes; but intricate characters are the *most* amusing. They have at least that advantage."
>
> "The country," said Darcy, "can in general supply but few subjects for such a study. In a country neighborhood you move in a very confined and unvarying society." (42–43)

What is continually enacted in particular instances throughout the novel is here more generally described: the psychological depth of "intricate" character is linked to the quantitative distribution of characters. The novel is full of more specific examples, such as when Elizabeth is received by the three Bingley siblings:

> She was received, however, very politely by them; and in their
> brother's manners there was something better than politeness;
> there was good humour and kindness. (33)

Again: the qualitative distinction between real politeness and what we might
call *politesse* is constructed only through a social comparison. In a similar
way, aesthetic criteria and distinctions are also not intrinsically grounded
but rely on exterior juxtaposition. In another example, a classic juxtaposition
of artificial and actual beauty, or "splendor" and "elegance," is socially
inflected: "Elizabeth saw, with admiration of his taste, that it was neither
gaudy nor uselessly fine; with less of splendor, and more real elegance, than
the furniture of Rosings" (246).

A dual process of discrimination—between physically real, specifically
located persons and between abstract, immaterial gradations of character—
is relentlessly repeated in Austen's universe.[7] Note how such a double
comparison asserts itself into a sentence, surfacing, almost as in afterthought,
in a subordinate clause: "To the civil enquiries which then poured in, and
amongst which she had the pleasure of distinguishing the much superior
solicitude of Mr. Bingley's, she could not make a very favourable answer"
(35). This dual understanding of character does not just inform individual
descriptions but underlies the larger structure of Austen's characterization.
The process of interior character development—embodied in the titles
Sense and Sensibility and *Pride and Prejudice*—is essentially a *via negativa*, a
dialectical process of rejecting different extremes (too much pride, too much
sensibility, etc.) to find a middle ground. This process accommodates itself
perfectly with an asymmetrical structure of characterization, as various minor
characters exemplify certain traits or ways of thinking that the protagonist
must learn to discard. This is the pattern in all of Austen's novels: dialectical
progress for the central protagonists, and the flattening, fragmentation, and
dismissal of many minor characters who facilitate this progress as negative
examples. The novels compel us not merely to aggregate the traits or
qualities of mind that are exemplified (this is too "fine"; this is too "gaudy")
but also to confront and evaluate what it means *to* exemplify, deriving these
abstracted traits through persons. The dismissal of each individual character
(along with the characteristics into which they are subsumed) points to a
larger process—the dismissal of an entire mode of character for another,
what we could see as the persistent transformation of characters as social
beings into character as the reflection of internal, abstract qualities. This
transformation, which we have seen in isolated sentences, is also enacted in
the narrative *as a whole*: through the derealization of minor characters.

It is only in this context that specific instances of parody can be seen in their full significance. Parody is the site of a human drama in Austen's novels, the transformation of human beings as specific individuals into attributes, characteristics, aspects of existence. The term "character" is a privileged word in Jane Austen's novels, appearing sixty-four times in *Pride and Prejudice* alone, and nearly as frequently in *Mansfield Park*, *Emma*, and *Persuasion*. Nor is the term used incidentally; all of these novels have key passages involving the word, and it appears most often toward the end. In *Pride and Prejudice* the term is always employed in the second sense: never "character" as a way of denoting a person, but always character as, precisely, what can be derived *from* a person.[8] And yet it is in just this relentless transformation of social relationships (between concrete, discrete persons) into psychological comparisons (between abstracted interior states) that the social significance of Austen's narrative emerges. As Duckworth puts it, in terms that now become more suggestive to us, the parody which underlies Austen's abstraction means that certain characters are laughed "out of existence." In *Pride and Prejudice*, this kind of departure, or expulsion, does not only take place when a character actually leaves the narrative, but, on the contrary, also occurs through the very *integration* of a character into the narrative totality, as this integration is accomplished in relation to the character's abstraction. And by rigorously representing the transformation of human beings into abstract qualities—and enacting this through the derealization of minor characters who, en masse, facilitate the development of the protagonist—Austen frames the very construction of the interior realm of personality, the space of the protagonist, as part of a profoundly social structure.

Notes

6. In fact, the putatively subtle distinction between Elizabeth and Jane *is* pointedly ironic: the rhetoric of balance ("more" than, "less" than) obscures how *both* Elizabeth's surfeit of quickness and lack of pliancy work to suggest that Jane is simply not as smart. Furthermore, the identification of Elizabeth with "more quickness" directly echoes Mr. Bennet's claim that Elizabeth has "something more of quickness than her sisters" in chapter 1, which, we will see, both sets in motion and anchors the basic asymmetric elaboration of the character-system. To complete this general claim in *specific* reference to Jane helps enfold the sister who might seem to partially challenge Elizabeth's lock on narrative centrality safely within the asymmetric structure. The subordinate clause in this sentence—"and with a judgment too unassailed by any attention to herself"—is also fascinating. Here the emphatic negative ("too unassailed") even more successfully conceals the actual charge of this sentence—not just less intelligent, Jane, distracted by the attention she receives, is somewhat self-absorbed, a combination that is usually quite fatal in an Austen novel. This clause also deviously increases the narrative attention *toward* Elizabeth precisely in terms of her own meritorious self-neglect.

7. A wonderfully elongated sentence from *Northanger Abbey* illustrates how this double-edged comparison propels the energy of Austen's early work: "Mrs. Thorpe, however, had one great advantage as a talker, over Mrs. Allen, in a family of children; and when she expatiated on the talents of her sons, and the beauty of her daughters—when she related their different situations and views—that John was at Oxford, Edward at Merchant-Taylors', and William at sea—and all of them more beloved and respected in their different stations than any other three beings ever were, Mrs. Allen had no similar information to give, no similar triumphs to press on the unwilling and unbelieving ear of her friend, and was forced to sit and appear to listen to all these material effusions, consoling herself, however, with the discovery, which her keen eyes soon made, that the lace on Mrs. Thorpe's pelisse was not half so handsome as that on her own" (32). This sentence, with its twenty clauses, shows a young writer experimenting with structure and taking pleasure in the "effusions" of fictional language. The sentence flows seamlessly between two kinds of comparison or discrimination: the "different situations" or "different stations" generated out of the dynamic structure of social reality, and the *interior elaboration* of this, in the comparison (through Mrs. Allen's free indirect discourse) that brings the sentence to a halt.

8. It is this abstraction that leads to the remarkable number of transitive verbs that "character" is coupled with in the novel. At various points character—always as the abstract qualities *of* a person—is described as something that can be considered (125), decided (11), developed (213), drawn (264), enquired of (206), exposed (174), fixed (231), given (258), illustrated (93), known (143), mistaken (258), misunderstood (273), praised (143), questioned (206), reestablished (227), respected (212), restored (326), sketched (94), studied (23), sunk (149), understood (22), unfolded (191), and valued (85). This relentless solidification of an abstraction is purchased only by the dematerialization of actual persons, who are subsumed into their characteristics.

CAROLE MOSES

Jane Austen and Elizabeth Bennet: The Limits of Irony

Critics have often remarked on the ostensible link between Elizabeth Bennet and her creator (Brownstein 54; Liddell 36; Mudrick 94). Elizabeth's wit and playfulness, the argument goes, reflect Austen's own personality. But this observation, innocuous as it seems, devalues the artistry of the novel, implying as it does a lack of design on the author's part: Jane Austen merely looked in a psychic mirror and reported the thoughts of the charming Elizabeth.[1] Even a critic who does not identify Austen and her character still finds an odd link between them. Barbara Hardy characterizes the narrative voice of *Pride and Prejudice* as "dry, caustic and not playful" (174) and conjectures that "all the playfulness has gone into Elizabeth Bennet, leaving none over for the narrator" (174). I hope to show that Elizabeth is not a psychic vampire, sucking the wit out of her passive author, but a carefully crafted character.[2] Indeed, Austen does several things with the ironic wit of her main character. By blurring the distinction between Elizabeth's voice and that of the omniscient narrator, she controls the reader's point of view. Austen tempts the reader to accept Elizabeth's initial assessment of Wickham and Darcy because Elizabeth sounds so much like the third-person onmiscient narrator. In this way, Austen forces the reader to experience the same errors that Elizabeth makes and to realize the difficulty of arriving at truth in a constantly shifting world. Elizabeth's ironic wit also defines nuances of her

From *Persuasions: The Jane Austen Journal* 25 (2003), pp. 155–164. © 2003 by the Jane Austen Society of North America.

character in ways that make her stand out from the more one-dimensional women in the novel: Caroline Bingley, Charlotte Lucas, Lydia, even Jane. And, ultimately, Elizabeth's wit defines theme as the novel develops a critique on the worth of an ironic worldview.

A. Walton Litz's comments are fairly typical of what critics say about point of view in the novel. Writing of an earlier experiment that heralds the style of *Pride and Prejudice*, he points out that Austen tells the story "from the point-of-view of one character while qualifying and expanding that viewpoint through dramatic irony and direct comment. Such a method ... combines in a limited form the omniscience of third-person narration with the immediacy of first-person narrative ..." (110). Although several critics have denied a distinctive authorial voice to the omniscient narrator (Hardy 66; Lascelles 173–174), I hope to show that both Austen and her character share the same ironic assumptions. Further, by associating the omniscient authorial voice with a detached ironic perspective, Austen leads the reader to accept Elizabeth's judgments. After all, she sounds like the omniscient narrator, so we expect of her the same reliability as that of her author. The narrative trick of the novel is that the onmiscient author is not reliable. Several writers have pointed out that Austen attempts to deceive the reader into believing Elizabeth's judgments of Darcy (Babb 113; Liddell 43). What has not been noted is the extent to which her deception is based on a shared voice with Elizabeth.[3] Commenting on the "general epistemological uncertainty" (454) of *Pride and Prejudice*, Tara Goshal Wallace notes that the reader must "puzzle out the truth from a mass of inconsistent data" (52). Interestingly, Robert Kellogg and Robert Scholes have shown that the decline of "full omniscience" (274) in the novel is linked to the rise of cosmic uncertainty:

> The whole movement of mind in Western culture from the Renaissance to the present—the very movement which spawned the novel and elevated it to the position of the dominant literary form—has been a movement away from dogma, certainty, fixity and all absolutes in metaphysics, in ethics, and in epistemology. (276)

Using the conventions of omniscient narration, Austen shows how difficult true perception is by blurring the distinction between her authorial voice and that of her erring main character. Like the reader of "The Heart of Darkness" or "My Kinsman, Major Molineux," the reader of *Pride and Prejudice* is faced with the task of extracting truth from very ambiguous narrative clues.[4]

Austen's famous opening sentence establishes the ironic narrative voice, and it is one the reader hears throughout the novel. Austen attributes Charlotte's acceptance of Mr. Collins to a "pure and disinterested desire of an establishment" (122); she refers to the "fire and independence" (121) of Mr. Collins in proposing to one woman the day after being rejected by another; she describes Mr. Bennet as a "true philosopher" (236) for making the best of an abysmal marriage by mocking his wife; and she refers to Mrs. Bennet's "gentle murmurs" (128) after Charlotte has accepted Mr. Collins. Clearly, Charlotte is not disinterested, Mr. Collins is hardly fiery; Mr. Bennet's so-called philosophy is based merely on his own amusement, and there is nothing gentle about Mrs. Bennet's complaints. Sometimes Austen's irony is a bit more indirect, leading to a generally wry tone. As she chronicles Elizabeth's feelings for Darcy; for example, she notes:

> If gratitude and esteem are good foundations of affection, Elizabeth's change of sentiment will be neither improbable nor faulty. But if otherwise, if the regard springing from such sources is unreasonable or unnatural, in comparison of what is so often described as arising on a first interview with its object, and even before two words have been exchanged, nothing can be said in her defence, except that she had given somewhat of a trial to the latter method, in her partiality for Wickham and that its ill-success might perhaps authorise her to seek the other less interesting mode of attachment. (279)

Surely, the long clause beginning "if otherwise" is tongue-in-cheek since the novel at this point has effectively demonstrated the dangers of love at first sight. And the wonderful phrase "less interesting mode of attachment" casts ironic light on her initial attraction to Wickham.[5]

John F. Burrows has analyzed "disjunction as a source of [Austen's] comic energy" (171), and this energy is often ironic and linked to the authorial voice. Although his travels do not extend beyond his home, Austen tells us that Sir William Lucas is "civil to all the world" (18). Lady Catherine has the meteorological power of "determin[ing] what weather they were to have on the morrow" (166), just as she "scold[s] [the cottagers] into harmony and plenty" (169). Treating weather and economic prosperity as if both are simply a matter of willpower creates an ironic dislocation. As the novel ends, Austen tells the readers that "Happy for all her maternal feelings was the day on which Mrs. Bennet got rid of her two most deserving daughters" (385). The implied callousness of the verb ("got rid of") when applied to its direct object ("her two most deserving daughters") casts an ironic light on the "maternal feelings" which open the sentence.

Like her author, Elizabeth has a keen sense of irony. Sometimes she says things she clearly does not mean; sometimes she juxtaposes words or phrases that produce absurdity. When Jane is discussing Bingley and his sisters' reluctance to accept her as a sister-in-law, Elizabeth says, "'if upon mature deliberation, you find that the misery of disobliging his two sisters is more than equivalent to the happiness of being his wife, I advise you by all means to refuse him'" (119), advice that is actually meant to eliminate Jane's scruples. The juxtaposition of emotionally charged language ("misery") with the more neutral "disobliging" underscores the irony.[6] Jane is clearly overreacting to the sisters, who will only be "disobliged" by Bingley's marriage to Jane. Commenting on her sister's attempts to exonerate both Wickham and Darcy by attributing their misunderstanding to an unnamed third party, Elizabeth tells her "'to clear them too, or we shall be obliged to think ill of somebody'" (85). Of course, the point is that "somebody" must be responsible for the enmity between the men, although at this point Elizabeth is deceived about who should bear the blame. Nevertheless, she intends to show Jane that in the real world not everyone can be exonerated of wrongdoing. Jane's later measured acknowledgement of Caroline Bingley's falsity prompts Elizabeth to comment "'That is the most unforgiving speech ... that I ever heard you utter'" (350). In one sense, Elizabeth merely speaks the truth—Jane is incapable of intense or prolonged anger—but her comment, by linking high emotion to Jane's temperate words, continues the light irony that Elizabeth so often uses.

By making absurd claims in a serious manner, Elizabeth often uses irony to make her point. After the Netherfield ball, Elizabeth responds to Jane's stated admiration for Bingley by saying, "'He is also handsome ... which a young man ought likewise to be, if he possibly can. His character is thereby complete'" (14). Discussing a handsome appearance as if it were a matter of willpower—and linking it to moral stature—subtly undermines the superficial basis of many social attractions in the novel. This passage reminds one of Lady Catherine "determining" the weather and, again, links Elizabeth to the authorial voice. Later in the novel, as Elizabeth reveals the truth to Jane about Wickham and Darcy, her sister, typically, tries to believe well of both men. Elizabeth's humorous response equates virtue with a physical entity that can shift and is her ironic way of admitting her previous false perception and her recent insight into the true nature of the two men: "'This will not do.... There is but such a quantity of merit between them; just enough to make one good sort of man; and of late it has been shifting about pretty much'" (225).[7]

As if further to identify the omniscient narrator and Elizabeth, Austen early in the novel blurs their thoughts. When describing Jane's praise of the Bingley sisters, Austen says "Elizabeth listened in silence, but was not convinced; their behaviour at the assembly had not been calculated to please in general; and with more quickness of observation and less pliancy of temper than her sister, and with a judgment too unassailed by any attention to herself, she was very little disposed to approve them" (15). Clearly, we are hearing Elizabeth's thoughts. But the passage goes on to recount their education and fortune, things only the omniscient narrator could know, ending in the ironic conclusion that "they were therefore in every respect entitled to think well of themselves, and meanly of others" (15). This seamless blending of Elizabeth's thoughts with Austen's knowledge prepares the reader to accept Elizabeth's views.

The identification of Elizabeth with the third-person narrator also appears in Austen's free indirect speech. This stylistic device occurs when the reader hears the character's thoughts, not in the style of the omniscient narrator, but in the idiom of the character being described. In other words, it is a character's thoughts, a prerogative of the omniscient author, but in the speaking style of the character. Dorrit Cohn notes that Austen was the "first extensive English practitioner" of this technique (108). But what is striking about *Pride and Prejudice* is that Austen and her character (Elizabeth) have essentially the same idiom. When, for example, Elizabeth is in agony over her aunt's slow pace at Pemberley and her embarrassment at having to make conversation with Darcy, the reader seems in Elizabeth's mind. But when the reader learns that "time and her aunt moved slowly" (257), the wryness could be Austen's or Elizabeth's. In fact, the reader has already heard Elizabeth equate virtue with a package that can "shift." This same linking of an intangible quality ("time") with a physical being ("aunt") therefore sounds as much like Elizabeth's style as Austen's third-person commentary. Earlier in this same chapter, when Elizabeth and the Gardiners meet Darcy, Elizabeth fears for his composure when he learns of their family relationship to her. The reader is told, however, that "he sustained it ... with fortitude" (255). Once again, language is being used comically as a quasi-militaristic noun ("fortitude") is used to describe a social situation. And, once again, the voice could be Austen's or Elizabeth's as filtered through free indirect speech. The reader has no way of knowing. Similarly, Elizabeth's later regrets about misjudging Darcy and rejecting his proposal are phrased in lightly ironic language as she thinks "no such happy marriage could now teach the admiring multitude what connubial felicity really was" (312). The self-mockery of the word choice ("admiring multitude") reveals Elizabeth's own mocking self-criticism, but, once again, the distinction between Austen's voice and Elizabeth's thoughts is blurred.

In addition to using irony to identify her character with narrative omniscience, Austen also uses irony as a sensitive barometer of Elizabeth's feelings. Elizabeth's irony (or lack of it) reflects a complex web of speaker, audience, purpose, and situation. She is not simply uniformly ironic. For instance, she is rarely ironic to certain characters: her mother, Lydia, Mr. Collins, Lady Catherine. The first two are so silly that irony would be wasted on them, and she is not especially close to either. Often she saves her irony for where it will do the most good: helping Jane to a better understanding of the world, for example. With Lady Catherine and Mr. Collins, she is usually trying to quell the impertinent queries of the former and to fend off the advances of the latter; irony would be out of place in accomplishing either goal. Thus, Elizabeth's irony differs from that of her father, whose ironic gibes—whether to his wife or daughters—only serve to reinforce his own sense of superiority and distance him still further from his family.

Barbara Hardy has compared Elizabeth and Darcy to Beatrice and Benedick in *Much Ado about Nothing* (55) but, unlike Benedick, Darcy is initially too haughty and then too smitten with Elizabeth to do verbal battle with the woman who attracts him. Elizabeth, however, shows a blend of flippancy and vulnerability that closely resembles that of Beatrice. Her irony clearly shows her complex emotional state. "When talking to Colonel Fitzwilliam at Rosings, she warns him to prepare to hear something "'very dreadful'" (175) about his cousin. This melodramatic opening leads to ironic deflation: Darcy has refused to dance at the Netherfield ball even though several women lacked partners. Elizabeth's irony accomplishes several things. It tweaks Darcy and thereby shows her independence. Being one of the women with whom he refused to dance, she shows how little she cares about his slight. It also allows her to lecture Darcy briefly on his aloofness and thus to hint that he would do well to examine his own character. Lastly, by turning the conversation to a mutual experience, she forces him to acknowledge a social relationship with her. Her playful jesting is thus a sign of her vulnerability, her attraction, and her determination not to assume a submissive role in whatever their relationship may become.

The same dynamic emerges when they finally do dance together. By treating the dance as if it is a game with rigid rules ("'It is your turn to say something now, Mr. Darcy.—I talked about the dance, and you ought to make some kind of remark on the size of the room, or the number of couples'" [91]), she shows him that she does not see his dancing with her as a great mark of condescension. Thus, she reserves her surface independence. Her response also masks her emotional vulnerability—he has, after all, refused to dance with her earlier—by using wit to camouflage potential awkwardness. And it teases him into further conversation, thus promoting their relationship while affecting nonchalance about it. Although at this point in the novel Elizabeth is still deceived about Darcy's character, thinking "Attention, forbearance, patience with Darcy, was injury to Wickham" (89), her witty repartee reveals an underlying attraction of which her conscious mind is unaware.

Elizabeth's occasional irony to other characters also defines her inner life. After her trip to Rosings, Wickham asks if Darcy has improved "'in essentials'" (234). She replies, "'Oh, no! ... In essentials, I believe, he is very much what he ever was'" (234). This is a potentially awkward encounter. Elizabeth wants him to know that she now realizes that Darcy was always the superior man, yet she does not want to cause a scene on the very day that Wickham's regiment is decamping. The indirect irony of her comment allows her to maintain an amicable relationship with him while alerting him to her recent knowledge. Her irony hits home since "Wickham looked as if scarcely knowing whether to rejoice over her words, or to distrust their meaning" (234).[8] When Jane asks her later in the novel when she began to love Darcy, she answers, "I believe I must date it from my first seeing his beautiful grounds at Pemberley'" (373). Her humorous assumption of materialistic motives dismisses with a laugh Jane's serious question. And when one considers how superior Elizabeth has felt to Jane throughout the novel and how she constantly tried to mold Jane's thinking to her own, one can understand why she treats her change of heart so lightly. The embarrassment of having to admit her own mistakes—even to someone as kind as her sister—is covered by her humor. And, to give Elizabeth her due, after the initial awkwardness of the question has passed, she reassures Jane how much she respects her husband-to-be.

Finally, Elizabeth's ironic voice raises thematic concerns about intellectual detachment and emotional engagement in the world. For when Elizabeth believes she is most detached and objective in judging Darcy, she is actually allowing her emotional reactions—to her sister's abandonment by Bingley and her own slighted sense of self-worth—to lead her astray. The recurring question in Austen criticism, whether she has a larger vision beyond marrying her heroines off happily,[9] actually posits a false dichotomy between wisdom and happy endings since happiness in marriage is not, as Charlotte believes, a "'matter of chance'" (23), but depends on an accurate assessment of self and others. Surely, this is the basis of most philosophical systems. As Tony Tanner has noted, *Pride and Prejudice* embodies the universal theme of recognition found in the "great tradition of Western tragedy—Oedipus Rex, King Lear, Phedre—albeit the drama has now shifted to the comic mode, as is fitting in a book which is not about the finality of the individual death but the ongoingness of social life" (105). Only when Elizabeth's distanced ironic view is balanced with her esteem for Darcy's true character does she become a whole person. Irony is thus an efficient tool in developing theme as well as portraying—to use Austen's word—one of the most "delightful" characters in literature.

Notes

1. Austen's identification with Elizabeth is, of course, reinforced by the comment she made about her novel's main character: "I must confess that I find her as delightful a creature as ever appeared in print, and how I shall be able to tolerate those who do not like her at least I do not know" (Tanner 105). But aside from Austen's partiality toward Elizabeth, the identification of the author with her characters seems part of a larger critical failure to judge Austen by the same standards as her male contemporaries. For an excellent overview of the way criticism has patronized Austen while claiming to celebrate her, see Claudia L. Johnson (xvi-xvii). And, although Elizabeth Bennet is the character most often discussed as Austen's surrogate, she is by no means the only one. Writing of Elinor's partially sympathetic response to Willoughby's narrative in *Sense and Sensibility*, Marvin Mudrick calls it a "Flagrant inconsistency," revealing "Jane Austen herself ... in a posture of yearning for the impossible and lost, the passionate and beautiful hero, the absolute lover" (85). Rather than seeing Elinor's sympathy as an element of her compassionate albeit principled nature, Mudrick paints Austen as the stereotypical frustrated spinster. In a less dismissive way, Sandra M. Gilbert and Susan Gubar see Emma as an "avatar of Austen the artist" (159), arranging marriages and generally treating her acquaintances the way an author treats his or her characters. While I am not arguing against the idea of Emma as a sort of author, I do question whether her presence shows "Austen's ambivalence about her imaginative powers" (158). Time and again, Austen criticism discusses her novels as extensions of the author's personality, not as autonomous works of art.

2. I am not concerned with whether Austen's art is consciously crafted or arises from her intuitive shaping of her materials. In either case, Elizabeth exists in a complex web of verbal, narrative, and thematic ambiguities.

3. Rachel M. Brownstein remarks on Elizabeth's resemblance to "the witty narrator" (54) but does not explore the way this resemblance tricks the reader. Mark M. Hennelly states that the readers "like Elizabeth herself; are constantly asked willingly to suspend ... disbelief; to reserve judgment and sympathy while [they] sort through all the visible evidence" (203). I contend that Austen makes it difficult for us to be distanced by forcing the reader to identify the narrative voice with that of Elizabeth.

4. Austen can be very direct and unambiguous: "Mr. Collins was not a sensible man" (70). The importance of this comment is not the information it conveys—no reader could mistake Mr. Collins for being sensible—but the implicit promise that the omniscient author will guide the reader through the novel. When no such guidance is given about Darcy and Wickham, the reader is left to rely on Elizabeth who, after all, sounds like the author. Early in the work, Austen has established her authorial role as guide in her assessment of Mrs. Bennet at the end of Chapter One: "She was a woman of mean understanding, little information, and uncertain temper. When she was discontented she fancied herself nervous. The business of her life was to get her daughters married; its

solace was visiting and news" (5). Once again, the assessment is less important than its promise of authorial judgment.

5. In *Sense and Sensibility*, Austen uses the same wry tone to describe Willoughby, the mysterious rescuer of Marianna. As he leaves the Dashwood house in suitably ominous weather, Austen notes that "he departed to make himself still more interesting, in the midst of an heavy rain" (42).

6. Although Darcy's voice is muted, he is capable of the same sort of ironic dislocation. When Caroline Bingley repeatedly interrupts his letter-writing with messages to his sister, Darcy asks "'leave to defer your raptures'" (48) over Georgiana's design for a table. The legalistic verb ("defer") and the emotionally charged noun ("raptures") underscore Darcy's irony.

7. One is reminded of Pope's address to Queen Anne in Canto iii of "The Rape of the Lock": "Here Thou, Great Anna! whom three realms obey,/Dost sometimes Counsel take—and sometimes Tea" (7–8). Putting tea and counsel on the same plane of reality as comestibles is much like Elizabeth's equating virtue with a physical package. In fact, John F. Burrows has discussed this pattern in an early Austen work (172). Augustan wit is often woven into the narrative texture of *Pride and Prejudice*. See, for example, Brower's comment that Austen's prose often achieves the "formal balance of the heroic couplet" and combines the "traditions of poetic satire with those of the sentimental novel" (62). And Kenneth L. Moler has noticed that Austen, Elizabeth, and Darcy all share the same reasonable speech patterns, using balanced phrases and abstract nouns. Such verbal similarities not only show Austen's debt to the Augustans but also reinforce the identification of Elizabeth and the onmiscient narrator. And they underscore the compatibility of Elizabeth and Darcy: quite literally, they speak the same language.

8. Like Elizabeth, Darcy can also use irony to discompose others. When Miss Bingley attempts to discredit Elizabeth by referring to her supposed strategies for succeeding with men, Darcy feigns agreement while letting her know that he sees through her own artifice: "'Undoubtedly ... there is meanness in all the arts which ladies sometimes condescend to employ for captivation. Whatever bears affinity to cunning is despicable'" (40). Like Elizabeth's barbed response to Wickham, Darcy's answer disconcerts his listener: "Miss Bingley was not so entirely satisfied with this reply as to continue the subject" (40).

9. Fortunately, Austen criticism is passing beyond the need to be defensive about the marriages at the end of her works. In fact, recent critics have focused on the ways Austen manages to exist in her time as well as go beyond it. As Jan Fergus notes, the novel can be read as a "Cinderella story" or as an "attack on romantic expectations" (86). Claudia L. Johnson has shown that Austen uses patriarchal conservative myths to question their very validity (91). And Oliver MacDonagh (35) points out that she allows many views of marriage to make their case in her works.

Works Cited

Austen, Jane. *The Novels of Jane Austen*. Ed. R. W Chapman. 3rd ed. Oxford: OUP, 1988.

Babb, Howard S. *Jane Austen's Novels: the Fabric of Dialogue*. Columbus: Ohio State UP, 1962.

Brower, Reuben Arthur. *The Fields of Light: an Experiment in Critical Reading*. New York: Oxford UP, 1951.

Brown, Lloyd W. *Bits of Ivory: Narrative Techniques in Jane Austen's Fiction*. Baton Rouge: Louisiana State UP, 1973.

Brownstein, Rachel. "*Northanger Abbey, Sense and Sensibility, Pride and Prejudice.*" *The Cambridge Companion to Jane Austen*. Ed. Edward Copeland and Juliet McMaster. Cambridge: CUP, 1997. 32-57.

Burrows, John F. "Style." *The Cambridge Companion to Jane Austen*. Ed. Edward Copeland and Juliet McMaster. Cambridge: CUP, 1997. 170-188.

Cohn, Dorrit. *Transparent Minds: Narrative Modes for Presenting Consciousness in Fiction*. Princeton: PUP, 1978.

Fergus, Jan. *Jane Austen: A Literary Life*. London: Macmillan Press, 1991.

Gilbert, Sandra M., and Susan Gubar. *The Madwoman in the Attic: The Woman Writer and the Nineteenth-Century Imagination*. New Haven: Yale UP, 1979.

Handler, Richard, and Daniel Segal. *Jane Austen and the Fiction of Culture*. Tucson: Arizona UP, 1990.

Hardy, Barbara. *A Reading of Jane Austen*. London: Peter Owen, 1975.

Hennelly, Mark M. "*Pride and Prejudice*: The Eyes Have It." *Jane Austen: New Perspectives*. New Series. 3. New York: Holmes and Meier Publishers, 1983.

Johnson, Claudia L. *Jane Austen: Women, Politics, and the Novel*. Chicago: CUP, 1988.

Lascelles, Mary. *Jane Austen and Her Art*. 1939. London: Oxford UP, 1963.

Liddell, Robert. *The Novels of Jane Austen*. London: Longmans, 1963.

Litz, A. Walton. *Jane Austen: A Study of Her Artistic Development*. New York: Oxford UP, 1965.

Macdonagh, Oliver. *Jane Austen: Real and Imagined Worlds*. New Haven: Yale UP, 1991.

Moler, Kenneth L. Pride and Prejudice: *a Study in Artistic Economy*. Boston: Twayne, 1989.

Morgan, Susan. *In the Meantime: Character and Perception in Jane Austen's Fiction*. Chicago: CUP, 1980.

Mudrick, Marvin. *Jane Austen: Irony as Defense and Discovery*. Princeton: PUP, 1952.

Pope, Alexander. *The Poems of Alexander Pope*. Ed. John Butt. New Haven: Yale UP, 1963.

Scholes, Robert, and Robert Kellogg. *The Nature of Narrative*. New York: Oxford UP, 1966.

Tanner, Tony. *Jane Austen*. Cambridge: Harvard UP, 1986.

Wallace, Tara Ghoshal. *Jane Austen and Narrative Authority*. New York: St. Martin's Press. 1995.

EMILY AUERBACH

The Liveliness of Your Mind:
Pride and Prejudice

Wit is more necessary than beauty; and I think no young woman ugly
who has it, and no handsome woman agreeable without it.
   —William Wycherley, *The Country Wife* (1673)

A chief event of life is the day in which we have encountered a mind that
startled us.
   —Ralph Waldo Emerson, *Character* (1844)

"My beauty you had early withstood.... Now be sincere; did you admire
me for my impertinence?"
   "For the liveliness of your mind, I did."
   —Elizabeth and Darcy in *Pride and Prejudice*

With *Pride and Prejudice* finally completed, Jane Austen wrote her sister
a mock-apology for its lack of depth. "I had had some fits of disgust.... The
work is rather too light & bright & sparkling;—it wants shade;—it wants
to be stretched out here & there with a long Chapter—of sense, if it could
be had, if not of solemn specious nonsense—about something unconnected
with the story; an Essay on Writing, a critique on Walter Scott, or the history
of Buonaparte—or anything that would form a contrast & bring the reader
with increased delight to the playfulness & Epigrammatism of the general

From *Searching for Jane Austen*, pp. 128–165. © 2004 by The Board of Regents of the University
of Wisconsin System.

stile.—I doubt your quite agreeing with me here—I know your starched Notions" (4 February 1813). Some critics have responded to this as evidence of Jane Austen's insecurity, concluding, "Jane Austen did not appear to have liked *Pride and Prejudice* nearly as much as we have. To her its 'playfulness and epigrammatism' appeared excessive and unrelieved."[1] Instead, I view this letter as yet another instance of Austen's ability to write a tongue-in-cheek disparagement of her work while actually celebrating its power. Austen knew full well that she needed no history of Napoleon or any "solemn specious nonsense" grafted onto her carefully crafted comic novel.

In fact, Austen demonstrates in *Pride and Prejudice* that one can have substance and sense without sacrificing playfulness or pleasure. After all, Jane Austen boasted to Cassandra in that same letter, "I am quite vain enough and well satisfied enough" with that "darling child," *Pride and Prejudice*. Generations of readers have agreed, hailing *Pride and Prejudice* as perhaps Jane Austen's all-time greatest creation. In this supposedly "too light, and bright, and sparkling" novel, Jane Austen introduces a dramatically different kind of young woman. Austen herself claimed that there had never been a heroine like Elizabeth Bennet, calling her "as delightful a creature as ever appeared in print" (29 January 1813). Austen creates a lively, intelligent young woman who thinks, reasons, argues, sparkles, and laughs her way through a series of absurd and unfair social circumstances. Many readers have found the witty Elizabeth to be much like Austen herself, yet such a link may obscure an equally important connection between Austen and the more problematic Mr. Bennet. Austen structures the novel so that we as readers initially share Mr. Bennet's point of view, yet she ultimately severs us—and perhaps herself—from his dangerously attractive cynicism. In *Pride and Prejudice* Austen calls into question the very nature of truth, rejects the notion of love at first sight, challenges notions of class, and explores the proper function of humor. Readers in search of Jane Austen can find in *Pride and Prejudice* her most probing analysis of the power and danger of her own comic art.

Before Austen introduces readers of *Pride and Prejudice* to her highly unconventional heroine, she forces them to question convention itself. The famous ironic opening of *Pride and Prejudice* ("It is a truth universally acknowledged, that a single man in possession of a good fortune, must be in want of a wife") invites us to rewrite the very first sentence of her novel. If we deduce that single women want husbands with fortunes, we simultaneously must conclude that ironic authors want readers with perception. From the start, Austen asks us to approach her whole novel in the spirit of intelligent and subversive questioning.

Too often the first sentence is quoted in isolation rather than in the important context of the paragraph that follows:

> It is a truth universally acknowledged, that a single man in possession of a good fortune, must be in want of a wife.
>
> However little known the feelings or views of such a man may be on his first entering a neighbourhood, this truth is so well fixed in the minds of the surrounding families, that he is considered as the rightful property of some one or other of their daughters. (3)

Before Austen ever introduces us to Elizabeth Bennet and other key characters in the novel, she calls our attention to the more general process of arriving at "truth."

Self-interested, materialistic inhabitants of this neighborhood, as yet unnamed, instantly seize on a "little known" man of good fortune as "property" for their daughters the minute he arrives in town ("on his first entering the neighbourhood"). Their assumption that the man will belong to "some one or other of their daughters" indicates a society where partners in marriages of convenience seem interchangeable pawns. To hide this reality, these neighbors construct false "universal truths" for all to implant in their minds with "well fixed" glue. *Pride and Prejudice* explores the conformity and blindness of communities, particularly small country villages unaware of their own provincialism. The "neighbourhood" (a term repeated far more frequently in *Pride and Prejudice* than any other Austen novel) transforms rumor and opinion into fact, unthinkingly perpetuating antiquated customs and rigid notions of class.

The neighborhood emerges as remarkably intrusive and unreliable. At varying points in *Pride and Prejudice*, Austen interrupts the story to remind us that private news, whether bad or good, accurate or false, rapidly permeates a neighborhood. A typical sentence reads, "The good news quickly spread through the house; and with proportionate speed through the neighbourhood" (309). Tell one neighbor and the whole town will know: "Mrs. Bennet was privileged to whisper it to Mrs. Philips, and *she* ventured, without any permission, to do the same by all her neighbours in Meryton" (350). This reminds us of Austen's quip in an early letter that Mr. Harvey's marriage "is a great secret, & only known to half the Neighbourhood" (5 September 1796).

In *Pride and Prejudice* Austen delays the tale of her principal characters in order to show how falsehoods start and multiply:

Mr. Bingley was obliged to be in town the following day.... [Mrs. Bennet] began to fear that he might be always flying about from one to another, and never settled at Netherfield as he ought to be. Lady Lucas quieted her fears a little by starting the idea of his being gone to London only to get a large party for the ball; and a report soon followed that Mr. Bingley was to bring twelve ladies and seven gentlemen with him to the assembly. The girls grieved over such a number of ladies; but were comforted the day before the ball by hearing, that instead of twelve, he had brought only six with him from London, his five sisters and a cousin. And when the party entered the assembly room, it consisted of only five altogether; Mr. Bingley, his two sisters, the husband of the eldest, and another young man. (10)

A paragraph like this leads some of my undergraduates to observe in dismay, "I've read three chapters of *Pride and Prejudice*, and *nothing's* happening!" The paragraph does indeed describe much ado about nothing. Why, instead of just telling us that Mr. Bingley arrived with two sisters, a brother-in-law, and a friend, does Austen delay the plot to tell us of the town's erroneous expectation of a large party, nineteen people, and other possibilities? As with the opening paragraphs of the novel, Austen calls to our attention the inaccurate and therefore wasteful nature of neighborhood discourse.

The population of Meryton tends to judge others too quickly and categorically, forming opinions collectively rather than individually. At first the crowd admires Mr. Darcy, but "the tide of his popularity" turns (10). "Every body" feels the same. "His character was decided. He was the proudest, most disagreeable man in the world, and every body hoped that he would never come there again," "every body [was] disgusted with his pride," "every body was pleased to think how much they had always disliked Mr. Darcy ... by every body else Mr. Darcy was condemned as the worst of men," "the general prejudice [was] against Darcy" (11, 78, 138, 226). In contrast, the "universally liked" Wickham quickly earns "the general approbation of the neighbourhood" (90, 206). The verdict on Wickham is unanimous: "the good opinion which *all* the neighbourhood had of him" (285). All Meryton functions as a unit, swayed too easily to label people as bad or good, villainous or angelic. Consider the town's response when Wickham changes from paragon to blackguard: "All Meryton seemed striving to blacken the man, who, but three months before, had been almost an angel of light.... Every body declared that he was the wickedest young man in the world; and every body began to find out, that they had always distrusted the appearance of his goodness" (86). Through the ridiculously illogical phrase "began to find out, that they had always," Austen exposes the way we rewrite our pasts to conceal our own mistakes.

Only Jane Bennet stands apart from the crowd, speculating that there must be additional circumstances "of which we can form no idea" and that conclusions might be drawn because "people have perhaps misrepresented" the facts. Rather than making up her mind, Jane determines that it is "impossible for us to conjecture the causes or circumstances": "It is difficult indeed—it is distressing.—One does not know what to think," Jane says. "I beg your pardon;—one knows exactly what to think," replies Elizabeth (86). One would expect that Austen would make her unconventional heroine, Elizabeth, the one to stand apart from the crowd, but she does not. She makes Elizabeth quick to censure and Jane quick to praise. The truth seems to lie somewhere between these two sisters.

Yet our focus never shifts between them, as it does in *Sense and Sensibility*. We rarely hear Jane's voice in this novel *except* in conversation with Elizabeth. The narrator clearly stays with Elizabeth, not Jane. When we do encounter Jane, she is often lying in bed apologizing for her illness, sitting and looking lovely, blushing deeply, consoling others, or trying to resign herself to permanent separation from Mr. Bingley. We never hear Jane talk to Mr. Bingley or Mr. Darcy in the course of *Pride and Prejudice*, an astonishing authorial choice on Austen's part. In contrast, Austen shows us the conversational sparks flying between Elizabeth and virtually every other character in the novel. Rather than easing into a marriage with an easy-mannered man, as Jane does, Elizabeth fights and argues her way from dislike to love in some of the most electrifying romantic scenes in literature. Both Jane and Elizabeth earn happy endings, but as Elizabeth quips, "I am the happiest creature in the world. I am happier even than Jane; she only smiles, I laugh" (383). From the opening chapter of this novel to its final paragraphs, Jane Austen celebrates her witty, energetic, and changing heroine, Elizabeth.

Austen introduces her heroine indirectly in the opening chapter by having the witty Mr. Bennet speak of her with affection ("my little Lizzy") and distinction ("something more ... than her sisters"), while the scatterbrained Mrs. Bennet puts her down ("not half so handsome as Jane, nor as good-humoured as Lydia"). Much as in *Northanger Abbey* Austen invites our sympathy for Catherine Morland by showing her waiting for a dance partner in Bath, so in *Pride and Prejudice* she elicits our response to Elizabeth by having her slighted by Mr. Darcy ("She is tolerable; but not handsome enough to tempt *me*"). Austen keeps the camera eye not on Jane happily dancing with Mr. Bingley but on Elizabeth sitting on the sidelines and overhearing humiliating conversations.

No wallower, Elizabeth transforms rejection into amusement: "Mr. Darcy walked off; and Elizabeth remained with no very cordial feelings towards him. She told the story however with great spirit among her friends; for she had a lively, playful disposition, which delighted in any thing ridiculous" (12). Elizabeth Bennet is the first Austen heroine to share her creator's love of narration ("She told the story") and wit. Elizabeth's response to this moment at the dance resembles Austen's own breezy tone in her letters when describing a dance: "I do not think I was very much in request—. People were rather apt not to ask me till they could not help it; ... There was one Gentleman ... who I was told wanted very much to be introduced to me;—but as he did not want it quite enough to take much trouble in effecting it, We never could bring it about" (9 January 1799). Elsewhere in her letters to her sister, Austen seems grateful to disagreeable neighbors for serving as comic fodder to her imagination: "Whenever I fall into misfortune, how many jokes it ought to furnish to my acquaintance in general, or I shall die dreadfully in their debt for entertainment" (22 January 1799). A niece's description of her aunt Jane Austen's "playful talk" and "playfulness of spirits" could apply equally well to Elizabeth Bennet, as could a nephew's comment that his aunt Jane's "unusually quick sense of the ridiculous led her to play with all the commonplaces of everyday life, whether as regarded places or things."[2] Humor can animate: two nieces recall that Jane Austen "would suddenly burst out laughing, jump up and run across the room" or "rub her hands, laugh to herself and run up to her room" to write.[3] Like her creator, Elizabeth Bennet delights in studying characters and can be moved by her observations to run and laugh. There is something sharp and impertinent about Elizabeth that makes us think she could, like Austen, write in a private letter that a neighbor's wife was "discovered to be everything that the Neighbourhood could wish her, silly & cross as well as extravagant" (18 December 1798).

How interesting that the sneering Miss Bingley condemns Elizabeth Bennet's lively expression with the same tone that some biographers even to this day have used to censure Jane Austen's appearance as presented in Cassandra's portrait: "I must confess that I never could see any beauty in her. Her face is too thin; her complexion has no brilliancy; and her features are not at all handsome. Her nose wants character ... and as for her eyes, which have sometimes been called so fine, I never could perceive any thing extraordinary in them. They have a sharp, shrewish look, which I do not like at all; and in her air altogether, there is a self-sufficiency without fashion, which is intolerable" (271). Now consider a recent critic's description of Jane Austen's portrait: "Cassandra's drawing [of Jane Austen] shows a woman more sharp-featured than appealing: the eyes are large and beautiful, glancing keenly ... and the mouth itself looks small and mean. She looks like a peevish hamster.... Her nose was narrow and possibly rather long."[4] Just as Miss Bingley criticizes Elizabeth for possessing "self-sufficiency," "abominable ... conceited independence," and "impertinence," so biographers at times have found Austen's prepossessing appearance disconcerting (271, 35–36).

Liveliness defines Elizabeth Bennet's character throughout *Pride and Prejudice*, from the first description of her "lively, playful disposition" to our final picture of her lively imagination, spirits, talents, and speech (12). Elizabeth uses a "lively, sportive" way of talking to Mr. Darcy, who "wants liveliness" and admits himself attracted to her precisely because of her "liveliness of mind" (387–88, 325, 380). This sets Elizabeth Bennet apart from other Austen heroines. In *Northanger Abbey* Catherine Morland is eager but too dense to share the lively Henry Tilney's intellectual repartee, and in *Sense and Sensibility* Elinor Dashwood cautions Edward Ferrars against mistaking Marianne's sparkling eyes for liveliness: "Gaiety never was a part of *my* character," says Edward. "Nor do I think it a part of Marianne's.... I should hardly call her a lively girl," replies Elinor (*SS*, 93). Marianne is too melancholy, Elinor too reserved to be called lively, and the men they marry are both in search of animation. Only in *Pride and Prejudice* does Austen let her heroine speak with unrepressed wit. No wonder she had trouble imagining any reader disliking her Elizabeth: "how I shall be able to tolerate those who do not like *her* at least, I do not know" (29 January 1813).

Liveliness allows Elizabeth Bennet to survive social circumstances full of as much ennui and pettiness as any dinner party in *Sense and Sensibility*. Sir John and Lady Middleton and John and Fanny Dashwood would feel at home in the neighborhood of Meryton, where the shallow Miss Bingley ironically complains of "the insipidity and yet the noise; the nothingness and yet the self-importance of all these people!" (27). On a twenty-four-mile carriage ride with the tedious Sir William Lucas and a daughter "as empty-headed as himself," Elizabeth has to listen to the conversation of two people with "nothing to say that could be worth hearing" offering "about as much delight as the rattle of the chaise" (152).

Unlike Marianne Dashwood, Elizabeth does not succumb to despair at this sort of inanity. Elizabeth survives such conversation by rallying her spirits, willing herself into better humor, and finding delight in absurdities. Even in the middle of Mr. Collins's long-winded marriage proposal to her, Elizabeth is "near laughing" at the ludicrous idea of his being run away with by his feelings (105). Throughout *Pride and Prejudice* Austen shows us "Elizabeth's spirits soon rising to playfulness again" (380). Personal disappointment also can be overcome through humor, as when she discovers Wickham's absence after she had dressed with special care for a ball: "She ... turned away with a

degree of ill humour, which she could not wholly surmount.... But Elizabeth
was not formed for ill-humour; and though every prospect of her own was
destroyed for the evening, it could not dwell long on her spirits.... she was
soon able to make a voluntary transition to the oddities of her cousin" (90).
The delightful absurdity of her cousin Mr. Collins again helps distract her
from disappointment about Wickham's absence.

Elizabeth's cheerful disposition helps her cope with change. Because
"it was her business to be satisfied—and certainly her temper to be happy,"
she can adjust to news that her much-anticipated trip to the Lakes has been
canceled (239). When the haughty Miss Bingley and Mrs. Hurst snub her,
Elizabeth counters their rudeness with laughter, repartee, and an energetic
exit:

> Then taking the disengaged arm of Mr. Darcy, [Miss Bingley]
> left Elizabeth to walk by herself. The path just admitted three.
> Mr. Darcy felt their rudeness and immediately said.—
> "This walk is not wide enough for our party. We had better go
> into the avenue."
> But Elizabeth, who had not the least inclination to remain
> with them, laughingly answered,
> "No, no; stay where you are.—You are charmingly group'd,
> and appear to uncommon advantage. The picturesque would be
> spoilt by admitting a fourth. Good bye."
> She then ran gaily off, rejoicing as she rambled about, in the
> hope of being at home again in a day or two. (53)

Throughout *Pride and Prejudice* Elizabeth jumps, springs, rejoices, smiles,
and laughs, causing conventional young women to gasp in horror. Miss
Bingley and Mrs. Hurst find her shockingly unladylike. Mrs. Bennet admits
that even though Elizabeth is twenty, she has maintained her girlhood right
to scamper, ramble, and "run on in a wild manner" (42). Austen's portrayal of
Elizabeth with muddy petticoats and a face glowing with exertion defies the
vision of a young woman portrayed in conduct books of the time. Elizabeth
Bennet seems not to have read Hannah More's *Essays on Various Subjects,
Principally Designed for Young Ladies* (1777): "That bold, independent,
enterprising spirit, which is so much admired in boys, should not, when it
happens to discover itself in the other sex, be encouraged, but suppressed."[5]

Elizabeth Bennet also ignores Hannah More's advice that "Girls
should be taught to give up opinions betimes, and not pertinaciously carry
on a dispute, even if they should know themselves in the right.... They
should acquire a submissive temper and a forbearing spirit."[6] Rather than

submitting, Elizabeth faces adversity with pertinacity and courage. When she arrives at Lady Catherine's formidable mansion, "Elizabeth's courage did not fail her" and she enters "without trepidation" (161). As Elizabeth puts it, "There is a stubbornness about me that never can bear to be frightened at the will of others. My courage always rises with every attempt to intimidate me" (174).

This courage also allows her to face her own mistakes and her own sorrows. When Elizabeth confronts real pain—her sister Lydia's disgrace, her sister Jane's heartache, her own feelings of mortification and self-reproach—she can no longer laugh her problems away, but her dauntless spirits do help her ward off depression. She refuses to let nostalgia or regret paralyze her, announcing that her philosophy is, "Think only of the past as the remembrance gives you pleasure" (369). Unlike Marianne Dashwood, who courted misery and nourished grief, Elizabeth refuses "to increase her vexations, by dwelling on them ... to fret over unavoidable evils, or augment them by anxiety" (232). Optimism, laughter, and courage seem the best medicines for keeping Elizabeth Bennet resilient, ready to go forward and encounter more of the world's folly and injustice.

Yet bold liveliness has its limits—and dangers. We can foretell Elizabeth Bennet's vulnerability if we remember that the charming scoundrel Willoughby in *Sense and Sensibility* is described as "very lively," with a lively imagination, lively spirits, and lively manner, and that the sensual Eliza Brandon is "so lively" before she falls into prostitution (*SS*, 50, 206). Austen will return to this theme in both *Mansfield Park* and *Emma* by presenting seductively attractive characters (Mary and Henry Crawford, Frank Churchill) possessing a store of liveliness to mask a shortage of steady principle. Just as Henry Tilney's lively wit in *Northanger Abbey* makes him better able to banter than to see life clearly, so Elizabeth Bennet's playful disposition can at times keep her from confronting the truth. Liveliness can be energy, brilliance, and animation, a zest for life; it also can connote a lightness and ease not altogether commendable. When confronting a terminal illness, would one want a lively nurse? Phrases that appear elsewhere in Austen such as "lively and ... thoughtless," "lively impudence," "talents for the light and lively," or "lively, and ... unthinking" suggest that Austen thought it possible to have a "too lively mind" (*NA*, 152; *E*, 369; *MP*, 350, 69).

Often in her novels Jane Austen uses minor characters as exaggerated versions of her protagonists' flaws, as if allowing them to view themselves in a distorted amusement park mirror. Just as the fallen Eliza stands as a warning to Marianne in *Sense and Sensibility*, so in *Pride and Prejudice* the "naturally lively" Lydia Bennet illustrates to Elizabeth that lively spirits, a sense of youthful playfulness, and the courage to defy authority are not enough unless governed by an educated mind, a loving, generous heart, and a moral conscience (284).

Austen goes to great lengths to draw parallels between Elizabeth and Lydia Bennet. The youngest of the five Bennet sisters, Lydia has "youth, health, and good humour," qualities she shares with Elizabeth (283). If Elizabeth is "almost wild," Lydia is off the charts (35). Like some of the hoydens in Austen's adolescent sketches, Lydia displays a "wild giddiness," "wild volatility," "exuberant spirits," and "all too natural ... high animal spirits" (213, 231, 45). She delights in unladylike behavior: "Dear me! We had such a good piece of fun the other day at Colonel Foster's.... What do you think we did? We dressed up Chamberlayne in woman's clothes, on purpose to pass for a lady,—only think what fun! ... Lord, how I laughed! ... And then when we came away it was such fun! ... And then we were so merry all the way home! We talked and laughed so loud" (221–22). Energy in young women may be refreshing, as in Catherine Morland's noisy and wild escapades on the green slopes, Marianne's outdoor rambles, and Elizabeth's brisk walks. But Lydia is little more than a silly, self-indulgent, obstreperous girl: "Lydia was Lydia still; untamed, unabashed, wild, noisy, and fearless" (315).

What are we to think of Lydia's fearlessness? Like Elizabeth, Lydia is undaunted by authority or convention. Lydia has a "sort of natural self-consequence" and is "self-willed" with a "disdain of all restraint" and an "ungovernable" temper (45, 231, 385). She is "absolutely resolved" to stay with Wickham, married or unmarried, because it pleases her to do so (322). Both Elizabeth and Lydia give their opinions decidedly for such young women and display a rebelliousness, irreverence, and audacity. We may admire Elizabeth for asserting herself against the dictatorial Lady Catherine, but what do we think when Lydia cavalierly disregards duty, honor, and gratitude in order to seek her own instant happiness?

Austen reinforces the parallels between Elizabeth and Lydia by showing them both attracted to the same seemingly charming man: Captain Wickham. "Whatever he said, was said well," Elizabeth thinks of Wickham, "and whatever he did, done gracefully" (84). Similarly, Lydia insists that Wickham "did every thing best in the world" (318). When Elizabeth first meets Wickham, she quickly shares with this handsome stranger her verdict on Mr. Darcy ("I think him very disagreeable") and Lady Catherine ("she is an arrogant, conceited woman"), thus joining her youngest sister in acting with a "total want of propriety" (77, 84, 198). When Wickham seems surprised by her vehemence and bluntness, Elizabeth boasts that she would deliver those opinions in almost any house in the neighborhood. Elizabeth comes to realize the danger of such frankness when she hears her own thoughts presented in Lydia's voice:

> Lydia laughed and said ... "There is no danger of Wickham's marrying Mary King.... I will answer for it he never cared three straws about her. Who could about such a nasty little freckled thing?"
>
> Elizabeth was shocked to think that, however incapable of such coarseness of *expression* herself, the coarseness of the *sentiment* was little other than her own breast had formerly harboured and fancied liberal. (220)

Elizabeth's shock here and elsewhere comes from recognizing a likeness in thinking between herself and her profligate younger sister. Like Lydia, Elizabeth has an unladylike tendency to be playful and teasing. Elizabeth speaks "laughingly" and makes glib comments in the early chapters of *Pride and Prejudice* that sound Lydia-like: "Did not you think, Mr. Darcy, that I expressed myself uncommonly well just now, when I was teasing Colonel Forster to give us a ball at Meryton?" (53, 24). *Both* Elizabeth and Lydia dearly love a laugh.

Austen distinguishes between the two by using the word "fun" only in association with Lydia, not Elizabeth. Lydia titters, "we had such fun," "it was such fun," "such a good piece of fun," and "very good fun" even when describing her own disgraceful behavior. A relatively new noun in Austen's day, *fun* connoted cheating and clowning and earned Dr. Samuel Johnson's condemnation as a "low cant word" to describe "high merriment" and "frolicksome delight."[7]

Lydia also laughs with as much readiness as a hyena. "You will laugh when you know where I am gone," she writes her friend after taking off with Wickham, "and I cannot help laughing myself at your surprise ... I can hardly write for laughing" (221–22). In her own letters Austen had mocked the hyperbolic expression, "'I could die of laughter at it,' as they used to say at school" (1 September 1796), and she gives this clichéd utterance to the giddy Lydia: "Lord! how I laughed! ... I thought I should have died ... I was ready to die of laughter" (221–22). Just as Elizabeth is constantly urged by her more sober older sister and by her aunt to respond to their questions seriously, so Lydia seems to take life as little more than a joke. Lydia carries this to an incredible extreme, taking not even her own future or the feelings of her family seriously: "What a good joke it future be! ... Good gracious! when I went away, I am sure I had no more idea of being married till I came back again! though I thought it would be very good fun if I was" (291, 316).

Unlike Elizabeth, who feels genuine sorrow, Lydia seems impervious to any emotions other than impatience and "fun." Austen's readers would have recollected a passage in Ecclesiastes: "Sorrow is better than laughter; for by the sadness of the countenance the heart is made better. The heart of the wise is in the house of mourning, but the heart of fools is in the house of mirth" (7:3–4). Elizabeth had previously defended laughter against the grave Mr. Darcy's attack on people "whose first object in life is a joke," but here in the figure of her own sister stands just such a heartless creature (57). Laughter has its place: and that place is not first.

Elizabeth recognizes the cause of her youngest sister's folly: "She has never been taught to think on serious subjects.... She has been given up to nothing but amusement and vanity. She has been allowed to dispose of her time in the most idle and frivolous manner" (283). Those strong words of Austen's Elizabeth Bennet about her sister sound surprisingly like Mary Wollstonecraft lamenting the state of degradation to which women are reduced: "The grand source of female folly and vice has ever appeared to me to arise from narrowness of mind.... Pleasure is the business of woman's life, according to the present modification of society, and while it continues to be so, little can be expected from such weak beings."[8] Austen's narrow-minded, uneducated Lydia Bennet has become idle and frivolous because she has been indulged by her mother, neglected by her father, and undervalued by society. Lydia is careless, ignorant, and vain, acting with impudence and imprudence.

In fact, this "silliest" girl in the county has such an "ignorance and emptiness of her mind" that she is literally "thoughtless, thoughtless Lydia" (29, 231, 292). It is easy to imagine Lydia Bennet today, skipping school in order to flirt shamelessly at a shopping mall in between credit card purchases and snacks paid for by others: "We mean to treat you all ... but you must lend us the money, for we have just spent ours at the shop.... Look here, I have bought this bonnet. I do not think it is very pretty, but I thought I might as well buy it as not.... Have you seen any pleasant men? Have you had any flirting?" (219, 221). Time moves slowly for a young woman with no inner resources: "Nothing less than a dance on Tuesday, could have made such a Friday, Saturday, Sunday, and Monday endurable" (88).

Not only her head but also her heart seems vacant. Not choosy about her dance partner, she seems ready to have any man who will flatter her vanity. Like many a bride-to-be today preoccupied with expensive wedding arrangements rather than the impending marriage, so Lydia on her wedding day worries only about whether Wickham will wear his blue coat (319). When she returns home as Mrs. Wickham, she ignores the disgraceful circumstances of her marriage and the pain she has caused others. She gloats about preceding her "old maid" sisters into the dining room: "Ah! Jane, I take your place now, and you must go lower, because I am a married woman" (317). Rather than facing the fact that she has married a profligate man who stays with her only because he is paid to do so, Lydia milks her moment of wedded importance: "Oh! mamma, do the people here abouts know I am married to-day? I was afraid they might not; ... so I ... took off my glove, and let my hand just rest upon the window frame [to show] the ring, and then I bowed and smiled like any thing" (316). In direct contrast to the loyal, affectionate Elizabeth, Lydia displays selfish indifference to her family and inattentiveness to her sisters' feelings.

Although Austen does not discuss religion in *Pride and Prejudice* as directly as she will in the later *Mansfield Park*, she seems to use Lydia Bennet to reveal the danger of a young woman having no moral principles, no conscience, and no belief in a higher power. Lydia's love of gambling—she is "extremely fond of lottery-tickets," "talk[s] incessantly of the lottery," and loves making bets—and Wickham's extensive gaming debts suggest they are fortune's fools, moving about restlessly without a higher purpose (76, 84). Lydia blithely uses the Lord's name in vain: "Lord how tired I am!" "Lord, how ashamed I should be of not being married before three and twenty! ... Lord! how I should like to be married before any of you ... Lord! how I laughed!" "Oh, Lord! yes" (103, 221, 317).

Why might Austen give us two Bennet sisters described as wild, bold, and laughing, one to admire and the other to censure? Perhaps, as Claudia Johnson suggests, Lydia serves for the reader as "a decoy who attracts the disapproval to which Elizabeth herself could otherwise be subject."[9] Austen's readers can accept Elizabeth's remarkable unconventionality, impertinence, impropriety, and violation of conduct-book standards because *compared to Lydia* she seems quite restrained, feminine, and virtuous. We see that Elizabeth, despite her muddy petticoats, self-confidence, and love of laughter, has both sense and sensibility, qualities woefully lacking in the unintelligent, unfeeling, and "absolutely uncontrouled" Lydia (231).

Yet how can we blame Lydia for her behavior when she has succeeded so marvelously in becoming like her mother? Much as she devoted many pages of *Sense and Sensibility* to showing the similarities between Marianne Dashwood and her equally romantic and imprudent mother, so Jane Austen makes it abundantly clear in *Pride and Prejudice* that "dear Lydia" is her mother's favorite daughter. Repetitions of words link daughter to mother. For example, the only times in *Pride and Prejudice* in which Austen uses *distracted* and *merry* are in conjunction with these two unthinkingly happy-go-lucky women:

"I should have gone quite distracted." (Lydia, 319)

"I shall go distracted." (Mrs. Bennet, 378)

"We were so merry all the way home!" (Lydia, 222)

"How merry we shall be together!" (Mrs. Bennet, 306)

Like her mother, Lydia has been raised to be a creature of appetite and pleasure without virtue or reason, and Austen leads us to suspect that the cycle will continue if the uneducated, unreformed, and unrepentant Lydia ever has daughters of her own.

Much as Lydia shows off her ring to passersby, so Mrs. Bennet focuses on the wedding clothes ("a privilege without which her marriage would scarcely seem valid"), boasts of Lydia's marriage to the whole neighborhood, and laments that the newspaper write-up is so brief (310). Her comments echo Jane Austen's joking remark in a letter, "One may as well be single if the Wedding is not to be in print" (late February 1815). Just as Lady Middleton and Fanny Dashwood argued over the heights of their sons in *Sense and Sensibility*, so Mrs. Bennet and her peers compete over their ability to land propertied husbands for their daughters.

But Austen sees to it that her readers understand rather than merely scorn Lydia and her mother. Denied education and power by society, Mrs. Bennet and Mrs. Wickham are left at the financial mercy of irresponsible husbands. Mrs. Bennet articulates the economic powerlessness of women when she notes of her husband's passive acceptance of the entail, "I am sure if I had been you, I should have tried long ago to do something or other about it" (62). In the last letter she writes in *Pride and Prejudice*, Lydia shrewdly uses her connections to try to *do something or other about* getting her feckless husband an income:

> "MY DEAR LIZZY,
> "I wish you joy.... It is a great comfort to have you so rich, and when you have nothing else to do, I hope you will think of us. I am sure Wickham would like a place at court very much, and I do not think we shall have quite money enough to live upon without some help. Any place would do, of about three or four hundred a year." (386)

Austen shows that despite their shallowness, Mrs. Bennet and Lydia at least take action and try to survive in economic circumstances stacked against them.

Just as "Lydia was Lydia still" at the end of the novel, unreformed and unimproved, so Mrs. Bennet remains exactly the same woman of "mean understanding, little information, and uncertain temper" whom we met at the beginning (315, 5). In one of the few narrative intrusions in *Pride and Prejudice*, Austen inserts her "I" voice to lament Mrs. Bennet's inability to grow: "I wish I could say [that she became] a sensible, amiable, well-informed woman for the rest of her life," but in fact Mrs. Bennet remains still "nervous and invariably silly" (385).

Like Mrs. Bennet and Lydia, Mary Bennet never grows or changes in the course of this novel. Yet her faults are profoundly different from theirs. "In consequence of being the only plain one" in the family, Mary spends her time practicing the piano, "always impatient for display" of her talent (25). She reads prose works so she can extract sayings of "thread-bare morality" for the edification of others (60). If Lydia is too flighty, Mary is too heavy: "Mary piqued herself upon the solidity of her reflections" (20). If we accept Blake's notion that to generalize is to be an idiot, then Mary's abstractions are another form of idiocy in a book filled with fools. Why talk generically of "virtue in a female" when scandal affects your youngest sister (289)? Mary only gives the illusion of having sense and sensibility; in fact, she has neither. Her musical performances display her lack of taste and genius, and her pompous reactions to her sisters demonstrate her dearth of compassion and empathy. Reading brings no wisdom, as Mary refers to pride and vanity without recognizing her own. Her remarks in fact plagiarize Hester Chapone's *Letters on the Improvement of the Mind* (1773), one of the many conduct books Austen debunked throughout her juvenilia.[10] In addition, Mary's comment about a woman's reputation being "no less brittle than it is beautiful" steals from Mr. Villars's insistence in a Fanny Burney novel that "the reputation of a woman ... is, at once, the most beautiful and most brittle of all human things."[11]

Perhaps Austen includes the prose-reading, pontificating Mary Bennet to prevent any reader from reaching easy conclusions about how to keep young women from following in Lydia's wild footsteps. Mary stands as a reminder to readers that the best way to raise daughters is not to feed them a diet of essays, conduct books, and sermons, forbid them from reading fanciful novels and lyrical poems, admonish them to avoid wit and laughter, and teach them to acquire fine arts for display rather than for their souls.

Again, Austen tempers her portrait of a female fool. She places Mary as the middle daughter out of five, thus excluded from both the close affection between Elizabeth and Jane and the camaraderie between the giddy Lydia and Kitty; she is the favorite of neither parent. Is it her fault that even though she "worked hard" at her music she has no innate talent (25)? Is it her fault that she is plain? What bad *luck* (a word repeated throughout this novel) that she was not first or second in line in the Bennet family to be married and that Elizabeth's mortifying rejection of Mr. Collins caused him to switch his "affections" to Charlotte Lucas. Mary actually *liked* Mr. Collins (she prizes his letters) and probably would have made an excellent wife for him. Perhaps Austen tells us of Mary's favorable response to Mr. Collins ("Mary might have been prevailed on to accept him") to remind us that coincidences, accidents, and sheer luck often influence just which women will capture those single men with large fortunes looking for wives (124).

Austen's final paragraph about this middle Bennet sister shows Mary continuing to moralize about others rather than developing herself. Her punishment is to be stuck permanently as the only daughter at home, forced therefore to keep Mrs. Bennet company. Mary's only comfort is that "she was no longer mortified by comparisons between her sisters' beauty and her own," a parting reminder from Austen that in a culture valuing appearance, Mary's destiny might have been different had she been blessed with a pretty face (386).

The fretful Kitty, who seems to have inherited her mother's frenzied nerves and Lydia's folly, has at least a chance of improvement, we are told, because she spends time with Elizabeth and Jane: "Kitty, to her very material advantage, spent the chief of her time with her two elder sisters. In society so superior to what she had generally known, her improvement was great.... she became, by proper attention and management, less irritable, less ignorant, and less insipid" (385). Give a young woman guidance ("management") and education and she can make great improvement, Austen suggests.

Austen frequently sets the "two elder sisters" apart from the rest of Meryton. When the regiment of officers leaves town, only Elizabeth and Jane respond sensibly: "All the young ladies in the neighbourhood were drooping apace. The dejection was almost universal. The elder Miss Bennets alone were still able to eat, drink, and sleep" (229). They are without question Mrs. Bennet's "two most deserving daughters," both possessing intelligence, compassion, virtue, and fortitude (385). Unlike the contrast Austen developed between Elinor and Marianne in *Sense and Sensibility*, Jane and Elizabeth join forces to conceal their sufferings and to keep their disordered family from further harm. Trying unsuccessfully but valiantly to act as surrogate parents, "Elizabeth had frequently united with Jane in an endeavour to check the imprudence of Catherine and Lydia" (213). In many ways, they function as husband and wife—like soul mates. Their close relationship perhaps reflects Jane Austen's own lifelong partnership with Cassandra. As a relative observed, "No one was equal to Jane in Cassandra's eyes. And Jane looked up to Cassandra as one far wiser and better than herself. They were as their mother said 'wedded to each other.'"[12] Austen's focus in *Pride and Prejudice* on two sisters' candid, animated, and supportive conversation may reflect her own joy in sharing with Cassandra "the pleasures of Friendship, of unreserved Conversation, of similarity of Taste & Opinions" (1 July 1808).[13] Of the 150 surviving Jane Austen letters, over 90 are addressed to Cassandra. Jane Austen clearly considers her sister a sympathetic, intelligent listener and acknowledges her superiority in a way reminiscent of Elizabeth Bennet's praise of Jane: "my only fear is of your being so agreeable, so much to [Mrs. Knight's] taste, as to make her wish to keep you with her for ever" (7 January 1807).

Like a married couple silently catching each other's eyes in public in order to find strength and comfort, "Jane and Elizabeth looked at each other" when stuck in a public place with the noisy, imprudent Lydia (221). At another point, a "glance from Jane invited Elizabeth to follow her upstairs" (116). Elizabeth admits that during hard times, she wants nothing better than to be with her sister: "I was very uncomfortable, I may say unhappy. And with no one to speak to, of what I felt, no Jane to comfort me and say that I had not been so very weak and vain and nonsensical as I knew I had! Oh! how I wanted you!" (226). At several points in this novel, Jane and Elizabeth rationally and feelingly discuss what action to take, using each other as a sounding board. When Elizabeth is away from home and news breaks of Lydia's disgrace, Jane deeply feels the loss of a partner to share the sorrow and plan the future: "I am truly glad, dearest Lizzy, that you have been spared something of these distressing scenes; but now as the first shock is over, shall I own that I long for your return?" (275). Elizabeth responds by feeling "wild to be at home—to hear, to see, to be upon the spot, *to share with Jane* in the cares that must now fall wholly upon her, in a family so deranged" (280; my italics). Austen makes sure readers not only hear extensive dialogue between the sisters but also are told that their reunion means "half the night spent in conversation" (374).

Too often labeled just a "courtship novel," *Pride and Prejudice* contains many passages demonstrating that Jane and Elizabeth care deeply about each other. Austen fills this novel with phrases such as "her thoughts naturally flew to her sister" or "the happiness of a most beloved sister" (262, 190). Jane's illness prompts Elizabeth's four-mile walk through the mud, and Elizabeth rejects Darcy in part because of his efforts to separate Jane from the man she loves. Throughout, Elizabeth maintains Jane's superiority, viewing her as "all loveliness and goodness" with "her understanding excellent, her mind improved, and her manners captivating" (186). In turn, Jane is quick to see why the wealthy Mr. Darcy would want to marry Elizabeth because of "the strong sisterly partiality which made admiration of Elizabeth appear perfectly natural" (224). Rather than competing, they love each other wholeheartedly: for example, instead of stewing about the fact that Jane had more dance partners and received more compliments than she did, Elizabeth "instantly read her feelings ... and every thing else gave way before the hope of Jane's being in the fairest way for happiness" (95). At another point, Elizabeth "felt Jane's pleasure" (12). Austen emphasizes the sisters' reciprocity of affection: "Each felt for the other" (334). Much as she ended *Sense and Sensibility* with a description of the closeness between two sisters, so Austen tells us in the closing chapter of *Pride and Prejudice* that "Jane and Elizabeth, in addition to every other source of happiness, were within thirty miles of each other" (385).

Why, then, if we have two intelligent, compassionate women who love each other do we not have two equal heroines? The first conversation Austen includes between Jane and Elizabeth answers that question:

> "I was very much flattered by his asking me to dance a second time. I did not expect such a compliment."
>
> "Did not you? *I* did for you. But that is one great difference between us.... He could not help seeing that you were about five times as pretty as every other woman in the room.... Well, he certainly is very agreeable, and I give you leave to like him. You have liked many a stupider person.
>
> "Dear Lizzy!"
>
> "Oh! you are a great deal too apt you know, to like people in general. You never see a fault in any body. All the world are good and agreeable in your eyes. I never heard you speak ill of a human being in my life." (14)

We cannot help but find Elizabeth more compelling, and we already know that the witty Mr. Bennet prefers her. Elizabeth is droll, self-deprecating, perceptive, and loving. And, as Austen expressed it in a letter, Elizabeth is more delightful than previous heroines, different from anything that "ever appeared in print." We may have encountered sweet, angelic, beautiful, modest Jane Bennets before in literature, but no one like Elizabeth. It is not surprising that Elizabeth troubled some in Austen's era, who felt Jane was the novel's true heroine. Author Mary Mussell Mitford, for instance, deplored Elizabeth Bennet for possessing an "entire want of taste" and for being "so pert, so worldly a heroine."[14]

Jane Bennet is too good to be true in two senses of the phrase—both in the conventional sense that she does not ring true to imperfect readers and also in the sense that her goodness keeps her from seeing the truth.

Elizabeth views her older sister as perfect in an imperfect world: "My dear Jane! You are too good. Your sweetness and disinterestedness are really angelic.... *You* wish to think all the world respectable, and are hurt if I speak ill of anybody. *I* only want to think *you* perfect" (134). Like the naive Catherine Morland who is so "warped by an innate principle of general integrity" that she fails for hundreds of pages to detect Isabella's dissembling manners and mercenary ulterior motives, the "honestly blind" but well-intentioned Jane Bennet persists for an unbelievably long time in finding the odious Miss Bingley and Mrs. Hurst charming, pleasing, friendly women (*NA*, 219; *PP*, 14). "Caroline is incapable of willfully deceiving anyone," Jane insists of the blatantly duplicitous Miss Bingley (119). Elizabeth quickly sees through this sneering, backstabbing woman because Elizabeth has "more quickness of observation and less pliancy of temper than her sister" (15).

Elizabeth has more "quickness" not only in terms of keenness of perception but also in terms of speed. It takes her one moment, not scores of chapters, to reject Miss Bingley and Mrs. Hurst. She does not share the sweet, steady Jane's cautious approach: "I would wish not to be hasty in censuring any one," Jane calmly states (14). Elizabeth's prejudice stems primarily from her tendency to jump to conclusions as quickly as she jumps over stiles. In a race, one definitely would bet on Elizabeth: "Away ran the girls ... Jane, who was not so light, nor so much in the habit of running as Elizabeth, soon lagged behind" (301). Elizabeth has to learn to form her own judgments more slowly and cautiously. "All I can promise you ... is not to be in a hurry" she eventually tells her aunt (145).

Jane is calmer than Elizabeth and fights against strong emotions like anger. The phrase "pliancy of temper" suggests the narrator's ambivalence about Jane Bennet (15). Certainly one would not wish to have a rigid, unyielding, utterly stubborn temper, but Jane's pliancy allows her to be too easily bent, influenced, and manipulated by others. She is constantly described as "sweet" and "mild," adjectives suggesting goodness but also a kind of feminine weakness. We cannot imagine Jane standing up so boldly to Lady Catherine, as Elizabeth does. Instead of pertinaciously fighting her adversaries with wit, Jane pliantly withdraws, stays composed, blames herself, and suffers stoically in silence, for "whatever she felt she was desirous of concealing" (129).

Interestingly, Austen shows us that the truth lies somewhere between Jane's steady faith in universal human goodness and Elizabeth's quick rush to total condemnation. When Elizabeth hears of Charlotte Lucas's engagement to Mr. Collins, she blasts her friend:

"Charlotte's marriage ... is unaccountable! in every view it is unaccountable!"

"My dear Lizzy, do not give way to such feelings as these. They will ruin your happiness. You do not make allowance enough for difference of situation and temper. Consider Mr. Collins's respectability, and Charlotte's prudent, steady character. Remember that she is one of a large family; that as to fortune, it is a most eligible match; and be ready to believe for everybody's sake, that she may feel something like regard and esteem for our cousin."

"... My dear Jane, Mr. Collins is a conceited, pompous, narrow-minded, silly man; you know he is, as well as I do; and you must feel, as well as I do, that the woman who marries him, cannot have a proper way of thinking.... You shall not, for the sake of one individual, change the meaning of principle and integrity, nor endeavour to persuade yourself or me, that selfishness is prudence, and insensibility of danger, security for happiness."

"I must think your language too strong in speaking of both," replied Jane, ... "But enough of this." (135–36)

Elizabeth speaks categorically, accusing Charlotte of sacrificing "*every* better feeling to worldly advantage." In fact, readers see that the unromantic, plain-faced Charlotte Lucas has made a practical choice with her eyes open, seeing an establishment with Mr. Collins as her "pleasantest preservative from want" (122–23). She pursues this marriage, setting out "to meet him accidentally in the lane" and making an effort to flatter him at the right time (121). Once married, the "sensible, intelligent ... prudent, steady" Charlotte develops her own coping strategy—encouraging Mr. Collins to garden so he will be out of the house and taking the worst room of the house so he will not bother her there (135). Jane may be wrong to think any regard or esteem can exist between this couple, but Elizabeth is too vehement in her scorn. Jane is in danger of blind optimism; Elizabeth of disillusionment.

Austen uses the husbands of Mrs. Bennet's "two most deserving daughters" to explore notions of gentlemanly behavior, a recurring theme in all six of her novels. Like the contrast Austen sets up between Elizabeth and Jane—Elizabeth quick to censure everyone whereas Jane finds only goodness—Mr. Darcy and his friend Mr. Bingley respond in radically different ways to the same social scene: "Between [Bingley] and Darcy there was a very steady friendship, in spite of a great opposition of character.... The manner in which they spoke of the Meryton assembly was sufficiently characteristic. Bingley had never met with pleasanter people or prettier girls in his life; every body had been most kind and attentive to him, there had been no formality, no stiffness, he had soon felt acquainted with all the room; and as to Miss Bennet, he could not conceive an angel more beautiful. Darcy, on the contrary, had seen a collection of people in whom there was little beauty and no fashion, for none of whom he had felt the smallest interest, and from none received either attention or pleasure" (16). Both are blind: Bingley sees no evil because of his easy, open temper; Darcy sees no good because of his overweening pride.

Like Mary Bennet ironically uttering reflections about vanity and pride without recognizing her own, Mr. Darcy speaks in humorless abstractions: "Nothing is more deceitful ... than the appearance of humility. It is often only carelessness of opinion, and sometimes an indirect boast" (48). "Yes, vanity is a weakness indeed. But pride—where there is a real superiority of mind, pride will be always under good regulation" (57). True, Lydia and Kitty Bennet spend far too much time thinking about the next merry dance, but does Darcy have to condemn it ("Every savage can dance") as primitive (25)? He moves in social circles with cold silence, "grave propriety," and formal bows that signal his disdain (26). He cannot take a joke ("Mr. Darcy is not to be laughed at!" Elizabeth notes) and seems full of self-love: "Mr. Darcy may hug himself," as Miss Bingley puts it (57).

Austen presents Darcy as a thinking, feeling man with a blunt core of integrity ("disguise of every sort is my abhorrence," he insists) who must learn in the course of the novel to behave with gentler manners and "perfect civility" to everyone, including those society deems beneath him (192, 251). Though no glib reciter of poetry or singer of duets, he has enough appreciation of the arts to enjoy Elizabeth's performances, to suggest dancing a reel to "a lively Scotch air," and to maintain the grounds of his Pemberley estate without ostentation in a style "neither formal, nor falsely adorned" (52, 245). Darcy's ability to nurture the natural beauty of his extensive grounds separates him from his aunt, a tasteless, showy woman, and from Mr. Collins, whose approach to houses and landscape is to count every item and calculate every price.

Darcy is, like Colonel Brandon, a gentleman in need of an animated woman. As Mrs. Gardiner concludes of Darcy, "His understanding and opinions all please me; he wants nothing but a little more liveliness, and *that* ... his wife may teach him" (325). Elizabeth already had reached that same conclusion: "It was an union that must have been to the advantage of both; by her ease and liveliness, his mind might have been softened, his manners improved, and from his judgment, information, and knowledge of the world, she must have received benefit of greater importance" (312). Austen suggests that marriage succeeds only if both partners become more whole, more complete, through the union.

As if to underscore the need for complementarity rather than similarity in marriage partners, Austen gives some of Elizabeth's qualities—liveliness, ease, good-humored playfulness—to Mr. Bingley but does not present Bingley and Elizabeth as attracted to each other. Bingley has the very strengths Darcy lacks: he can laugh at himself, act graciously to others, take pleasure in any surroundings, and democratically accept as his equals those with less money. He is a newly made gentleman whose family fortune came from trade, not inherited titles and estates, but he has not acquired the nouveau riche hauteur of his sisters nor the aristocratic pride of his friend, Mr. Darcy. Bingley is a respectable "good-looking and gentlemanlike" man with "a pleasant countenance" and "perfect good breeding," a man others call "sensible, good humoured, lively" with "unaffected cordiality ... a greater sweetness of address, and a stronger desire of generally pleasing than any other man" (10, 14, 16, 261).

Bingley is the only character Austen ever describes as possessing a "ductility" of temper, a word reminding us of Jane Bennet's pliancy and tractability (16). Unlike Darcy (to whom nothing comes easily), Bingley has "easy, unaffected manners," "so much ease," an "easiness of temper," "good-humoured ease," and "ease and cheerfulness" (10, 14, 15, 133, 261, 345). Like *lively*, the term *ease* is loaded with ambivalence. Bingley's ease suggests his relaxed informality and cheerful social poise, but it also indicates a too ready acceptance of whatever happens (such as Darcy sending him away from Jane) and an almost lazy resignation to his gentlemanly lot. "I am an idle fellow," he confesses (38). Elizabeth bemoans Bingley's "want of proper resolution which now made him the slave of his designing friends," and Darcy admits of his easygoing friend, "He had a stronger dependence on my judgment than on his own" (133, 199). Bingley speaks with wit (he jokes with his sisters and joshes Darcy), but he never takes *action* unless directed to do so by Darcy. Bingley and Jane may live happily, easily, and sweetly ever after, but they will remain passive and at the mercy of others. As Mr. Bennet puts it to Jane, "Your tempers are by no means unlike. You are each of you so complying, that nothing will ever be resolved on; so easy, that every servant will cheat you" (348).

As in *Sense and Sensibility*, Austen suggests in *Pride and Prejudice* that idleness and easy wealth threaten to make men effeminate. If Bingley is too pleasing and pliant, Wickham is downright soft, resembling what Austen knew to be the negative stereotype of a woman: "His appearance was greatly in his favour; he had all the best part of beauty, a fine countenance, a good figure, and very pleasing address," "a captivating softness ... in manners," "every charm of air and address," "every charm of person and address," "He smiled, looked handsome, and said many pretty things" (72, 180, 206, 284, 330). Like Bingley, Wickham is "a young man of most gentlemanlike appearance" who seems all that is "amiable and pleasing," with an "easy assurance," "easy address," and "good-humoured ease" (72, 152, 315, 316). Austen's repetition of identical phrases for Bingley and Wickham seems designed to draw readers' attention to the similarities—and ultimately the key differences. To a *far* greater extent than Bingley, Wickham has acquired the exterior of a gentleman without ethics. Bingley is a rather weak but good man, whereas Wickham is a downright scoundrel, a man whose "vicious propensities—the want of principle" propel him into "a life of idleness and dissipation" (200, 201).

Austen expands her exploration of the gentleman in *Pride and Prejudice* by introducing a gallery of minor male characters with various degrees of gentlemanliness. Mr. Hurst, for instance, "merely looked the gentleman" but is "an indolent man, who lived only to eat, drink, and play at cards" (35). Colonel Fitzwilliam is "not handsome," but his well-informed mind and manner of conversing make him "most truly the gentleman" (170–71). The only titled gentleman in *Pride and Prejudice* is Sir William Lucas, a knight with "the complaisance of a courtier" who is little more than a timid, unintelligent man in awe of the nobility (126). Joining Sir William Lucas in his adulation of the rich and titled is William Collins, a ridiculous "mixture of pride and obsequiousness, self-importance and humility" who utters "pompous nothings" and allows himself to be slavishly ruled by the opinions and decrees of Lady Catherine de Bourgh (70). Mr. Collins is more than stupid: he is mean-spirited. As a way of punishing Elizabeth for refusing his offer, he takes pleasure in spreading the gossip about Lydia and in gloating in his letters to Mr. Bennet that he has not married into their pitiful family: "Let me advise you then, my dear Sir, to console yourself as much as possible, to throw off your unworthy child from your affection for ever, and leave her to reap the fruits of her own heinous offence" (297). Austen shows this clergyman using biblical language ("reap the fruits") to preach a lack of mercy and forgiveness. This is no gentleman, just as this is no man of God.

Although Mr. Bennet can see Mr. Collins's pomposity, he fails to overcome his *own* failings as a gentleman. Mr. Bennet casually ignores his daughters' plight due to the entail and seeks merely "leisure and tranquillity," not the proper discharge of his duties (71). Yes, he is literate ("with a book he was regardless of time"), but he approaches life's vicissitudes with "calm unconcern" (12, 111). His neglect of his giddy daughters and ridicule of his wife in part contribute to Lydia's disgrace. Mr. Bennet sums up his laissez-faire approach to the world when he quips, "I am quite at leisure" (377).

By placing into Mr. Bennet's mouth a rhetorical question—"For what do we live, but to make sport for our neighbours and laugh at them in our turn?"—Austen indirectly steers us toward a different conclusion (364). Mr. Bennet has too little sense of duty or responsibility.

Mr. Bennet's brother-in-law, Mr. Gardiner, would answer that a gentleman lives to help his family and neighbors, not to laugh at them. Austen describes Mr. Gardiner as "a sensible, gentlemanlike man, greatly superior to his sister [Mrs. Bennet] as well by nature as education," a "well-bred and agreeable" man with "intelligence ... taste and ... good manners" who marries an equally well-bred, sensible, and loving woman, functions as a loving husband, father, brother, and uncle, and takes dignified action to help the Bennet family with their Lydia troubles (139, 255). Although, horror of horrors, he "lived by trade, and within view of his own warehouses," Mr. Gardiner is more gentlemanly in manner and deed than those considered his social betters (139). In passages throughout *Pride and Prejudice* describing "gentlemanlike" behavior, Austen warns readers not to view handsome, leisured men as gentlemen until their just principles, informed understanding, liberal generosity, and active discharge of duties prove them worthy of the name.

One form of prejudice Austen explores in *Pride and Prejudice* is our tendency to prejudge men and women by "First Impressions," as the novel was originally called—in particular, by first impressions based on appearance. Mary Bennet and Charlotte Lucas know full well that they have fewer options because of their plain faces, while Mrs. Bennet has been able to land herself a good husband solely because of her youth and beauty. Bingley instantly gravitates toward Jane because she is the most beautiful woman in the room, and Elizabeth finds Wickham charming and virtuous simply because he is handsome. When Elizabeth and Jane consider the true nature of Darcy and Wickham, they marvel at the difference between semblance and substance, the fact that "one has got all the goodness, and the other all the appearance of it" (225). Elizabeth had labeled Wickham "the most agreeable man I ever *saw*," a phrase suggesting she has judged with her eyes rather than her mind (144).

In answer to Marvell and Shakespeare's question, "Who ever lov'd that lov'd not at first sight?" (Marvell's *Hero and Leander*, 1.176, quoted by Shakespeare's Phebe in *As You Like It*, 3.5.82), Austen could have answered, the hero and heroine of *Pride and Prejudice*. Austen rejects the notion of love at first sight—both the emphasis on appearance and the emphasis on speed—by showing the slow-developing relationship between Elizabeth and Darcy. Discussions of haste and hurry throughout the novel make readers conscious of the need for love to develop slowly and thoughtfully. Unlike

Laura and Edward of the adolescent "Love and Freindship," who marry within two minutes of meeting each other, Elizabeth and Darcy take their time. As Elizabeth explains to Jane, "It has been coming on so gradually, that I hardly know when it began" (373).

Darcy shares this, bewildered inability to pinpoint the moment when love began. He confesses to Elizabeth, "I cannot fix on the hour, or the spot, or the look, or the words, which laid the foundation. It is too long ago. I was in the middle before I knew that I *had* begun" (380). I do not recall a passage like this in any previous literary work. It seems a deliberate rejection on Austen's part of the love-at-first-sight formula expected of courtship romances. Darcy moves from regarding Elizabeth as "not handsome enough to tempt" him, to finding Elizabeth's face "rendered uncommonly intelligent" by her sparkling eyes, to considering in general that a truly accomplished woman must possess "something more substantial, in the improvement of her mind by extensive reading," to discovering that he has indeed become "bewitched" by Elizabeth's lively mind and playful spirit (12, 23, 39, 52). Darcy clearly wants a woman with a mind, not just a pretty face or superficial skills. Despite his gravity, Darcy cannot help but smile at several points because of Elizabeth's pointed retorts. Like Henry Tilney in *Northanger Abbey*, Elizabeth Bennet mocks conventional small talk: "It is *your* turn to say something now, Mr. Darcy.—*I* talked about the dance, and *you* ought to make some kind of remark on the size of the room, or the number of couples" (91). Austen notes here and at many other moments after Elizabeth speaks, "Darcy smiled." Elizabeth thinks quickly and perceptively, as in her response to Darcy's justification for his antisocial behavior:

> "I certainly have not the talent which some people possess," said Darcy, "of conversing easily with those I have never seen before. I cannot catch their tone of conversation, or appear interested in their concerns, as I often see done."
>
> "My fingers," said Elizabeth, "do not move over this instrument in the masterly manner which I see so many women's do. They have not the same force or rapidity, and do not produce the same expression. But then I have always supposed it to be my own fault—because I would not take the trouble of practising. It is not that I do not believe *my* fingers as capable as any other woman's of superior execution."
>
> Darcy smiled and said, "You are perfectly right." (175–76)

Elizabeth insists on her inalienable right to banter: "it belongs to me to find occasions for teazing and quarreling with you as often as may be" (381). She makes Darcy think, challenges his complacency, and thus enlivens him. Darcy falls in love with Elizabeth because she is "a rational creature speaking the truth from her heart" with wit and perception (109).

In fact, if we try to find the precise moment when Darcy becomes "bewitched" by Elizabeth and is prompted through a very un-Darcy-like impulse to ask her to "seize ... an opportunity of dancing a reel," we discover that the conversation right before this pits the two against each other like skilled lawyers in a courtroom (52). In a passage worth quoting at some length, Darcy argues the "case" with Elizabeth against Bingley's yielding personality until Bingley finally protests the dispute. Darcy says,

> "Your conduct would be quite as dependant on chance as that of any man I know; and if, as you were mounting your horse, a friend were to say, 'Bingley, you had better stay till next week,' you would probably do it, you would probably not go—and, at another word, might stay a month."
>
> "You have only proved by this," cried Elizabeth, "that Mr. Bingley did not do justice to his own disposition. You have shewn him off now much more than he did himself." ...
>
> "You expect me to account for opinions which you chuse to call mine, which I have never acknowledged. Allowing the case, however, to stand according to your representation, you must remember, Miss Bennet, that the friend who is supposed to desire his return ... has merely desired it, asked it without offering one argument in favour of its propriety."
>
> "To yield readily—easily—to the *persuasion* of a friend is no merit with you."
>
> "To yield without conviction is no compliment to the understanding of either."
>
> "You appear to me, Mr. Darcy, to allow nothing for the influence of friendship and affection. A regard for the requester would often make one readily yield to a request, without waiting for arguments to reason one into it...."
>
> "Will it not be advisable, before we proceed on this subject, to arrange with rather more precision the degree of importance which is to appertain to this request, as well as the degree of intimacy subsisting between the parties?" ...
>
> "Arguments are too much like disputes [Bingley later interjects]. If you and Miss Bennet will defer yours till I am out of the room, I shall be very thankful." (49–51)

Indeed, Elizabeth and Darcy do enjoy arguing, much as professional chess players suffering through matches against amateurs would feel grateful to find formidable opponents to challenge their skills. Austen reinforces our perceptions of Elizabeth and Darcy as equals by giving them matching amounts of speaking time. In addition to the debate about Bingley's personality, there are over a dozen other major dialogues between Darcy and Elizabeth.[15] Readers hear Elizabeth and Darcy talk as intellectual equals far more than any other pair of lovers in Austen's novels. What a far cry the animated Elizabeth–Darcy exchanges are from the mismatched opening "conversation" between Mr. and Mrs. Bennet. One reason Mr. Bennet misses Elizabeth so much when she is away from home is that she functions as his substitute soul mate, the one person with whom he can engage in verbal sparring and a witty exchange of ideas.

By getting to know and respect Elizabeth's mind and heart, Darcy moves from coldly dismissing her appearance (Darcy is reported to have said, "*She* a beauty!—I should as soon call her mother a wit") to admiring her as "one of the handsomest women" he has met (271). This is love at fourth or fifth sight, perhaps—and not just by sight. Darcy attributes his attraction to the liveliness of Elizabeth's *mind*, not to the liveliness of her eyes or delicacy of her features. His attraction is not just cerebral, though, as he seems struck in part by Elizabeth's intense affection for Jane. Like Elizabeth, Darcy values the love of a sister. He has faithfully loved Georgiana, trying to protect her honor and nurturing her growing intimacy with Elizabeth.

Elizabeth takes many more chapters to fall in love and has to overcome active dislike of Darcy as "the last man in the world whom [she] could be prevailed on to marry" (193). In Elizabeth's list of attributes that eventually attract her to Darcy, his height and "noble mien" get nary a mention (10). For Elizabeth, Darcy's natural taste, educated mind, moral judgment, and honorable conduct reveal his gentlemanliness. Unlike her father, infatuated by beauty, Elizabeth will not form a hasty "unequal marriage" leaving her the "grief" of being "unable to respect [her] partner in life" (376).

Austen intrudes as narrator to tell us that a gradually developed love between a man and a woman, in this case Darcy and Elizabeth, may be less romantic to write about but more satisfying in its depth: "If gratitude and esteem are good foundations of affection, Elizabeth's change of sentiment [toward Darcy] will be neither improbable or faulty. But if otherwise, if the regard springing from such sources is unreasonable or unnatural, in comparison of what is so often described as arising on a first interview with its object, and even before two words have been exchanged, nothing can be said in her defence, except that she had given somewhat of a trial to the latter method, in her partiality for Wickham, and that its ill-success might perhaps authorise her to seek the other less interesting mode of attachment" (279). Much as in *Northanger Abbey* Austen pretended to apologize for the ways Catherine failed to resemble heroines in other books, so here she pretends that her description of mature love based on a solid foundation is "less interesting" than the love at first sight which "is so often described" in typical romances.

As if to emphasize that she is more interested in the *process* of falling in love than the romance itself, Austen again chooses to withdraw the camera lens (or at least turn off the sound equipment) right as Darcy proposes to Elizabeth: "he expressed himself on the occasion as sensibly and as warmly as a man violently in love can be supposed to do" (366). Here Austen uses the clichéd expression ("violently in love") she called into question earlier in the novel as "so hackneyed, so doubtful, so indefinite, that it gives ... very little idea," a phrase "as often applied to feelings which arise from an half-hour's acquaintance, as to a real, strong attachment" (140–41). By the time we are told in the third volume that Darcy is "violently in love," we know it is the latter, more slowly grown and therefore genuine form of attachment; it is not based on beauty (Mr. Bennet), convenience (Mr. Collins), or sensuality and money (Wickham), but rather esteem.

It is easy (to use a Bingley term) to be so charmed by the growing love between Elizabeth and Darcy that we fail to recognize the radical social nature of their marriage—and of the novel as a whole. In *Sense and Sensibility* Marianne marries a man with an annual income of two thousand pounds, but she was the daughter of a gentleman from a long-established, respectable family with no vulgar relations in the closet. In contrast, Elizabeth Bennet secures a man worth ten thousand pounds per year and can offer him little besides an embarrassing assemblage of relatives. Not only that but Darcy has noble, titled ancestors while Elizabeth has the taint (also called "pollution" and "impurities") of relatives in trade and in the law (141, 388). As Austen economics expert Edward Copeland notes, this is "a Cinderella match of great wealth and comparative poverty, across significant social lines," a union of "dizzying" stakes between "potentially one of the most impoverished" heroines and the wealthiest Austen hero.[16]

There is no denying that Austen turns the class system upside down and inside out in this novel. Why else would she go to such lengths to show that the woman at the top of the social ladder—the aristocratic Lady Catherine de Bourgh—has less breeding than the lowly, totally untitled Mrs. Gardiner, the novel's true "lady"? Mrs. Gardiner is "an amiable, intelligent, elegant woman" who shares with her husband "affection and intelligence," or sensibility and sense (139, 240).

Aristocracy based on birth gives power to those who may not deserve it, Elizabeth Bennet recognizes, and she refuses to feel afraid of Lady Catherine simply because of her title: "Mere stateliness of money and rank, she thought she could witness without trepidation" (161). Elizabeth feels unafraid of Lady Catherine because she possesses no talents or virtues that justify her title and rank. Elizabeth probably shared the thoughts of Figaro in his daring monologue from *Marriage of Figaro*: "Because you're a great lord, you think you've a great mind as well! Nobility, fortune, rank, power, it makes a man proud. What have you done to deserve all that? You went to the trouble of being born, nothing more."[17] Although Lady Catherine enjoys condescending to her social inferiors and "likes to have the distinction of rank preserved," she occupies a superior position merely through accident of birth, not through any talent or merit of her own (161). Mr. Collins is sure that Elizabeth will temper her "wit and vivacity" when she comes face to face with the great Lady Catherine ("the silence and respect which her rank will inevitably excite"), but Elizabeth in fact responds by voicing her opinions and registering her lack of awe (106). She feels herself to be Lady Catherine's equal, despite Lady Catherine's noble line and insistence that Elizabeth is "a young woman of inferior birth, of no importance in the world" (355). In her interchanges with Lady Catherine, Elizabeth's firm insistence on equality marks a glorious instance of civil disobedience. An iconoclast, Elizabeth is "the first creature who had ever dared to trifle" with the formidable Lady Catherine (166). As if proving Mary Wollstonecraft's assertion that women can think and reason, Elizabeth uses calm logic in her pointed arguments with the enraged Lady Catherine.

In some ways, Austen presents Lady Catherine as an upper-class version of Mrs. Bennet. Darcy feels "ashamed of his aunt's ill breeding" much as Elizabeth feels mortified by her mother's vulgarity (173). Both women shamelessly put forward their daughters, lack taste and depth, and oppress others with their interference. Both make ridiculously absurd remarks that show they do not know themselves or their own limitations. When it rains and Jane must therefore stay with the Bingleys, Mrs. Bennet acts "as if the credit of making it rain were all her own" (31). Similarly, Lady Catherine is happy to gather a party around her so she can "determine what weather they were to have on the morrow" (166). Mrs. Bennet claims that nobody suffers the way she does, while Lady Catherine insists, "Nobody can feel the loss of friends more than I do" (210). Why might Austen create these parallels? Perhaps she wishes readers to sense that class and wealth are mere accidents of birth and no guarantees of refinement. Give Mrs. Bennet a title, a showy estate, and a sickly unmarried daughter and she could fill Lady Catherine's elegant shoes admirably.

Mrs. Bennet, however, only has the power to make her own family cringe. Lady Catherine inflicts herself on the entire multitude around her, a sort of heartless cross between Louis XIV and Marie Antoinette sallying forth to the poor in order to "silence their complaints, and to scold them into harmony and plenty" (169). Like contemporary bosses micromanaging every aspect of their employees' lives, Lady Catherine gives authoritative commands about everything from the arrangement of furniture to the proper size of joints of meat. She cannot bear Elizabeth's obstinacy, her refusal to kowtow to authority, her upstart ideas, and her nerve in thinking she could marry into such a noble family. In a telling exchange Lady Catherine says to Elizabeth,

> "My daughter and my nephew are formed for each other. They are descended on the maternal side, from the same noble line; and, on the father's, from respectable, honourable, and ancient, though untitled families. Their fortune on both sides is splendid. They are destined for each other by the voice of every member of their respective houses; and what is to divide them? The upstart pretensions of a young woman without family, connections, or fortune. Is this to be endured! But it must not, shall not be. If you were sensible of your own good, you would not wish to quit the sphere, in which you have been brought up." ...
>
> "Whatever my connections may be," said Elizabeth, "if your nephew does not object to them, they can be nothing to *you*.... How far your nephew might approve of your interference in *his* affairs, I cannot tell; but you have certainly no right to concern yourself in mine." ...
>
> "Are the shades of Pemberley to be thus polluted?" (356–57)

This is an extraordinarily revolutionary scene. As if to underscore the political overtones of this clash, Austen uses terms like *dictatorial, magistrate, power, rights, commands,* and *authoritative* to describe the conflict between the imperial Lady Catherine and her defiant subject, Elizabeth. We hear echoes of Lady Catherine in Gilbert and Sullivan's absurdly haughty Pooh-Bah, The Lord High Everything Else in *The Mikado*: "I can trace my ancestry back to a protoplasmal primordial atomic globule. Consequently, my family pride is something inconceivable. I can't help it. I was born sneering."[18]

Austen does not simplify her presentation of class by implying that all people in lower classes are worthy. Yes, Elizabeth has the very well-bred Aunt and Uncle Gardiner, more deserving of praise than their upper-class "betters," but she also has Aunt and Uncle Phillips, characterized by their vulgarity and strong smell of port. Whether she turns her eyes on aristocrats or those of the middle class, Austen suggests each case must be judged (not prejudged) on its merits.

Rather than concluding *Pride and Prejudice* with a paragraph describing Darcy and Elizabeth's romantic love for each other, Austen chooses to end with an emphasis on the breakdown in walls between the classes. Formerly, Elizabeth had assumed that a marriage to Darcy would have meant separation from her relatives in trade ("my aunt and uncle would have been lost to me"); the Gardiners, she assumes, would be unable to visit Pemberley because of their lower social status (246). The final paragraphs of this novel assure readers that in fact such visits are welcomed:

> Lady Catherine was extremely indignant on the marriage of her nephew.... But at length ... she condescended to wait on them at Pemberley, in spite of that pollution which its woods had received, not merely from the presence of such a mistress, but the visits of her uncle and aunt from the city.
>
> With the Gardiners, they were always on the most intimate terms. Darcy, as well as Elizabeth, really loved them; and they were both ever sensible of the warmest gratitude towards the persons who, by bringing her into Derbyshire, had been the means of uniting them. (388)

Darcy's ability to overcome his snobbish sense of superiority in order to accept Elizabeth as his equal and to measure her relatives (and his own) by worth rather than birth marks perhaps the greatest personal evolution any Austen hero undergoes.

Darcy has not finished evolving by the end of the novel, though: he has just *begun* to learn how to be laughed at. Laughter is a leveler, so Elizabeth's teasing will keep Darcy from ever becoming a Lady Catherine de Bourgh who condescends to scowl at those of "inferior" ranks. If a wife can laugh at her husband, she claims a kind of equality and security; a right to judge. She is no doormat or admiring doll that, like many a political candidate's wife, claps and smiles no matter how inane her husband's speech. She has a mind of her own and the courage to give voice to her thoughts, however subversive.

To be able to laugh at oneself is to admit weaknesses; to recognize therefore the possibility of change. Could Mrs. Bennet ever laugh at her whininess, Mary at her pedantry, or Mr. Collins at his pomposity, they would be on their way to improvement.

To laugh at others, however, can border on cruelty. For example, Miss Bingley and her sister "indulge their mirth" at Elizabeth's expense, utter "witticisms" designed to skewer her, and display a kind of liveliness: "They could describe an entertainment with accuracy, relate an anecdote with humour, and laugh at their acquaintance" (37, 46, 54). The phrase "laugh at" says it all. Elizabeth may laugh at follies and nonsense whenever she can, but she will not join Miss Bingley in laughing at other people in a mean, disloyal, or cutting way.

Like Caroline Bingley, Mr. Bennet likes "set downs" of others (13). He humiliates his daughter Mary by saying "you have delighted us long enough" when her musical performance wearies others, a sharp remark that makes Elizabeth feel sorry for her sister (101). He makes sarcastic jokes at Mrs. Bennet's expense, thus "exposing his wife to the contempt of her own children," and copes with his disastrous marriage through his "powers of entertainment": "To his wife he was very little otherwise indebted, than as her ignorance and folly had contributed to his amusement" (236). For Mr. Bennet, laughter serves as an escape vent, not a means for reform. Elizabeth realizes that her father's approach to his silly youngest daughters does much harm: "Her father, contented with laughing at them, would never exert himself to restrain the wild giddiness of his youngest daughters" (213). Instead of caring that Mr. Collins will evict the Bennet women from Longbourne, Mr. Bennet only seems glad to discover that he has a relative stupid enough to be amusing: "Mr. Bennet's expectations were fully answered. His cousin was as absurd as he had hoped, and he listened to him with the keenest enjoyment" (68).

As she considers her father's inappropriate use of humor, Elizabeth realizes she must check her own tendency to put down others. She knows that one reason she likes disliking Darcy is because it gives her a chance to display her wit: "I meant to be uncommonly clever in taking so decided a dislike to him, without any reason. It is such a spur to one's genius, such an opening for wit to have a dislike of that kind. One may be continually abusive without saying any thing just; but one cannot be always laughing at a man without now and then stumbling on something witty" (226). Like her father, Elizabeth also is so keenly aware of the world's folly that she veers toward cynicism. "Stupid men are the only ones worth knowing, after all," Elizabeth quips on her way to visit Mr. Collins, a man "who has not one agreeable quality, who has neither manner nor sense to recommend him" (154). Mrs. Gardiner warns her at that point, "Take care, Lizzy; that speech savours strongly of disappointment." Like Mr. Bennet taking refuge from his disappointing marriage in witty barbs, Elizabeth "delight[s] in any thing ridiculous" and "loves absurdities" (12, 152). "Follies, nonsense, whims and inconsistencies *do* divert me," she admits, "and I laugh at them whenever I can" (57).

But unlike her father, Elizabeth grows in her understanding that humor can be abused. Mr. Bennet's response to Jane's grief at Bingley's departure is to joke about how women like to be jilted ("I congratulate her. Next to being married, a girl likes to be crossed in love a little now and then"), a remark demonstrating no compassion or understanding of genuine emotion (137). Elizabeth cannot get her father to take seriously her remonstrances about how Lydia and Kitty are behaving in discreditable, harmful ways. Late in the novel, Mr. Bennet assumes Elizabeth will still be diverted by his comments about the foibles of Lady Catherine, Mr. Collins, and Mr. Darcy, not sensing that he has "most cruelly mortified her" by his remarks and has made her feel "It was necessary to laugh, when she would rather have cried" (369). She recognizes that her father's witty repartee indicates an "ill judged ... direction of talents" (237).

In searching for Jane Austen in *Pride and Prejudice*, we find her not only in the witty, lively, good-humored voice of her heroine but also in the more destructive sarcasm of Mr. Bennet. Austen goes to great lengths in this novel to place her readers in the same position as Mr. Bennet. Like Mr. Bennet, we laugh at the absurdity of fools so blind that they seriously utter hilariously ironic remarks. Miss Bingley yawns directly after saying she never tires of a book and accuses Elizabeth of practicing "a paltry device, a very mean art" of putting down women in order to captivate men, the very act Miss Bingley is guilty of herself (40). Lady Catherine boasts of her musical superiority (and her daughter's) while revealing that neither can play a note.

And how can we not help sharing Mr. Bennet's delight in Mrs. Bennet's absurdity? She accuses the Lucases of being artful people "all for what they can get" without recognizing that she has competed for the same wealthy sons-in-law (140). When Mrs. Bennet says, "I should not mind any thing at all," "I am frightened out of my wits," or "I shall go distracted," we chuckle to ourselves that she has no mind at all and has gone witless and distracted long ago (130, 288, 378). We appreciate our narrator's wit in informing us that Lady Lucas is "not too clever to be a valuable neighbour to Mrs. Bennet" (18). Some of Mrs. Bennet's unconsciously funny comments are priceless:

"She is a selfish, hypocritical woman, and I have no opinion of her." (6)

"I told you ... that I should never speak to you again, and you will find me as good as my word.... Not that I have much pleasure indeed in talking to any body. People who suffer as I do from nervous complaints can have no great inclination for talking. Nobody can tell what I suffer!—But it is always so. Those who do not complain are never pitied." (113)

"I am determined never to speak of it again to anybody. I told my sister Philips so the other day." (227)

"My comfort is, I am sure Jane will die of a broken heart, and then he will be sorry." (228)

We feel indebted to Mrs. Bennet for comic relief, just as Mr. Bennet credits his wife for contributing to his amusement.

Austen shows off her own Mr. Bennet-like ability to use words as weapons. She can produce brilliant oxymorons that capture the split between image and reality. Lady Catherine radiates "dignified impertinence" and is "all affability and condescension," Miss Bingley displays "sneering civility" and is "all that was affectionate and insincere," and Mrs. Bennet can do no better than to be "restored to her usual querulous serenity" (166, 157, 269, 383). It seems to me that Austen leads her readers into a trap. We share in Mr. Bennet's ironic vision and laugh along with him at the follies and inconsistencies of his relatives and neighbors, but suddenly we find ourselves uncomfortable with his irresponsible and insensitive behavior. Like Elizabeth, we as readers are forced to check our laughter—and think about it.

Pride and Prejudice, begun as "First Impressions" only a few years after the juvenilia, perhaps marks Austen's departure from the high-spirited, rollicking hilarity of her adolescent works, where murders are funny if described wittily enough. One acquaintance of Austen remembered her as being much like Mr. Bennet: "I remember her as a tall thin spare person, with very high cheek bones great colour—sparkling Eyes not large but joyous & intelligent ... her keen sense of humour I quite remember, it oozed out very much in Mr. Bennett's [sic] Style."[19] One early critic describes Austen's biting humor in a way that could apply to Mr. Bennet: "Jane Austen was always to delight in her fools: without compunction she mocks their follies so as to get all the amusement out of them she can."[20] But by showing Elizabeth and her father taking different comic bends in the road, Austen asks readers and perhaps herself to question that amusement—to consider the proper and improper uses of humor. Be on guard, she seems to say, against humor that divides, pains, or destroys. Austen would have known the saying that laughter is the work of the devil.

Yet most of all, *Pride and Prejudice* celebrates not the damning but the redeeming power of comic fiction; its ability to educate and entertain its readers, to expand their definition of humanity and their knowledge of themselves. When Mr. Collins boasts that he "never read[s] novels," he echoes Reverend Fordyce's attack on novels as an "infernal brood of futility and lewdness" that should be avoided because "Instructions they convey none."[21] However, readers are left thinking that Mr. Collins would have been better off putting down Fordyce's *Sermons* and picking up an insightful novel like *Pride and Prejudice* (68). Austen adds additional humor by reminding readers of a scene in Richard Brinsley Sheridan's *The Rivals*: a hairdresser uses pages of Fordyce's *Sermons* as curling-papers, and a heroine named Lydia Languish reads novels instead of preachy essays.[22] Mrs. Bennet would probably agree with Sheridan's Mrs. Malaprop, "I would by no means wish a daughter of mine to be a progeny of learning. I don't think so much learning becomes a young woman." By echoing Sheridan, Fordyce, and other male authors, Austen demonstrates that learning becomes a woman writer, particularly one with the ability to give earlier works a witty twist. No wonder Sheridan called *Pride and Prejudice* "one of the cleverest things he ever read."[23]

Our narrator makes it clear that she is writing no mere travelogue ("It is not the object of this work to give a description of Derbyshire, nor of any of the remarkable places through which their route thither lay") and no love-at-first-sight romance (240). Instead *Pride and Prejudice* fits exactly the description Austen had given of novels in *Northanger Abbey*, bought but not published at this point: "'It is only Cecilia, or Camilla, or Belinda'; or, in short, only some work in which the greatest powers of the mind are displayed, in which the most thorough knowledge of human nature, the happiest delineation of its varieties, the liveliest effusions of wit and humour are conveyed to the world in the best chosen language" (*NA*, 38).

In that passage from *Northanger Abbey*, Austen refers to *Cecilia* by Fanny Burney, and it is interesting that she takes the title of *Pride and Prejudice* from that novel. "The whole of this unfortunate business," says Dr. Lyster in *Cecilia*, "has been the result of PRIDE and PREJUDICE.... Yet this, however, remember; if to PRIDE AND PREJUDICE you owe your miseries ... to PRIDE AND PREJUDICE you will also owe their termination."[24] In Burney's novel, however, only the hero was guilty of pride and prejudice while the heroine was faultless from the beginning, much like Jane Bennet. The narrative voice of *Cecilia* is hardly funny. In contrast, Austen writes a witty novel that claims for both men and women the right to be flawed and struggling, to experience evolutionary and revolutionary moments like Elizabeth's sense of mortification: "She grew absolutely ashamed of herself.— ... she had been blind, partial, prejudiced, absurd. 'How despicably I have acted! ... I, who have prided myself on my abilities! ...

How humiliating is this discovery!... Till this moment I never knew myself'"
(208). Mr. Bennet only feels self-reproach for a few brief moments and then
lapses back into cynicism, noting that he will see to it that Kitty spends at
least ten minutes a day in a rational manner. Elizabeth has learned to balance
her amused, detached stance with serious reflection and self-knowledge.

Austen may ask us to check our laughter, but definitely not stop
it altogether. In fact, she closes *Pride and Prejudice* with the young, shy
Georgiana Darcy learning from her new sister-in-law, Elizabeth, that a
woman may adopt a lively, sportive manner with her husband and "take
liberties" with him (388). The humor between Elizabeth and Darcy will
enrich, not polarize, their union.

In *Pride and Prejudice* Austen celebrates a marriage of sorts in her own
approach as author—what Twain would later call "seriously scribbling to
excite the laughter of God's creatures."[25] Like Elizabeth and Darcy blending
liveliness and judgment, Austen's own fiction offers sparkling amusement
and serious instruction, barbed wit and gentle wisdom.

Notes

1. Johnson, *Jane Austen*, 73.
2. Caroline Austen, *My Aunt Jane Austen*, 5, 16.
3. Honan, *Jane Austen*, 184.
4. Myer, *Jane Austen*, 1.
5. Hannah More, *Essays on Various Subjects, Principally Designed for Young Ladies* (1775; reprint, London: Wilkie & Cadell, 1777), 145. See a discussion of Austen and More in Armstrong, *Sense and Sensibility*, 61.
6. More, *Essays on Various Subjects*, 145.
7. Samuel Johnson, *A Dictionary of the English Language* (1755; reprint, London: Reeves & Turner, 1877), 504.
8. Wollstonecraft, *Vindication of the Rights of Woman*, 144–45.
9. Johnson, *Jane Austen*, 76–77.
10. Hester Chapone, letter 4 (On the Regulation of the Heart and Affections), *Letters on the Improvement of the Mind*, cited in Frank Bradbrook's explanatory notes in the Oxford World Classics edition of *Pride and Prejudice* (Oxford, 1990), 348.
11. Compare *PP*, 289, and vol. 2, letter 8 of Fanny Burney's *Evelina* (Oxford: Oxford World Classics, 1982), 164.
12. Honan, *Jane Austen*, 186.
13. I am indebted for this idea to Ruth Perry's "Home at Last: Biographical Background to *Pride and Prejudice*," in *Approaches to Teaching Pride and Prejudice*, ed. Marcia Folsom (New York: Modern Language Association, 1993), 46–56.
14. Letter of December 1814 to Sir William Elford, *The Letters of Mary Russell Mitford*, ed. R. Brimley-Johnson (New York: Dial Press, 1925), 121–22.
15. Penny Gay, *Jane Austen's Pride and Prejudice* (Sydney: Sydney University Press, 1990), 27.
16. Edward Copeland, "The Economic Realities of Jane Austen's Darcy," in Folsom, *Approaches to Teaching Pride and Prejudice*, 43–45.

17. Pierre de Beaumarchais, *The Marriage of Figaro*, 5.3, in *The Three Figaro Plays*, trans. David Edney (Ottawa: Dovehouse, 2000), 324.

18. *The Complete Plays of Gilbert and Sullivan* (New York: Norton, 1941), 303.

19. Charlotte-Maria Middleton in Le Faye, *Jane Austen*, 178.

20. Lord David Cecil, *A Portrait of Jane Austen* (New York: Hill, 1978), 62.

21. James Fordyce, "On Female Virtue," in *Sermons to Young Women* (1766; reprint, London: T. Cadell, 1792), 1: 148–49.

22. Richard Brinsley Sheridan, *The Rivals*, 2.2, in *Masterpieces of the Drama*, ed. Allison, Carr, and Eastman (New York: Macmillan, 1957), 289. I am indebted for the link between Lydia Bennet and Lydia Languish to Honan, *Jane Austen*, 34. Honan reminds us that Austen's brothers acted out *The Rivals*.

23. Le Faye, *Jane Austen*, 175.

24. Fanny Burney, *Cecilia: or Memoirs of an Heiress* (London: Virago, 1986), 908.

25. Letter to Orion and May Clemens, 19–20 October 1865, in *Mark Twain's Letters* (Berkeley: University of California Press, 1988), 1: 323.

DARRYL JONES

Pride and Prejudice

I. FAIRYTALES

The first thing to say about *Pride and Prejudice* is that it is a fairytale. The fact that it is set in the village of Meryton, or 'Merry Town', provides the first clue to this. Setting the novel here is akin to setting it in Happy Valley or Pleasantville, an untroubled community reflective of a larger, idealised polity: all is well with the world.[1] We are, ostensibly at least, in Little (conceivably even in 'Merrie') England, where the famous aphorism with which the novel opens, however ironically presented it may be, is nevertheless vindicated by its close: 'It is a truth universally acknowledged, that a single man in possession of a good fortune, must be in want of a wife' (PP, 3). Its fairytale narrative economy, in which Opposites Attract, and in which a feisty, intelligent heroine in financially straitened circumstances overcomes the opposition of a backward-looking tradition and authority, as well as the preconceptions about class and money to which her own sceptical intelligence has initially predisposed her, to win the hand of a man who is effectively the richest man in England, provides the template for innumerable subsequent redactions upon the same theme. It is, I would suggest, *the* major source for most subsequent romantic comedies, particularly movies in the Hollywood tradition.

From *Critical Issues: Jane Austen*, pp. 93–112. © 2004 by Palgrave Macmillan.

It is also this fairytale element which has led to *Pride and Prejudice*'s being the most enduringly popular of all Jane Austen's novels. 'The Republic of Pemberley', the astonishing fan-based Austen website named, of course, for Darcy's Derbyshire residence, provides a good example of this. On the Internet, websites such as the Republic of Pemberley have potentially democratised the literary canon by opening Austen up to a fan-base going public for the first time with theories and interpretations of beloved novels, and also offering a forum for fan-fiction in the form of new versions, sequels, continuations, homages, available for all to read. However, rather than opening up interpretation, the traditional 'Janeism' of many of these responses—hostile as it often is to academic discourse—might paradoxically be said to shore up and confine interpretations.

The power of the stranglehold *Pride and Prejudice* has on the popular imagination is very graphically demonstrated by a search of the Republic of Pemberley's 'Bits of Ivory', its extensive and ongoing collection of submitted Austen sequels and spin-offs. At the time of writing (September 2003), all five of the ongoing stories take their lead from *Pride and Prejudice*. Thus, for example, Louise Barada's *An Encounter at Netherfield* juxtaposes two conversations, one between Darcy and Bingley, the other between Elizabeth and Jane, both reporting Darcy's successful proposal of marriage: the first ends, fancifully but rather touchingly, with Bingley planning 'a double wedding. We are to be brothers the same day'—a conclusion which is, frankly, at least as satisfying and plausible as the authentic doubled resolution of *Sense and Sensibility*. Each sequel in its turn is the subject of vigorous discussion, which tends to be naïve and uncritical, though again touchingly supportive. Thus, for example, 'HopeElyse' responds 'Lovely! Simply lovely. There is not much more too [*sic*] say', 'Else' comments 'I've loved every word of it! Thank you so much!' while 'Judith O' says, 'you've done an excellent job with this story. Very like the original, and I can picture each scene in my imagination. Please do continue!' More strikingly still, the Bits of Ivory archives contain more stories based on *Pride and Prejudice* than on all the other Austen novels combined—a whopping 316 completed stories, compared with 27 for *Persuasion*, 26 for *Sense and Sensibility*, 23 for *Emma*, 14 for *Mansfield Park*, and a meagre 8 for *Northanger Abbey*. A search of the Republic of Pemberley's archives did not merely confirm my suspicions about *Pride and Prejudice*'s cultural dominance, it spectacularly outdid them.

Part of *Pride and Prejudice*'s appealing fairytale quality also lies in the ways in which the novel touches upon many of the issues which recur in other Austen novels as thorny, difficult, oppressive or ideologically contradictory, but does so smoothly, in ways which render them untroubling, easily resolved. Here, certainly, the realist novel's tendency towards consensus, identified by

Ermarth, Watson and Seeber and discussed in detail in the previous chapter, seems uncomplicated and absolute. While the appeal of this tactic is obvious, and makes *Pride and Prejudice* Austen's most harmonious novel, it also makes it her most glib, a condition which might be said to apply *a fortiori* in the case of academic critics trained to sniff out difficulties and ambiguities: 'We will certainly,' writes Claudia Johnson, 'misrepresent [Austen's] accomplishment if we posit this singular novel as the one against which the others are to be judged.'[2] There is, however, and self-evidently, a considerable readerly pleasure to be gained from having one's generic expectations *precisely* confirmed, and this is the kind of pleasure which *Pride and Prejudice* seems to afford.

The novel begins from the same premise as *Sense and Sensibility*, the unfair treatment afforded women under primogeniture. The celebrated opening sentence is one of the subtlest instances of Austen's use of free indirect speech, as it is really only to Mrs Bennet that this 'truth universally acknowledged' obtains this early. The most materially pressing truth is this:

> Mr Bennet's property consisted almost entirely in an estate of two thousand a year, which, unfortunately for his daughters, was entailed in default of heirs male, on a distant relation; and their mother's fortune, though ample for her situation in life, could but ill supply the deficiency of his. Her father had been an attorney in Meryton, and had left her four thousand pounds. (PP, 28)

Mr Bennet, then, has no male heir, and therefore in accordance with its entail, his Longbourn estate devolves to 'my cousin, Mr Collins, who, when I am dead, may turn you out of this house as soon as he pleases' (PP, 61). Recognising that this form of disinheritance is likely to cast her daughters adrift effectively penniless, like the Dashwood girls, Mrs Bennet 'continued to rail bitterly against the cruelty of settling an estate away from a family of five daughters, in favour of a man whom nobody cared anything about' (PP, 62). She is quite correct, of course, and even Lady Catherine de Bourgh says that she sees 'no occasion for entailing estates from the female line' (PP, 164). The fact that Mr Collins is an objectionable buffoon, 'a conceited, pompous, narrow-minded, silly man' (PP, 135), serves only to underline this. It is precisely these iniquitous laws of inheritance whose consequences are so devastating to the Dashwoods, and which have here, no less seriously, conspired to drive Mrs Bennet insane (which she undoubtedly is): 'I am sure I do not know who is to maintain you when your father is dead.—*I* shall not be able to keep you' (PP, 113), she says to Elizabeth after her rejection of Mr Collins's proposal of marriage. The famous exchange between the Bennets on the subject of Mrs Bennet's nerves is certainly clever and amusing, but it is also indicative of a rather callous disregard for women on Mr Bennet's part, a refusal of imaginative sympathy with his wife and a refusal to acknowledge his own dereliction of paternal duty towards his daughters:

> 'Mr Bennet, how can you abuse your children in such a way? You take delight in vexing me. You have no compassion for my poor nerves.'
>
> 'You mistake me, my dear. I have a high respect for your nerves. They are my old friends. I have heard you mention them with consideration these twenty years at least.' (PP, 5)

This discussion draws on an Enlightenment tradition of medical speculations about the function of the nervous system, particularly in women, its relation to sensibility and therefore its presence in theories of the novel.[3] This is a rich and complex subject, and one which elsewhere, even in another Austen novel, would have been treated with the seriousness it merits. Thus, in a manner characteristic of the novel's tendency to smooth over differences and difficulties, the conditions which were to predicate *Sense and Sensibility*, making it Austen's gloomiest novel, are here deflected, rendered ideologically safe by being made the vehicle for an admittedly funny joke. But Mrs Bennet's obsession with marrying off her daughters at all costs stems from real practical parental concern—if they do not marry, they may starve, especially given that Mr Bennet himself has made no provision for his daughters' futures but seems instead to be in a form of denial—he retreats to his library. This amounts to a condition every bit as pathological, and considerably more culpable, than his wife's, as even Elizabeth eventually comes to recognise:

> Elizabeth, however, had never been blind to the impropriety of her father's behaviour as a husband ... that continual breach of conjugal obligation and decorum which, in exposing his wife to the contempt of her own children, was so highly reprehensible. But she had never felt so strongly as now, the disadvantages which must attend the children of so unsuitable a marriage, nor ever been so fully aware of the evils arising from so ill-judged a direction of talents; talents which rightly used, might at least have preserved the respectability of his daughters, even if incapable of enlarging the mind of his wife. (PP, 236–7)

This is potentially grim stuff, and in *Sense and Sensibility* it makes for actually grim stuff. *Pride and Prejudice*, however, elides the implications of these issues by making for the two oldest Bennet girls, at least, marriages which are, by any standards, spectacularly lucrative, but which serve yet again to demonstrate the novel's tendency towards compromise.

II. PROPERTIES

Bingley is 'a young man of large fortune from the north of England' with 'four or five thousand a year' (PP, 4): he is, that is to say, new money, the cash-rich heir of an industrial family from the north of England. Bingley was and is a mill-town just to the north of Bradford, which was a major centre for the manufacture of textiles during the industrial revolution, when the invention of the flying shuttle (1733), the spinning jenny (1770) and 'Crompton's Mule' (1779), revolutionised the industry. Bradford in particular became a boom-town after the introduction of the first steam-powered mill in 1798 made large-scale factory-systems possible here as elsewhere across the north. Bingley, then, is a textile magnate whose family, at least, wish to launder their fortune through marriage into the gentry: thus Caroline Bingley has designs on Darcy, 'a gentleman' (as Elizabeth reminds Lady Catherine de Bourgh), while Bingley himself marries Jane, 'a gentleman's daughter' (PP, 356). Bingley's social mobility is symbolically represented, as it was later to be in *Persuasion*, through the fact that he lives in rented accommodation:

> Mr Bingley inherited property to the amount of nearly an hundred thousand pounds from his father, who had intended to purchase an estate but did not live to do it.—Mr Bingley intended it likewise, and sometimes made choice of his county; but as he was now provided with a good house and the liberty of a manor, it was doubtful to many of those who best knew the easiness of his temper, whether he might not spend the remainder of his days at Netherfield, and leave the next generation to purchase. (PP, 15)

The 'property' which he inherits, a vast fortune, is presumably in factories, and he initially thinks of buying his way into the gentry through purchase of property: 'I will buy Pemberley itself if Darcy will sell it.... I should think it more possible to get Pemberley by purchase than imitation' (PP, 38).

Pemberley itself is the most straightforwardly symbolic of Austen's great houses, the nearest she comes to the tradition of great Country House literature, of Ben Jonson's Penshurst and Andrew Marvell's Appleton House, whose significance in mythologising a national polity (the management of the estate represents the management of the state) Raymond Williams has analysed in *The Country and the City*.[4] In the England of the 1790s, and through to the end of the Napoleonic Wars, this image of the estate as a microcosm for the nation and an expression of the ideal of English polity gained further topical currency because of its use by Edmund Burke as a recurring image in *Reflections on the Revolution in France*, that powerful formulation of English conservatism, as that which needs shoring up as a protection against revolutionary Jacobinism:

> You will observe, that from the Magna Charta to the Declaration of Right, it has been the uniform policy of our constitution to claim and assert our liberties, as an *entailed inheritance* derived to us from our forefathers, and to be transmitted to our posterity; as an estate specially belonging to the people of this kingdom without any reference whatsoever to any other more general or prior right. By this means our constitution preserves an unity in so great a diversity of its parts. We have an inheritable crown, an inheritable peerage; and an house of commons and a people inheriting privileges, franchises, and liberties, from a long line of ancestors.[5]

Almost immediately, the landed estate became a discursively contested site to a degree even greater than it had been across the eighteenth century: in 1793, Charlotte Smith's *The Old Manor House*, in a conscious Jacobin counterblast to Burke, presented *its* landed estate, Rayland Hall, as a crumbling pile peopled by antiques and relics, badly in need of ideological renovation. The complexities and ambiguities of estate management and improvement which, as the next chapter will demonstrate, bedevil *Mansfield Park* are nowhere in evidence, however, in *Pride and Prejudice*. While it is the case that the Bennets' entailed estate devolves out of their hands to Mr Collins, and that there is in this an implied critique of Mr Bennet's familial mismanagement, the outrageously successful marriages of Elizabeth and Jane magically overcompensate the family for this loss, embedding them further still within Burke's model Tory constitution.

The great eighteenth-century exemplar of virtuous masculinity, Samuel Richardson's Sir Charles Grandison, is in part Austen's model for Darcy, not least in his management of his estate, Grandison Hall, which, as Edward Malins has suggested, bears all the hallmarks of Capability Brown's handiwork:[6]

> This large and convenient house is situated in a spacious park; which has several fine avenues leading to it.
>   On the north side of the park, flows a winding stream, that may well be called a river, abounding with trout and other fish;

the current quickened by a noble cascade, which tumbled down its foaming waters from a rock, which is continued, to some extent, in a kind of ledge of rock-work rudely disposed.

The park itself is remarkable, for its prospects, lawns, and rich-appearing clumps of trees of large growth; which must therefore have been planted by the ancestors of the excellent owner; who, contenting himself to open and enlarge many fine prospects, delights to preserve, as much as possible, the plantations of his ancestors; and particularly thinks it a kind of impiety to fell a tree, that was planted by his father.

On the south side of the river, on a natural and easy ascent, is a neat, but plain villa, in the rustic taste, erected by Sir Thomas; the flat roof of which presents a noble prospect. The villa contains convenient lodging-rooms; and one large room in which he used sometimes to entertain his friends.

The gardener's house is a pretty little building. The man is a sober diligent man, he is in years: Has a housewifely good creature of a wife. Content is in the countenance of both: How happy they must be![7]

Pride and Prejudice's version of Sir Charles's happy gardener is Mrs Reynolds, Darcy's happy housekeeper, who swears that:

'He is the best landlord and the best master ... that ever lived. Not like the wild young men now-a-days who think of nothing but themselves. There is not one of his tenants or servants but will give him a good name. Some people call him proud, but I am sure I never saw anything of it. To my fancy, it is only because he does not rattle away like the other young men.' (PP, 249)

Elizabeth's visit, with the Gardiners, to Pemberley, provides, after Darcy's letter to Elizabeth, the novel's second narrative *peripeteia*. The description of the grounds, influenced according to John Dixon Hunt and Peter Willis by Humphry Repton, provides a veritable pornography of estate management, designed to display its owner not only, as Elizabeth notes, in 'an amiable light' (PP, 249), but in the most sensational of lights:[8]

The park was very large, and contained great variety of ground. They entered it in one of the lowest points, and drove for some time through a beautiful wood, stretching over a wide extent.

Elizabeth's mind was too full for conversation, but she saw and admired every remarkable spot and point of view. They gradually ascended for half a mile, and then found themselves at the top of a considerable eminence, where the wood ceased, and the eye was instantly caught by Pemberley House, situated on the opposite side of a valley, into which the road with some abruptness wound. It was a large, handsome, stone building, standing well on rising ground, and backed by a ridge of high woody hills;—and in front a stream of some natural importance was swelled into greater, but without any artificial appearance. Its banks were neither formal, nor falsely adorned. Elizabeth was delighted. She had never seen a place for which nature had done more, or where natural beauty had been so little counteracted by an awkward taste. They were all of them warm in their admiration; and at that moment she felt, that to be mistress of Pemberley might be something! (PP, 245)

Indeed. And the end of the novel has Elizabeth confessing to Jane that it is precisely this visit to Pemberley which has made all the difference:

'Will you tell me how long you have loved him?'
    'It has been coming on so gradually, that I hardly know when it began. But I believe it must date from my seeing his beautiful grounds at Pemberley.' (PP, 373)

Pemberley, landscaped and improved 'but without any artificial appearance' enacts in bricks and mortar, wood and water, the novel's synthesising, ameliorating middle way: 'There is,' Alistair Duckworth writes, 'a kind of scenic *mediocritas* about the estate, a mean between the extremes of the improver's art and uncultivated nature.'[9] So too with the events at Pemberley, and the social inclusiveness which they symbolise. When Darcy initially proposes to Elizabeth, he deplores 'the inferiority of [her] connections' (PP, 192)—the Gardiners, who 'lived by trade, and within view of [their] own warehouses' in Cheapside (PP, 139) (that is, they have not begun to gentrify themselves through the renting of a country estate, as Bingley has). However, in Pemberley, Darcy encounters Elizabeth and the Gardiners on a symbolically unifying 'simple bridge' (PP, 253), and a class rapprochement begins, a rapprochement which closes with the novel itself, whose last words are not specifically of Elizabeth and Darcy, but of the importance of the Gardiners to their lives:

With the Gardiners, they were always on the most intimate terms. Darcy, as well as Elizabeth, really loved them; and they were both sensible of the warmest gratitude towards the persons who, by bringing her into Derbyshire, had been the means of uniting them. (PP, 388)

III. LETTERS

If *Pride and Prejudice* is a novel about a house, then it is also a novel about a letter: Darcy's letter to Elizabeth, which takes up most of Volume 2 Chapter 12 (Chapter 35 in some modern editions), and on which the entire text hinges. In an archaeological account of Austen's novels, B. C. Southam suggests a possible explanation for the prominence of this letter. Remarking that, in the novel, 'a very credible system of letters [carries] much of the story in an epistolary version', Southam suggests that '*Pride and Prejudice* was originally a novel-in-letters'.[10] Certainly, the novel's crucial narrative event is a piece of writing, and Darcy's letter has the status of an autonomous and co-existent parallel text which effects a rewriting of much which has proceeded it. As readers, in effect, Darcy's letter causes us to read the first half of the novel *twice*. Darcy's letter operates as a synoptic device within the text, a kind of narrative split-screen effect. The purpose of this is to allow for Elizabeth's negotiation between two simultaneous stories, which now occupy the same narrative space, and its outcome is that Elizabeth effects a renegotiation of the terms of her own story, and concludes that 'actions were capable of a very different construction' (PP, 258). 'Can there be any other opinion on the subject?' Jane asks when she and Elizabeth offer each other very different interpretations of another letter, Caroline Bingley's to Jane. 'Yes there can,' Elizabeth replies, 'mine is totally different' (PP, 118).

The whole novel offers Elizabeth an exercise in interpretation; Darcy's letter sets about dismantling her confidence in the fixity of the meaning of these interpretations: 'How differently did everything now appear' (PP, 207), she thinks after reading it, 'Till this moment I never knew myself' (PP, 208). *Pride and Prejudice*'s initial working title, 'First Impressions', itself suggests the significance of the 'second impression': the letter, then, allows the text formally to enact its own ideological 'double vision', to have it both ways. At Pemberley, a major symbolic component in the novel's double vision, Elizabeth 'admired ... every point of view' (PP, 245), thus enacting in spatial terms Elizabeth's new-found capacity for a generous understanding of its owner.

A number of critics have in fact made reference to Austen's, and specifically to *Pride and Prejudice*'s 'double vision',[11] this in the sense of the novel's 'balancing act',[12] its tendency to accommodate or smooth over ideological differences which can amount to a refusal or inability to subscribe to a single narrative or political position (Johnson suggests that the novel's every argument is undercut by 'a built-in countervailing argument').[13] Elizabeth herself has frequently been read as a female fantasy figure, but she embodies a contradictory double fantasy. She is, on the one hand, as several critics have pointed out, 'a fantasy of female autonomy', a heroine willing and able to articulate effective resistance to the power-structures of class, money and gender: a radical, therefore, or even potentially a revolutionary heroine.[14] Conversely, as Marilyn Butler, ever eager to read a Tory Austen, has noted, *Pride and Prejudice* contains the archetypal plot of the conservative novel: 'An impulsive or mistaken protagonist, frequently someone whose first choice in love was rash, now uses sober judgement and external evidence to select a partner in marriage.'[15] Marriage, furthermore, the novel's 'double vision' shows, to a man who, though proud abroad, dispenses from his Pemberley estate a Grandisonian largesse. Darcy, then, is a genuine conservative model of the benign aristocracy, an embodiment of a social organisation straight out of Edmund Burke. But it is he and not Elizabeth who articulates the nearest that the novel comes to open Jacobinism, an Enlightenment feminist programme for women's education which echoes Wollstonecraft's call for a redefinition of women's education in the *Vindication of the Rights of Woman*, and one which sets him explicitly against the conservative conduct-book moralising of Mr Collins and of Mary Bennet. Darcy suggests a programme so radical in its implications that Elizabeth refuses to believe it possible. In the *Vindication*, Wollstonecraft writes witheringly of the limitations inherent in the series of 'alluring' accomplishments which comprised the standard female education, and which have served effectively to cretinise generations of women, denying them a stake in the Enlightenment:

> The conduct and manners of women, in fact, evidently prove that their minds are not in a healthy state; for, like the flowers which are planted in too rich a soil, strength and usefulness are sacrificed to beauty; and the flaunting leaves, after having pleased a fastidious eye, fade, disregarded on the stalk, long before the season when they ought to have arrived at maturity. One cause of this barren blooming I attribute to a false system of education, gathered from the books written on this subject by men who, considering females rather as women than human creatures, have been more anxious to make them alluring mistresses than affectionate wives and rational mothers; and the understanding of the sex has been so bubbled by this specious homage, that the civilized women of the present century, with a few exceptions, are only anxious to inspire love, where they ought to cherish a nobler

ambition, and by their virtues exact respect.... It is acknowledged that [women] spend many of the first years of their lives acquiring a smattering of accomplishments; meanwhile, strength of body and mind are sacrificed in libertine notions of beauty, to the desire of establishing themselves—the only way women can rise in the world—by marriage.[16]

Miss Bingley, who certainly wishes to establish herself and rise in the world by marriage to Darcy, offers a conventional account of women's accomplishments, to which Darcy adds a crucial Wollstonecraftean condition:

> 'I cannot boast of knowing more than half a dozen [women], in the whole range of my acquaintance, that are really accomplished.'
>
> 'Nor I, I am sure,' said Miss Bingley.
>
> 'Then,' observed Elizabeth, 'you must comprehend a great deal in your idea of an accomplished woman.'
>
> 'Yes; I do comprehend a great deal in it.'
>
> 'Oh! certainly,' cried his faithful assistant [Miss Bingley], 'no one can be really esteemed accomplished, who does not greatly surpass what is usually met with. A woman must have a thorough knowledge of music, singing, drawing, dancing, and the modern languages, to deserve the word; and besides all this, she must possess a certain something in her air and manner of walking, the tone of her voice, her address and expressions, or the word will be but half deserved.'
>
> 'All this she must possess,' added Darcy, 'and to all this she must yet add something more substantial, in the improvement of her mind by extensive reading.'
>
> 'I am no longer surprised at your knowing *only* six accomplished women. I rather wonder now at your knowing *any*.'
>
> 'Are you so severe upon your own sex, as to doubt the possibility of all this?'
>
> '*I* never saw such a woman. *I* never saw such capacity, and taste, and application, and elegance, as you describe, united.' (PP, 39–40)

The irony here, of course, is that it is precisely Elizabeth herself who does unite all of these qualities, as a version of the Wollstonecraftean heroine.

In a novel which, from its very opening sentence, makes marriage for the Bennet sisters an imperative of overpowering (in Mrs Bennet's case, crushing) financial importance, the ultimate fantasy may not be Elizabeth's acts of verbal rebellion but the fact that she manages to make herself such an astonishingly good match. More precisely, of course, these apparently contradictory impulses, of rebellion and conservatism, are brought together as the novel offers a synthesis of ideological opposites, a proto-Hegelian social dialectic which succeeds in uniting desirable qualities from both sides, having the best of both worlds, having it both ways through the elision or harmonising of discord. Little wonder, then, that the novel has proven so popular: it is calculatedly Austen's most inoffensive work. Critics, predictably, have divided along party lines when faced with this tendency, with Butler and Johnson as ever, it seems, articulating interpretive poles: either *Pride and Prejudice* is 'a categorically happy novel' (Johnson, for once voicing an opinion which the good folks of the Republic of Pemberley would only too happily endorse), or it closes at an impasse with its own intentions, in 'moral limbo' (Butler).[17]

The novel closes by resolving, as it were magically, what is initially a conflict of imperatives, the sexual and the economic. In purely financial terms, even marrying Mr Collins would, given the entail which hangs over the Bennet family, be a prudent move for Elizabeth. In a conversation significantly placed immediately after the ball in which Elizabeth confirms her unfavourable 'First Impression' of Darcy, she and Charlotte Lucas, discussing Jane and Bingley's burgeoning relationship, and through that the pragmatics of the marriage market in general, reveal very different outlooks:

> 'Jane [says Charlotte] should make the most of every half an hour in which she can command his attention. When she is secure of him, there will be leisure for falling in love as much as she chuses.'
>
> 'Your plan is a good one,' replied Elizabeth, 'where nothing is in question but the desire of being well married; and if I were determined to get a rich husband, or any husband, I dare say I should adopt it. But these are not Jane's feelings; she is not acting by design.' ...
>
> 'Well,' said Charlotte, 'I wish Jane success with all my heart; and if she were married to him tomorrow, I should think she had as good a chance of happiness, as if she were studying his character for a twelve-month. Happiness in marriage is entirely a matter of chance. If the dispositions of the parties are ever so well known to each other beforehand, it does not advance their felicity in the least. They always grow sufficiently alike afterwards to have their share of vexation; and it is better to know as little as

possible of the defects of the person with whom you are to share your life.' (PP, 22–3)

Elizabeth, despite her denial of the primacy (even, perhaps, the necessity) of financial security in marriage, is forced to negotiate between a desire which includes the sexual (mutual attractiveness, compatibility, knowledge) and 'the desire of being well married', that is, of getting 'a rich husband'. The two other marriages which take place during the course of the novel illustrate the danger of veering too close to either pole of desire, and if they do so somewhat schematically it is because they are narrative devices, there to point up Elizabeth and Darcy's own centralising course.

'I certainly *have* had my share of beauty' (PP, 4), says Mrs Bennet, and the Bennets' marriage is entirely down to her youthful sexiness, wherein lies the problem:

> [Mr Bennet] captivated by youth and beauty, and that appearance of good humour, which youth and beauty generally give, had very early in their marriage put an end to all real affection for her. Respect, esteem, and confidence, had vanished for ever; and all his views of domestic happiness, were overthrown. (PP, 236)

Mrs Bennet admits, with a kind of touching honesty which belies her husband's, and the novel's, antipathy towards her as 'a woman of mean understanding, little information, and uncertain temper' (PP, 5), that 'When a woman has five grown up daughters, she ought to give over thinking of her own beauty' (PP, 4). Amongst these 'five grown up daughters' it is Lydia who has inherited her mother's status as a teenage sex-bomb:

> Lydia was a stout, well-grown girl of fifteen, with a fine complexion and good-humoured countenance.... She had high animal spirits, and a sort of natural self-consequence, which the attentions of the officers, to whom ... her easy manners recommended her, had increased into assurance. (PP, 45)

The handsomest of these officers is Wickham, 'the happy man towards whom every female eye was turned' (PP, 76). Elizabeth is certainly susceptible to his magnetism: 'Whatever he said, was said well; and whatever he did, done gracefully. Elizabeth went away with her head full of him. She could think of nothing but Mr Wickham' (PP, 84). Elizabeth is shocked at Lydia's shameless lack of remorse when she returns from her elopement married to Wickham, a marriage whose strong mercenary element Lydia is aware of and perhaps even collusive in. As Susan Staves notes in her study of 'seduced maidens', seduction *could* be a collusive act: a correspondent to the *Gentleman's Magazine* wrote in 1773, 'Oh, ye powers, did you not give the lovely Sophia less love, or more resolution to resist.'[18] In the same way, in *Sense and Sensibility*, Willoughby attempts to justify his treatment of Eliza Brandon to Elinor:

> 'I do not mean to justify myself, but at the same time cannot leave you to suppose that I have nothing to urge—that because she was injured she was irreproachable, and because *I* was a libertine, *she* must be a saint. If the violence of her passions, the weakness of her understanding—I do not mean, however, to defend myself.' (SS, 322)

Like the lovely Sophia, Lydia has little or no 'resolution to resist'.

'Happiness in marriage,' Charlotte, we remember, tells Elizabeth, 'is entirely a matter of chance' (PP, 23). Despite Elizabeth's confidence in telling Charlotte 'that you would never act in this way yourself' (PP, 23), Charlotte marries Mr Collins. It is of course a marriage for security's sake, a settlement based on not so much 'the desire ... to get a rich husband' and the desire to get 'any husband': 'marriage was the only honourable provision for well-educated young women of small fortune, and however uncertain of giving happiness, must be their pleasantest preservative from want' (PP, 122–3). Charlotte is 'twenty-seven, without ever having been handsome' (PP, 123), and when Mrs Bennet says to Bingley, 'Not that I think Charlotte so *very* plain—but then she is our particular friend' (PP, 44), we know that it is in her interest to downplay Charlotte's desirability in order to boost her own daughters', but nevertheless all honest readers will acknowledge that 'plain' is here and remains a euphemism for ugly. Charlotte is an ugly woman approaching thirty, and the novel registers her family's 'apprehension of Charlotte's dying an old maid' (PP, 122). While, two novels later, *Emma* will show its heroine adamant that a wealthy young woman should have no particular need for marriage, here Charlotte quite unambiguously accepts Mr Collins's proposal 'solely from the pure and disinterested desire of an establishment' (PP, 122), as aware as Elizabeth is that her husband-to-be is, in the words of Lilian S. Robinson, 'a schmuck'.[19] Here, Charlotte is again under no illusions: 'I am not romantic, you know' (PP, 125), she tells Elizabeth, indicating a willingness to efface her own sexuality—indeed, of the positive desirability under these circumstances, which obtained for many women, of as low a sex-drive as possible. Elizabeth considers it 'humiliating' and 'disgracing' that Charlotte has 'sacrificed every better feeling to worldly advantage' (PP, 125)—including, unquestionably or even perhaps primarily, the 'better feelings' of sex. Nevertheless, the patrilineal imperative which drives Mr Collins to marry means that the marriage must be consummated, an heir produced. But to minimise her contact with her husband, Charlotte's marriage becomes a kind of game of 'musical rooms': as often as possible Charlotte ensures that, wherever Mr Collins is, she is somewhere else, deliberately spending much of her time in an uninviting room or suggesting that he tend his garden: 'To work his garden was one of his most respectable pleasures; and Elizabeth admired the command of countenance with which Charlotte talked of the healthfulness of the exercise, and owned she encouraged it as much as possible' (PP, 156). Interestingly, then, the Gardiners aren't the novel's only gardeners: the future, this passage implies, belongs to Mr Collins too.

Mr Collins's status as a potential lover has led to some fascinating critical speculations. Robinson draws our attention to the fact that 'whether Jane Austen wishes to remember it or not, the repulsive Mr Collins cannot be avoided in bed'.[20] Dorothy Van Ghent went further, offering a memorably grotesque fantasy of Mr Collins's 'grampus-like erotic wallowings'![21] In Robert Z. Leonard's MGM production of *Pride and Prejudice* (1940), Mr Collins is played with terrific sliminess by Melville Cooper. Perfect casting, but Cooper was not the only actor up for the role. In what could have been an inspired choice, the young Phil Silvers—Sergeant Bilko himself!—was also up for the part. In his autobiography, *The Man Who Was Bilko*, Silvers recalls how, dressed in a wig last worn by Edward G. Robinson in Howard Hawks's *Tiger Shark* and affecting an accent he'd picked up from conversations with Robert Morley, he tested for the English casting director:

> me: My dear Dame Elizabeth, your modesty does you no dissoivice—
>
> basil: Cut. It's dis-service, Mr Silvers.
>
> me: Okay ... dis-service in my eyes. You can hardly doubt the poipuss—
>
> basil: Cut. Purr-pose, Mr Silvers.
>
> me: ... purr-pose of my discourse. My attentions have been too marked to be avoided. (On my knees.) Oh! forgive this passion.

He didn't get the part, but, Silvers recalls, 'These three minutes were perhaps the funniest I've done.'[22]

Elizabeth's dominant mode, in the first half of the novel at least, is a verbal irony which Darcy characterises as 'easy playfulness' (PP, 23). The purpose and function of this irony is to deflect meaning (in this she is her father's daughter, as both acknowledge), and the meaning deflected is predominantly sexual, the advances of Mr Collins and (at first) Darcy. One of Elizabeth's commonest discursive strategies to deflect Darcy's signification in the first half of the novel is to 'speak for' him, anticipating his discourse and mimicking it, turning the gaze of his 'satirical eye' (PP, 24) back upon himself: 'You expect me,' he says, 'to account for opinions which you chuse to call mine, but which I have never acknowledged' (PP, 50). For example, at the Netherfield ball, Darcy asks her to dance:

> She smiled, but made no answer. He repeated the question, with some surprise at her silence.
>
> 'Oh!' said she, 'I heard you before, but I could not immediately determine what to say in reply. You wanted me, I know, to say "Yes", that you might have the pleasure of despising my taste, but I always delight in overthrowing those kind of schemes, and cheating a person out of their premeditated contempt. I have therefore made up my mind to tell you, that I do not want to dance a reel at all—and now despise me if you dare.' (PP, 52)

(Alice Chandler reads a sexual innuendo here: 'The word *reel* did have a sexual connotation in Jane Austen's time. The phrases "the reels o' Bogie", "the reels of Stumpie" [!] and "dance the miller's reel" are all slang terms for sexual intercourse.' This being the case, one might want to render Elizabeth's put-down in the modern vernacular as something like 'I wouldn't have sex with you if you were the last man on earth'.[23]) This verbal agility, Elizabeth's second-guessing of Darcy's speech, allows her consistently to evade his meaning, to reinterpret his motives, and to misinterpret them, to turn the first half of the novel into a series of misreadings. Thus, when Elizabeth tells Darcy that his 'defect' is 'a propensity to hate every body', Darcy replies ('with a smile') that hers 'is wilfully to misunderstand them' (PP, 58). In effect, Elizabeth will not allow Darcy to speak to her. 'I beg your pardon,' she tells him, 'one knows exactly what to think' (PP, 86), and when dancing in conspicuous silence, Darcy, ostensibly talking about books, suggests to Elizabeth that 'We may compare our different opinions', she simply turns him down: 'No—I cannot talk about books in a ball-room; my head is always full of something else' (PP, 93).

Darcy's letter does not put a total stop to Elizabeth's self-authorising ironic discourse, thank heavens, but it *does* effect a diminishing or tempering of it. By the end of the novel, Elizabeth countenances restraint in her repartee with Darcy: 'she checked herself. She remembered that he had yet to learn to be laught at, and it was rather too early to begin' (PP, 371).

Early in the novel, she famously states that 'follies and nonsense, whims and inconsistencies do divert me, I own, and I laugh at them whenever I can' (PP, 57). But Elizabeth comes to an awareness of her own 'inconsistencies', and realises, as Emma Woodhouse never does, that 'nonsense' can contain meaning. When eventually, towards the novel's close, Elizabeth and Darcy engage in a dialogue which *does* signify, they discuss his letter:

> Darcy mentioned his letter, 'Did it,' said he, 'did it *soon* make you think better of me? Did you go on reading it, give any credit to its contents?'
>
> She explained what its effect on her had been, and how gradually all her former prejudices had been removed. (PP, 368)

One thing the letter does not contain is a better phrased reiteration of Darcy's botched proposal: Elizabeth's witheringly accurate elucidation of her reasons for not wanting to marry him have put paid to that. The purpose of the letter is rather to clear Darcy of the 'two offences of a different nature, and by no means equal magnitude ... laid at my charge' (PP, 196)—his separation of Bingley from Jane on account of the unsuitability of the Bennet family, and his having 'blasted the prospects of Mr Wickham ... Wilfully and wantonly' (PP, 196).

It's no surprise, perhaps, that Darcy should find Mrs Bennet's 'total want of propriety' to be 'objectionable' (PP, 198). It *is* objectionable. The novel itself, through its narrative voice (largely speaking from Elizabeth's point of view), has asserted this from the opening chapter, we have seen, with its seemingly dispassionate account of her 'mean understanding, little information, and uncertain temper'. Elizabeth certainly feels this way, and the narrative records her feelings on one of the occasions which led to the formation of Darcy's opinion about Mrs Bennet: 'Her mother would talk of her views in the same intelligible tone. Elizabeth blushed and blushed again with shame and vexation' (PP, 100). At the same gathering, Elizabeth's views of other members of her family foreshadow Darcy's denunciation: Mary's singing has her 'in agonies' (PP, 100). Like most families, perhaps, the Bennets can be excruciatingly embarrassing. Darcy's real 'offence' may have been his refusal to accommodate, to suppress this awareness in his actions, to keep his opinions to himself. Elizabeth's family pride, her sense of being 'a gentleman's daughter' (PP, 356), is offended by Darcy's actions—but then again the Bennets are not, as things stand, his family. The novel's equalising 'balancing act' sees to it that Darcy, too, is provided with an embarrassing relative, Lady Catherine de Bourgh, every bit as cringe-making as Mrs Bennet, and considerably more malicious. Here, a familial imperative analogous to Elizabeth's obliges him to stifle his overt reaction to her equally 'objectionable' behaviour, which Elizabeth is quite properly willing to challenge with all her verbal resources: 'Mr Darcy looked a little ashamed of his aunt's ill breeding, and made no answer' (PP, 173).

The more serious offence with which Elizabeth charges Darcy is his effective disinheritance of Wickham. Given that Darcy's and Wickham's account of the same events radically contradict each other, this is simply a case of whose evidence is the more believable: 'on both sides it was only assertion' (PP, 205). Reuben A. Brower, in what for me remains the finest single piece ever written on *Pride and Prejudice*, suggests that 'The passages in which Elizabeth reviews the letter present an odd, rather legalistic process ... [in which] the evidence on both sides is weighed and a reasonable conclusion is reached.'[24] This seems perfectly true: 'She put down the letter, weighted every circumstance with what she meant to be impartiality, deliberated on the probability of each statement' (PP, 205). But there is nothing necessarily 'odd' about this legalistic process: rather, Elizabeth responds in kind to the terms of Darcy's letter, whose vocabulary ('justice', 'offences', 'charge') quite clearly places the affair in terms of a criminal trial, with Elizabeth as judge: 'I demand of [this letter] your justice,' he writes (PP, 196). This response in kind presupposes on Elizabeth's part a nascent willingness to do what had previously been unthinkable, accept Darcy's point of view. Wickham also appeals to Elizabeth to accept the veracity of his own version of events through the adoption of legal discourse: 'I have known [Darcy] too long and too well to be a fair judge. It is impossible for *me* to be impartial' (PP, 77); 'I cannot do justice to [Darcy's father's] kindness' (PP, 79). 'Why did you not seek legal redress?' Elizabeth asks him (PP, 79).

Elizabeth initially considers Wickham 'A young man ... whose very countenance may vouch for [his] being amiable' (PP, 80–1). The letter provides an awareness of 'inconsistencies' of which Elizabeth was not aware, and which she could not 'laugh at':

> Again, she read on. But every line proved more clearly that the affair, which she had believed impossible that any contrivance could so represent, as to render Darcy's conduct in it less than infamous, was capable of a turn which must make him entirely blameless throughout the whole. (PP, 205)

Elizabeth re-reads Wickham: 'She could see him instantly before her, in every charm of address, but could remember no more substantial good than the general approbation of the neighbourhood, and the regard which his social powers had gained him in the mess' (PP, 206). She comes to realise that Darcy's 'character was by no means so faulty, nor Wickham's so amiable, as they had been considered in Hertfordshire' (PP, 258). Darcy's letter, and Elizabeth's subsequent visit to Pemberley, allow her to place *him*, conversely, 'in an amiable light' (PP, 249). Stuart M. Tave has discussed the significance for Austen of the amiable (as opposed to the merely 'agreeable'):[25] in *Emma*, Mr Knightley, as Chapter 5 will discuss more fully, sets great store by Frank Churchill's being only '"ammable"', 'very agreeable', rather than genuinely 'amiable' (E, 149). Darcy's letter enables Elizabeth to distinguish the sincerely 'amiable' from that which is, like Wickham, whose countenance vouches for it, only amiable-looking.

Pride and Prejudice, then, might be described as a bipartite novel, pivoting on Darcy's letter. Austen can only move into the second half of her novel, in which a synthesis is achieved, desire consummated, a marriage contracted, by effectively handing control of her narrative over to Darcy. Darcy's letter is pure meaning, signification unmediated by the narrative's tendency towards ironic deflection or deferral. Without rupturing the narrative to interpose the story which it has not been allowing Darcy to tell, this 'categorically happy novel' might never have ended so evidently to the satisfaction of (almost!) all.

Notes

1. R. W. Chapman (PP, p. 416) identifies Meryton as occupying the same geographical space as Hemel Hempstead, which must be nice for the good people of that town.

2. Johnson, *Women, Politics and the Novel*, p. 93.

3. For a lengthy discussion of this subject, see Barker-Benfield, *The Culture of Sensibility*, pp. 1–36.

4. Raymond Williams, *The Country and the City* (London: Hogarth Press, 1993).

5. Edmund Burke, *Reflections on the Revolution in France*, ed. Conor Cruise O'Brien (Harmondsworth: Penguin, 1968), p. 119.

6. Edward Malins, *English Landscaping and Literature 1660–1840* (London: Oxford University Press, 1966), p. 110.

7. Samuel Richardson, *The History of Sir Charles Grandison*, ed. Jocelyn Harris (Oxford: Oxford University Press, 1986), 7:272–3.

8. John Dixon Hunt and Peter Willis (eds), *The Genius of the Place: The English Landscape Garden 1620–1820* (Cambridge, MA, and London: MIT Press, 2000), p. 372. I am indebted to my former student Jean O'Mahony for the phrase 'pornography of estate management' as a description of Pemberley—it seems to me precisely right (which is why I stole it).

9. Alistair M. Duckworth, *The Improvement of the Estate: A Study of Jane Austen's Novels* (Baltimore and London: Johns Hopkins Press, 1971), p. 123.

10. Southam, *Jane Austen's Literary Manuscripts*, p. 62.

11. Most notably in the classic account by Reuben A. Brower, 'Light, Bright and Sparkling: Irony and Fiction in *Pride and Prejudice*', in Ian Watt (ed.), *Jane Austen: A Collection*

of Critical Essays, Twentieth-century Views series (Englewood Cliffs, NJ: Prentice-Hall, 1963), pp. 62–75. See also Sandra M. Gilbert and Susan Gubar, *The Madwoman in the Attic: The Woman Writer and the Nineteenth-century Literary Imagination* (New Haven, CT: Yale University Press, 1979), p. 154; Hudson, *Sibling Love and Incest*, p. 68.

12. Johnson, *Women, Politics and the Novel*, p. 89.

13. *Ibid.*, p. 77.

14. Judith Lowder Newton, *Women, Power and Subversion: Social Strategies in British Fiction, 1770–1860* (London and New York: Methuen, 1985), p. 62. Similarly, Johnson, *Women, Politics and the Novel*, p. 76, considers the novel 'almost shamelessly wish-fulfilling'.

15. Butler, *War of Ideas*, p. 214.

16. Mary Wollstonecraft, *A Vindication of the Rights of Woman*, ed. Miriam Brody (Harmondsworth: Penguin, 1975), pp. 79, 83.

17. Johnson, *Women, Politics and the Novel*, p. 73; Butler, *War of Ideas*, p. 218.

18. *Gentleman's Magazine*, 43 (1773), 603. See Staves, 'British Seduced Maidens', 109, for an account of this.

19. Lilian S. Robinson, 'Why Marry Mr Collins?', in *Sex, Class and Culture* (London and New York: Methuen, 1986), p. 178.

20. *Ibid.*, p. 178.

21. Dorothy Van Ghent, *The English Novel: Form and Function* (New York: Harper and Row, 1953, rpt 1961), p. 103.

22. Phil Silvers, with Robert Saffron, *The Man Who Was Bilko* (London and New York: W. H. Allen, 1974), pp. 85–6.

23. Alice Chandler, '"A Pair of Fine Eyes": Jane Austen's Treatment of Sex', *Studies in the Novel*, 7 (1975), 103n12.

24. Brower, 'Light, Bright and Sparkling', p. 71.

25. Stuart M. Tave, *Some Words of Jane Austen* (Chicago and London: University of Chicago Press, 1973), pp. 117–20.

JILLIAN HEYDT-STEVENSON

The Anxieties and "Felicities of Rapid Motion": Animated Ideology in Pride and Prejudice

*P*ride and Prejudice's kinetic energy resists its evocation of an idyllic society at the height of a calm, country perfection; everyone in this novel is physically, and often extravagantly in motion: fleeing to London, scurrying to Brighton, flying from Pemberley or hastening toward it. Elizabeth remarks that "people themselves alter so much, that there is something new to be observed in them for ever" (43). Even so fundamental a fact as the population of local society fluctuates as the news about Bingley's number of guests varies wildly; and rumors speed through the town as it alters its opinions about Darcy (9–13). Motion propels marriage and generation. The subject of balls "always makes a lady energetic" (24): "to be fond of dancing was a certain step towards falling in love" (9). Bingley boasts that his "ideas flow so rapidly that [he has] not time to express them" (48). The brisk Mr. Collins means to find a bride during a visit of only one week—and he succeeds. Darcy's own restless evolutions drive him to change his mind in favor of Elizabeth just as he has decided against her (26), though a moment later he accuses Caroline of jumping to conclusions when he charges that "a lady's imagination is very rapid" in marching toward thoughts of matrimony (27). Elizabeth's own busy mind works dynamically, as when conjectures, "rapid and wild," about the reason why Darcy attended Lydia's wedding were "hurried into her brain" (320). Elizabeth's *immobility*—sitting out two dances without a

From *Austen's Unbecoming Conjunctions: Subversive Laughter, Embodied History*, pp. 69–102. © 2005 by Palgrave Macmillan.

partner—becomes a sign of rejection and casualty that offends Darcy: he is in no mood "at present" to humor girls that other men reject (12); that "at present," though, suggests he will change his mind, and, indeed, he soon finds Elizabeth's animation magnetic: the "easy playfulness" of her manners, the "light and pleasing" quality of her figure, as well as "the brilliancy ... [of] her complexion" (23, 33).

These examples speak to a consistent sense of "embodied subjectivity" (Grosz 22), that is, a synergetic relation between mind and body. A common reading of Austen in general and *Pride and Prejudice* in particular, however, discounts the physical, contending instead that the narrative bifurcates body and mind, accentuating mental constraint and repression over bodily excess. Tending to track the heroine's growth in terms of her mind and understanding, readers have often found the novels to be a classic *bildungsroman*. One consequence of such a perspective has been to insist that Austen's fiction lacks sex (Susan Morgan even titles one chapter "Why There is no Sex in Jane Austen"). The idea that elegance and maturity require Austen and her heroines to harness their feelings and curb their bodies traces its genealogy to Charlotte Brontë's extraordinary, but by this time shopworn, declaration that "The Passions are perfectly unknown to [Austen].... [E]ven to the Feelings she vouchsafes no more than an occasional graceful but distant recognition; too frequent converse with them would ruffle the smooth elegance of her progress" (qtd. in Dennis Allen 425). Such a declaration occludes an investigation of the body's role in the novel—except for its criminal element (Mrs. Bennet and Lydia, for example)—by enforcing the idea that Austen advocates inhibition over expression. John Wiltshire claims, for example, that Mrs. Bennet's "unabashed sexuality is a demonstration of everything the novel assumes, but keeps otherwise implicit and under wraps," and wonders if her "baffled energies [are] a distorted, bizarre version of [Elizabeth's] transgressive high spirits—this daughter who runs everywhere?" ("Mrs. Bennet's" 185). Yet evidence indicates instead that all the characters unabashedly appraise sexual and physical appeal. Even a quick gathering of examples suggests that *Pride and Prejudice*'s world allows for more expansive expressions of physicality than just aberrant energy or the discipline of that excess. William Deresiewicz contends that "Austen transforms the process of courtship as she found it in her novelistic predecessors, making it both more conscious and more emotionally profound.... [Love], no longer an ecstasy antithetical or ... unrelated to friendship, ... becomes instead a form of friendship" (519). In general I agree, though this primary emphasis on dispassionate friendship discounts how these metamorphoses in self-knowledge sink in somatically. I want to highlight how the novel acknowledges the body's joyful effusions, its transgressions, the violations it endures and inflicts, and its function as an epistemic barometer. Instead of interpreting the body as a passive tool that mind fills up and out, or, in Locke's sense, of a possession or property that the mind controls, I argue that the narrative addresses the "bodily dimension of consciousness" (Grosz 22)—a dynamic, psychophysical process of expression—and dramatizes how the body materializes the ideologies it has absorbed.

KNOWING THROUGH THE BODY

Other considerations besides Jane's illness entice Elizabeth to walk six miles. Mary Poovey contends that "when [Elizabeth] bursts into Netherfield to see her sick sister ... the mud on her skirts becomes completely irrelevant beside the healthiness of her unself-conscious concern for Jane" (195). I think, however, that the chance for action also lures her as she "cross[es] field after field at a quick pace, jumping over stiles and springing over puddles with impatient activity, and finding herself at last within view of the house, with weary ancles, dirty stockings, and a face glowing with the warmth of exercise" (32). When Caroline sniffs a moment later that Elizabeth has "no stile" (35), her word reminds us that in catapulting styles as well as stiles, her physical flights *are* her mental flights. Darcy's famous appreciation of her brilliant complexion takes on greater significance when linked to medical discourse that associated exercise with a sharper and stronger intelligence, and also with a woman's ability to conceive: *Aristotle's Master-piece* warns that a "want of exercise and idleness are very great enemies to the work of generation, and indeed are enemies both to the soul and body.... A moderate exercise ... opens the pores, quickens the spirits, stirs up the natural heat, strengthens the body, sense and spirits, comforts the limbs, and helps nature in all its exercises" (42). The synchronism between her body and mind suggests that although the heroine loves her sister, the pleasure of conversing and engaging in perhaps more than "moderate" exercise pulls her toward Netherfield. Once there, the drawing-room conversation launches her body out of her chair and away from the still perusal of a book: with a mind that races like her body, "Elizabeth was so much caught by what passed, as to leave her very little attention for her book; and soon laying it wholly aside, she drew near the card-table, and stationed herself between Mr. Bingley and his eldest sister, to observe the game" (38).

A psychical corporeality energizes Elizabeth and Darcy's conversations, which always exceed the merely cerebral. For example, when Elizabeth rejects his proposal, Austen tabulates his reactions so as to suggest that the body-mind works together to articulate the physics of the moment: "[h]is complexion became pale with anger, and the disturbance of his mind was visible in every feature. He was struggling for the appearance of composure, and would not open his lips, till he believed himself to have attained it" (190). His color "heighten[s]," and he "walk[s] with quick steps across the room" when he exclaims, "And this ... is your opinion of me!" (191–192). His proposal and the heated argument that follows exact a heavy physical toll: "[s]he knew not how to support herself, and from actual weakness sat down and cried for half an hour" (193). "Air and exercise" help her recover from her "indisposition" and only after physical release restores her strength can she comprehend the information from Darcy's letter (195):

> She read, with an eagerness which hardly left her power of comprehension, and from impatience of knowing what the next sentence might bring, was incapable of attending to the sense of the one before her eyes.... [W]hen she had gone through the whole letter, though scarcely knowing any thing of the last page or two, put it hastily away, protesting that she would not regard it, that she would never look in it again.... In this perturbed state of mind, with thoughts that could rest on nothing, she walked on; but it would not do; in half a minute the letter was unfolded again.... After wandering along the lane for two hours, giving way to every variety of thought [,] re-considering events, ... fatigue ... made her at length return home. (204–209)

Here, her mental revelation coincides with—even depends upon— physical movement: the truth about Wickham "unfolds" before her as she folds and unfolds the letter, and her eyes sprint so impatiently that their movement incapacitates cognition. Her "variety of thought" and "thoughts that could rest on nothing" convey the corporeal aspect of ideas. In contrast to her earlier walk to Netherfield, an act of jouissance that heightens her vitality, here Elizabeth walks her way to exhaustion and understanding at the same time.

Darcy and Elizabeth engage in what Peter Brooks has called "the project of knowing the body and knowing through the body, essentially by way of erotic experience, since eroticism makes the body most fully sentient and also most 'intellectual,' the most aware of what it is doing and what is being done to it" (Brooks 278). The characters cherish good figures and erotic magnetism with a nonchalance that allows, indeed expects, the reader to take sexual appeal for granted and to connect it with romance and romance with marriage. By treating erotic passion openly, and without embarrassment or alloy, the novel normalizes it, rendering it almost invisible. For example, Mrs. Bennet encourages Jane and then Elizabeth to join a group of young, mixed company for almost a week unchaperoned. If other novels of the period (Burney's *The Wanderer*, Edgeworth's *Belinda*, or Scott's *Waverley*, for example) are to be given any credit for verisimilitude about moral expectations, the Bennet sisters' freedom from adult supervision of their chastity is remarkable. Attentive to the allure of the flesh, "the gentlemen pronounc[e] [Darcy] to be a fine figure of a man" (10); Mrs. Bennet avows the sexual appeal of a red coat (29); Wickham has "all the best part of beauty," including "a good figure" (72).[1] Darcy's physical discomfort, registered in his unpolished manners—staring at Elizabeth, visiting her without speaking and so on—suggests that his attraction manifests itself in his very presence. Though the Bingley sisters are untrustworthy, they convey a sense of how Elizabeth joins Lydia in possessing "high animal spirits" (45).

> "She really looked almost wild."
> "She did indeed, Louisa. I could hardly keep my countenance. Very nonsensical to come at all! Why must she be scampering about the country because her sister had a cold? Her hair so untidy, so blowsy!"
> "Yes, and her petticoat; I hope you saw her petticoat, six inches deep in mud, I am absolutely certain; and the gown which had been let down to hide it, not doing its office." (35–36)

"Abusing" Elizabeth for her vitality, Caroline and Louisa associate that exhilaration with sexual drive, associating her with profligate women, such as gypsies and prostitutes, and thereby collapsing her body's motility with her mind's immoral migrations. Elizabeth's playful banter on the efficacy of poetry in driving away love gives the body priority over wit (though she does so in a witty way): "I have been used to consider poetry as the *food* of love," said Darcy. Elizabeth retorts: "Of a fine, stout, healthy love it may. Every thing nourishes what is strong already. But if it be only a slight, thin sort of inclination, I am convinced that one good sonnet will starve it entirely away" (44–45). The mere idea of love, given form but not a real body in a sonnet, offers nothing but starvation to a consumptive lover. For Elizabeth, no Platonist, the body is the ground of love, and ideas feed it, not the other way around.

Though usually roped off from interpretations of the novel or collapsed into the category of the kind of unbridled and unsuitable activity that Austen condemns are the "vulgar" pursuits of Elizabeth's aunt, Mrs. Philips: she watches the handsome Wickham through her front window for an hour "as he walked up and down the street" and "Kitty and Lydia would certainly have continued the occupation, but unluckily no one passed the windows now" worth gazing at (74). This kind of voyeurism could be dismissed as the coarse behavior of the novel's marginalized, since it is Mrs. Philips and Lydia who are the flashy participants, but when Darcy acts in a similar fashion, his behavior underscores how the narrative affirms the power of knowing through physical appeal. Austen thus augments the list of those who enjoy the erotic gaze beyond men or those of lower rank or intelligence. Longing for Darcy's gaze and frustrated that he ignores her, Caroline moves from one physical "attitude" to another when she exclaims,

> "Miss Eliza Bennet, let me persuade you to follow my example, and take a turn about the room.—I assure you it is very refreshing after sitting so long in one attitude."
> Elizabeth was surprised, but agreed to it immediately. Miss Bingley succeeded no less in the real object of her civility; Mr. Darcy looked up. He was as much awake to the novelty of attention in that quarter as Elizabeth herself could be, and unconsciously closed his book. (56)

Austen may be satirizing Caroline by alluding here to the infamous originator of "the art of the attitude," Lady Emma Hamilton, who amused private audiences with a kind of pantomime in which scantily clad, she "shifted from one figure taken from classical myth to another, always freezing into a pose that recalled that of a famous statue" (Cox 171).[2] As if in on the joke of Caroline and Elizabeth as actors performing attitudes for his sake, Darcy reminds the women that they want him to admire their figures and that he is delighted to gratify their desire:

> He was directly invited to join their party, but he declined it, observing, that he could imagine but two motives for their chusing to walk up and down the room together, with either of which motives his joining them would interfere.... "You either chuse this method of passing the evening because you are in each other's confidence and have secret affairs to discuss, or because you are conscious that your figures appear to the greatest advantage in walking;—if the first, I should be completely in your way; and if the second, I can admire you much better as I sit by the fire." (56)

Caroline's remark—"Oh, shocking!"—spoken with mock horror, reveals how she basks in his plainspoken bawdy talk rather than registering it as an insult to her propriety. In this episode, Austen reiterates how well the characters understand their world's sexually charged atmosphere and how boisterously they participate in situations that the novel, at least, does not characterize either as *de trop* or as requiring censure.

VIOLATING THE BODY

It is unlikely that anyone reading Austen today would agree with Leslie Stephen's 1876 comment that her humor is "so excessively mild" (*Critical Heritage* 2, 174), or with J. I. M. Stewart, that her world is "drastically purged of almost everything alarming and mysterious in the human situation" (Southam, *Essays* 130), or with H. W. Garrod that she "describes everything in the youth of women which does not matter" (Southam, *Essays* 130). Instead, she invokes one of the "alarming and mysterious" aspects of the "human situation"—one of the aspects that "does ... matter": the mistreatment of the body, an arena of experience that becomes visible in *Pride and Prejudice* once we acknowledge the novel's physicality. Erotic attraction, physical abuse, and institutional ideologies intersect throughout the novel, underscoring how the "body's history" partakes of "the history of bodily violation" (Lefkovitz 1). For example, Austen fuses these three matters when Lydia and Catherine recount their activities during the elder girls' absence: "Much had been done, and much had been said in the regiment since the preceding Wednesday; several of the officers had dined lately with their uncle, a private had been flogged, and it had actually been hinted that Colonel Forster was going to be married" (60). The disturbing nonchalance with which the younger sisters mention flogging here suggests that it was common: an anecdote from the *Entertaining Magazine* (1803) treats the subject as a joke (and with a stereotypical slighting of the Irish): "An Irish drummer being employed to flog a deserter, the sufferer, as is usual in such cases, cried out 'Strike higher! Strike higher!' the drummer, accordingly, to oblige the poor fellow, did as he was requested. But the man still continuing to roar out in agony—'Devil burn your bellowing!' cried Paddy; 'there is no pleasing of you, strike where one will!'" (135). Though not in the racist way that the anecdote does, Austen capitalizes on the comic potential of forming a discordant catalogue by inserting flogging between these social activities. Her flat equation of disparate matters calls attention to buried connections among these unlike phenomena: the reference to marriage has the effect of sexualizing both dining and flogging; and the reference to flogging conflates marriage with punishment.

The catalogue's elements, far from grating, correspond. That flogging was punishment for, among other "crimes," slaves who rebelled and men who chose men as sexual partners, reinforces a sense of the intrusion of patriarchal power into all areas of private life. In his discussion of humiliation, William Ian Miller points out that because "victimizers, according to our common notions, will tend to be male, and victims, if not female to the same extent as victimizers are male, will in many settings, be gendered female nonetheless. A male victim is a feminized male" (55). That women and slaves were equated needs no explanation; nor that flogging was common in early nineteenth-century life; nor that Austen would have been familiar with public whippings and graphic accounts in descriptions of colonial life, at the least from her reading of Thomas Clarkson's *History of the Abolition of the Slave Trade* (1808), which, as part of the antislavery campaign, utilized verbal and visual images of flogging to influence abolitionist legislation. As Mary Favret argues, "the white woman was repeatedly invited to view the representation of racial and sexual violence," asked "to fix [her] eyes on 'the strong marks of slavery'": "'Be not afraid,' wrote one tract, 'we do not ask you to do anything, to incite in anything unbecoming to your sex'" (Flogging 39, 40). The hope was that when women looked, they filtered out the pornographic gaze—cleansing the image with their own mercy. But those same images also offered women a chance "to participate vicariously in sexual excesses otherwise denied to proper gentlewomen" (Favret 41).

The uninflected clustering of these three activities—dining, flogging, and marrying—in one sentence (and a prominent sentence at that, since it closes a chapter) comments on how often women becomes "slaves" in courtship and marriage and how a coupling that promises to provide material security (the dining side of this triangle), can lacerate a woman's identity. In other words, Lydia and Catherine's story provides an example that dramatizes, at the most basic level, the negative impact that marriage can have on the body. The constellation of marriage and flogging provides a context for the full irony of Collins's reference to the "violence of [his] affection" (106) when he proposes to Elizabeth, and problematizes his comment when he anticipates that Lady Catherine will find Elizabeth's "wit and vivacity ... acceptable ..., especially when tempered with the silence and respect which her rank will inevitably excite" (106). By silencing her wit, such a marriage promises to demolish the cornerstone of Elizabeth's intelligence and life force. Favret, drawing on Shenstone's "The School Mistress" (1742), whose mission it was "to illustrate the secret connexion betwixt *Whipping and Rising* in the world," highlights how, in eighteenth-century education, "flogging" was linked with learning (26), and thus with social mobility. Extrapolating from this, it is appropriate that Austen would conjoin flogging and marriage, since matrimony was the only way for women to "rise" in this world. As I discuss throughout this book, Austen's novels investigate how her heroines register through their bodies the experience of knowing and being known in courtship and marriage, and one important subset in that experience is sexual attraction. Mr. Collins illustrates Henri Bergson's point that the attitudes, gestures, and movements of the human body are laughable in proportion as the body acts like a machine (10). Collins's mental and physical inelasticity—his inability to hear Elizabeth's rejections of his proposals and his failure to use language in such a way that it correlates to the experience at hand—makes him funny. Needlessly worrying that this blockhead might lose momentum in his courtship of her, Charlotte plans her strategy for love: her

> object was nothing less, than to secure [Elizabeth] from any return of Mr. Collins's addresses, by engaging them towards herself. Such was Miss Lucas's scheme; and appearances were so favourable that when they parted at night, she would have felt almost sure of success if he had not been to leave Hertfordshire so very soon. But here, she did injustice to the fire and independence of his character, for it led him to escape out of Longbourn House with admirable slyness, and hasten to Lucas Lodge to throw himself at her feet.... Miss Lucas perceived him from an upper window as he walked towards the house, and instantly set out to meet him accidentally in the lane. But little had she dared to hope that so much love and eloquence awaited her there. (121)

Charlotte's spontaneous "scheme," the couple's "accidental" meeting in the lane, and Mr. Collins's "fire and independence" when he "throws" his body at her feet, amuse because they employ the mechanical gestures of beings programmed to enact the ideology of romantic love. They ape dynamic sexual energy here in a robotic way—hilarious in its brittleness, but pointing by contrast to the kind of knowledge that might be found in spontaneous physical attraction.

Charlotte's union, with Collins is horrible to imagine not only because he is vengeful and mean, but also because she will have to endure a marriage suffused with physical aversion. In a displaced way, we get an insight into this aspect of their future when Elizabeth's dances with Collins produce what Austen describes as a sort of inverted orgasm: dancing with the clergyman brings nothing but "distress; they were dances of mortification. Mr. Collins, awkward and solemn, apologising instead of attending, and often moving wrong without being aware of it, gave her all the shame and misery which a disagreeable partner for a couple of dances can give. The moment of her release from him was exstasy" (90).[3] Charlotte thinks to herself that "the stupidity with which he was favoured by nature, must guard his courtship from any charm that could make a woman wish for its continuance" (122); her awareness of that fact ironically emphasizes that although she can control the length of courtship, she will have no such power in marriage, in which there will be no "ecstatic" release from his touch, from those "conjugal duties"[4] that Mr. Collins will expect to be fulfilled, given that his second reason for marrying is that it "will add very greatly to [his] happiness" (105). I thus disagree with Ruth Perry, who, arguing that "sexual disgust was an invention of the eighteenth century," claims that because Charlotte "is a vestigial character, left over from an era of pragmatic rather than romantic matches ... the physical repugnance that we in the present century feel at the idea of sleeping with Mr. Collins is entirely absent in Jane Austen's treatment of the matter.... There is not the slightest whiff of sexual disgust about the matter; not from Charlotte, nor from Elizabeth, nor from the narrator" (121, 120).[5] The novel, however, delineates sexual attraction; and if that is identifiable, so too is physical revulsion, regardless of whether or not Charlotte is "vestigial" in her thinking.

Collins's bumbling body and insensitivity suggest that Charlotte does indeed experience disgust, insofar as her union with him disables her senses, shutting down at least three avenues of perception: touch, as I have suggested above; sound, since Charlotte "wisely did not hear" his shameful retorts (156); and sight, since to keep Collins out of her radius in her new house, Charlotte takes the inferior room:

> The room in which the ladies sat was backwards. Elizabeth at first had rather wondered that Charlotte should not prefer the dining parlour for common use; it was a better sized room, and had a pleasanter aspect; but she soon saw that her friend had an excellent reason for what she did, for Mr. Collins would undoubtedly have been much less in his own apartment, had they sat in one equally lively. (168)

Sitting "backwards" (i.e., in the back portion of the house) cuts her off from the "pleasanter aspect"—a wider view onto the road and the world outside— but this is the price that Charlotte accepts for avoiding her husband. Beyond these perspectival and sensory deprivations, however, marriage with him also obliterates that most significant element of consciousness, memory: to reduce his irritation on her nerves and brain, Charlotte lives in such a way that Mr. Collins is "often forgotten" (157). Elizabeth's parting thoughts about her friend's marriage spotlight how evanescent are the bewitching promises of marriage's material security, the comforts Lydia and Catherine's catalogue implied in its reference to "dining." Charlotte's "home and her housekeeping, her parish and her poultry, and all their dependent concerns, had not *yet* lost their charms" (216, emphasis added). The alliteration here, rare in Austen, reinforces the grim puns inherent in parish (perish) and poultry (paltry), all of it inadequate compensation for the loss of plastic and responsive mindfulness.[6] In order to "dine," Charlotte marries, only to face being flogged with corrosive stupidity every day of her life.

Elizabeth's marriage, by contrast, heralds the efflorescence of her senses, a process that begins with Darcy first making himself *known* to Elizabeth by wounding and marking her body—"he looked for a moment at Elizabeth, till catching her eye, he withdrew his own and coldly said, 'She is tolerable; but not handsome enough to tempt *me*; and I am in no humour at present to give consequence to young ladies who are slighted by other men'" (11–12). The "catching" of her eye suggests the sharp aim of the whipping words that follow, words that represent the collective male appraisal that rejects a woman "not handsome enough," a woman who is only "tolerable"—or just bearable. In objectifying her body he fragments her sense of self, but she fights back: as she later tells Darcy, "My courage always rises with every attempt to intimidate me" (174). Grosz argues that the body, "as well as being the site of knowledge-power ... is thus also a site of resistance, for it exerts a recalcitrance, and always entails the possibility of a counterstrategic reinscription, for it is capable of being self-marked, self-represented in alternative ways" ("Inscriptions" 64–65). From the moment he insults her, Elizabeth reinscribes his attacks: she retells the "story ... with great spirit among her friends; for she had a lively, playful disposition, which delighted in any thing ridiculous" (12). The problem, though, is that this counterstrategy fails since she remains irate through much of the novel, and that anger provides no effective way to resist Darcy's advances since he refuses to read her dislike as such. She may playfully protest that he is ridiculous, but her resentment reveals she is far from playfully amused.

Darcy's change of mind about Elizabeth's beauty and intellectual appeal is unmistakable; why then is Elizabeth, even though she dislikes him—the novel's famous and eponymous "prejudice"—unable to detect his crush on her? He tries to flirt with her by asking if she

"feel[s] a great inclination ... to seize such an opportunity of dancing a reel?"

She smiled, but made no answer. He repeated the question, with some surprise at her silence.

"Oh!" said she, "I heard you before; but I could not immediately determine what to say in reply. You wanted me, I know, to say 'Yes,' that you might have the pleasure of despising my taste;

but I always delight in overthrowing those kind of schemes, and cheating a person of their premeditated contempt. I have therefore made up my mind to tell you, that I do not want to dance a reel at all—and now despise me if you dare."

"Indeed I do not dare."

Elizabeth, having rather expected to affront him, was amazed at his gallantry; but there was a mixture of sweetness and archness in her manner which made it difficult for her to affront anybody; and Darcy had never been so bewitched by any woman as he was by her. (52)

She registers flirtation as another affront to her sexuality, since he implies that she has such a passion for dancing that she would "seize" any opportunity (even a country dance) to act like a "savage" (to quote his comment earlier that "every savage can dance") (25). She takes this insult to heart since it implies that her physicality coarsely embodies her "taste." When she declines in a manner that she expects will "affront him," her behavior instead enthralls him. Grosz explains that there is an "enormous investment in definitions of the female body in struggles between patriarchs and feminists: what is at stake is the activity and agency, the mobility and social space, accorded to women. Far from being an inert, passive, noncultural and ahistorical term, the body may be seen as the crucial term, the site of contestation, in a series of economic, political, sexual, and intellectual struggles" (*Volatile Bodies* 19). How can a woman know her own body or another's under the thumb of such a system?

Because of Darcy's confidence and the narrator's statement that "there was a mixture of sweetness and archness in her manner which made it difficult for her to affront anybody" (52), the novel makes it hard to see or to take her settled disapprobation for him seriously. The contradiction between Darcy's and Elizabeth's interpretation of her reactions to him provides an example of how her body becomes "the site of contestation" in the novel. She has expressed her aversion so well and to so many that when she decides to marry Darcy, she has trouble convincing her family that she loves him: Jane cries, "You are joking, Lizzy. This cannot be!—engaged to Mr. Darcy! No, no, you shall not deceive me.... I know how much you dislike him" (372); and her father reminds her, "have not you always hated him?" (376). In contrast, because he loves Elizabeth, Darcy misreads her choler, at least until his first proposal. Does he differ so much from Collins in construing Elizabeth through the ideological filter that says that women flirt, but they do not get angry? What feels to her like outrage sounds to him like delightful, coquettish wit. When Darcy says she "find[s] great enjoyment in occasionally professing opinions which in fact are not your own" (174), ironically, like Collins, he assumes that like a conduct book heroine, she dissimulates, and does so for his pleasure, engaging in that "sweet, reluctant amorous delay" that Milton assigns Eve in *Paradise Lost*. As I alluded to earlier, Darcy admits that because Elizabeth's and Caroline's "figures appear to the greatest advantage in walking, [he] can admire [them] much better as [he] sit[s] by the fire" (56). Miss Bingley wants to know how they shall "punish him for such a speech"? Elizabeth answers by instructing Caroline to "'Teaze him—laugh at him.—Intimate as you are, you must know how it is to be done.' 'But upon my honour I do *not*. I do assure you that my intimacy has not yet taught me *that*'" (56). Elizabeth, the passage suggests, already has the secret for punishing—witty words that carry their own physical charge. Laughter embodies an aggressive purpose here, providing an outlet for both her hostility and perhaps her sexual attraction to him. Elizabeth says that if you want to punish, then, there is "Nothing, so easy, if you have but the inclination," and *she* is inclined to find release in such a way from the power Darcy holds over her sister and family. In this sense, her wit intends (as Regina Gagnier has argued feminist comedy aims to do) to be "metasemiotic, casting in doubt ... cultural codes" (139). Darcy's attraction to her, however, nullifies her feminist gestures of revolt, since he interprets her remarks as appeals toward his body, toward a collapsing of subject and object; from Darcy's point of view, Elizabeth's laughter draws him closer.

In these varying responses—the fact that she "never knew" herself (208), that her mother and the Bingley sisters read her as "wild"; that her father and sister believe she "hates" Darcy; that the narrator discloses that she is, underneath it all, "sweet and arch"; that Darcy finds her "bewitching"; and that she herself believes that she articulates a transparent state of "immoveable dislike" (193)—a question emerges about her self-knowledge as well the knowledge about her that others might have. The context of the *bildungsroman* provides an insufficient answer since the characters' diverging interpretations of Elizabeth expose the tension between her own agency and social pressures: the difficulty of reading identity outside of an ideological lens renders her growth curve more ineffable and labyrinthine than a movement from "a" to "b" ("until this moment I never knew myself"). As Katherine Canning emphasizes, "embodied practices are always contextual, inflected with class, ethnic, racial, gender, and generational locations" (87). Can Elizabeth read her own body, know her attraction to him—those signals that seem so clear in her playful wit—or do social constructions of gender preclude Darcy, and the narrator, from interpreting her humor as a real resistance to his attempt to mark her, markings so obvious, he believes, that she cannot be surprised that he proposes to her?

As if to reinforce the idea that a man's aggression is always pellucid, the novel renders Darcy's own truculence toward those he dislikes palpable. In the episode in which Caroline Bingley tries to make herself known to Darcy by flattering his epistolary style, he responds to her with the same hostility he had earlier directed toward Elizabeth. Miss Bingley irritates Darcy by complimenting him for writing to his sister, for writing "fast," and for writing "many" letters, including those of business, and for passing along from her a message to Georgiana in his letter (47). Unable to inspire a satisfactory response with her flattery, and incapable of grasping "the perfect unconcern with which her praises were received" (47), she shifts strategy and offers to be serviceable: "I am afraid you do not like your pen. Let me mend it for you. I mend pens remarkably well." Perhaps in desperation she here unconsciously tries to engage Darcy with a powerful metonymy of phallic power and feminine submission. Apparently recognizing the double entendre, whether she does or not, Darcy wittily invokes autoeroticism when he answers, "Thank you—but I always mend my own" (47). A common pun, the pen as phallus occurs throughout literature written before the nineteenth century, especially in Shakespeare. For example, in *The Merchant of Venice* Gratiano says to his wife, Nerissa, "I'll mar the young clerk's pen" (V.i.237), when she threatens to tryst with the clerk.[7] And from Sir George Lyttelton's *A Collection of Poems*, comes this little poem, playing on the same idea: Epigram VIII, "On Mrs. Penelope," by Gilbert West. "The gentle Pen with look demure, / Awhile was thought a virgin pure; / But Pen as ancient poets say, / Undid the night of work by day" (2:230).

Whether Caroline understands the pun she has made or the one Darcy throws back at her, she does suggest one way women did serve men at the time, that is by making and repairing pens, and that historical context illuminates the power dynamics implicit in this exchange. John Savigny's *Instructions at Large for Making and Repairing Pens* (1786) relates that he has "instructed many young ladies, who at first entertained an idea of the difficulty of attainment, who, notwithstanding, are now capable of making pens for the most capital prize-writing ..." (lviii). Savigny encourages young ladies to master this skill: "It cannot be imagined they can be capable of feeling a more exquisite degree of pleasure, than in finding the perfection of their faculties able to supply a remedy for the decay" of their parents' aging eyes. Savigny, devoted to his cause, wants all who write to "have it in their power to accommodate themselves with pens"; the treatise implies, however, that a woman's ability to make and repair these instruments might also be useful to the young gentleman, who a week after having "le[ft] the seminary, with the reputation of being a fine writer, ... greatly disappoints his friends by his performance when he uses the pens he finds at home, or of such as may be purchased ready made" (lv). His strong moral tone in pleading for the handcrafted over the mechanically produced and consumed article of capitalist enterprise recalls the Romantic-era sentimentalization of objects explored earlier in my discussion of the production of hair jewelry. Savigny's morality also emerges in his sentimental picture of young female eyes helping deteriorating parental vision and in the anecdote he relates about a gentlewoman who "omitted sending her sister a letter for one whole month" because "her cousin, who used to make her pens, happened to be at Bath" (lx). The treatise reveals an unsteady union between its promise of empowerment for the women who gain this knowledge and the subordination of that skill to domestic duties: when one is "once rendered capable of making a fine pen, [one] will soon discover the proper means of suiting it to all the different hands now in use" (83). Though Savigny speaks literally here about the fit between a pen and an individual hand, he also implies that there are differences between the purposes a man or woman might put a pen to. Women should enable others to write.

This sense in the treatise that a woman should subordinate her initiative and knowledge to good service parallels Caroline's self-subjection, but it also reflexively recalls Austen's agency as a writer. Caroline wants to serve Darcy with her pen-making skill; Austen has a pen that fits her own hand quite well indeed, and she empowers her writing by her subversive pun on that word. The scene embodies female submission and male dominance; however, the fact that a woman has written this episode agitates that clear power balance. If it is impossible to believe that Austen knew she was making such a pun, perhaps she becomes, like Elizabeth, a site of contestation in which regardless of how legible her own anger may be (though couched in a witty double entendre), she must perforce be characterized as having a "sweetness and archness in her manner which made it difficult for her to affront anybody" (52). Lisa Merrill argues that "in feminist comedy, we are no longer cast as an omniscient audience laughing at a character 'unknowingly betraying' herself[;] rather, the context and the character interact in such a way as to stir our empathy as much as our amusement" (279). Feminist comedy, as Austen employs it, expands beyond Merrill's definition. In offering a bawdy witticism, the novelist expresses her hostility toward the kind of traditional female subordination that Caroline embodies here, and if she does empathize with Miss Bingley insofar as she exposes the social genetics that spawned such behavior—the kind of conduct-book discourse that permeates Savigny's treatise—Austen's empathy does not tenderize her hostility. Austen has "made" her own pen, and in doing so shows another way that feminist comedy might empower women. Darcy's aggressive humor, when directed toward Caroline, provides both him and Austen the opportunity to displace bellicose feelings with flogging double entendres that the public may or may not tolerate from a woman.

TRANSGRESSION

Lori Hope Lefkovitz argues that "as the body acquires new definition, what it means to transgress its boundaries changes accordingly" (1). The novel asks in a number of ways what it means when female bodies transgress the precincts apportioned to them, and those transgressions vary from Elizabeth's walk to Netherfield to Lydia's illicit days in Meryton and London. The novel's arresting reference to cross-dressing constitutes one fecund example of those transgressions: Lydia exclaims that

> we had such a good piece of fun the other day at Colonel Forster's. Kitty and me were to spend the day there, and Mrs. Forster promised to have a little dance in the evening; (by the bye, Mrs. Forster and me are *such* friends!) and so she asked the two Harringtons to come, but Harriet was ill, and so Pen was forced to come by herself; and then, what do you think we did? We dressed up Chamberlayne in woman's clothes, on purpose to pass for a lady,—only think what fun! Not a soul knew of it, but Col. and Mrs. Forster, and Kitty and me, except my aunt, for we were forced to borrow one of her gowns; and you cannot imagine how well he looked! When Denny, and Wickham, and Pratt, and two or three more of the men came in, they did not know him in the least. Lord! How I laughed! And so did Mrs. Forster. I thought I should have died. (221)

The women dress an officer up as a "lady," hoping, no doubt, to trick the unknowing men into a romantic advance; because of the context, Austen's choice of names for Lydia's friend, Pen, perhaps short for Penelope, also suggests subversive gender play—with more "pens" in female hands, the cross-dressing now goes in the other direction. The narrator blandly explains that "with such kind of histories of their parties and good jokes, did Lydia, assisted by Kitty's hints and additions, endeavour to amuse her companions all the way to Longbourn. Elizabeth listened as little as she could, but there was no escaping the frequent mention of Wickham's name" (222). The narration here suggests that although she does not enjoy Lydia's stories, references to Wickham upset Elizabeth more than the "histories of their parties and good jokes." Dennis Allen argues that the incident hints that "romantic or sexual desire can ignore society's heterosexual imperative, leading to a homosexual eros which in effect obliterates the cultural distinction of male and female.... Lydia's trick suggests that desire has the potential to violate the logical foundations of her society, ... [to threaten] a nihilistic dissolution of the social order that fully justifies Austen's fear of it" (438–439). I would argue, instead, as I will do in my analysis of *Northanger Abbey*, that Lydia's trick does not reveal Austen's "fear" of desire, but rather her recognition that people consciously act out many gender characteristics. The episode, for example, satirizes the gender status of the military, which supposedly embodies masculinity, and the male virtues of courage and volition. That certain members of the regiment and their wives enjoy cross-dressing as a form of recreation illustrates Wollstonecraft's link in the *Vindication* between idle women and a standing army—far from being purposeful, both are groups with nothing to do. Using comedy to raise insistent questions about gender constructions, the novel trumpets how the military uniform itself performs a role: both a disguise and a costume, it constitutes "another form of female attire" (Beerbohm, qtd. in Garber 55). In uniform, a soldier already dresses in drag. Marjorie Garber points out that "whatever the specific semiotic relationship between military uniforms and erotic fantasies of sartorial gender, the history of cross-dressing within the armed services attests to a complicated interplay of forces, including male bonding, acknowledged and unacknowledged homosexual identity, carnivalized power relations, [and] the erotics of same-sex communities ..." (55–56). Mrs. Bennet, recalling "the time when I liked a red coat myself very well" (29), reinforces how military men wear, indeed in a sense *are*, costumes that provide a veritable fashion show for civilians.

This episode also introduces questions about the understanding and reception of homosexuality (as I have pointed out, the Romantic era collapsed the transvestite and the homosexual into one category), an issue also implied in the possible allusion to sodomy I analyzed above, with the flogging of the private. I discuss later in the book how male transvestism had become a "burlesque or grotesque" (Senelick 81). Here, Lydia's triumph—"you cannot imagine how well he looked!"—unveils how the afternoon's "fun" also provides a moment for Chamberlayne (itself a pointed act of naming; the chamberlain was the intimate servant of the bedchamber) to feel "at home" in his body and career, unrecognizable as a *man* to five or six of his peers. Many other Romantic novels include instances of cross-dressing, Scott's *Redgauntlet*, for example, but rarely do women attire men. This episode bears out Cixous and Clement's argument that "Laughter breaks up, breaks out, splashes over.... It is the moment at which the woman crosses a dangerous line, the cultural demarcation beyond which she will find herself excluded.... An entire fantastic world, made of bits and pieces, opens up beyond the limit, as soon as the line is crossed" (*Newly Born Woman* 33). In including transvestism, Austen undermines firm conceptions of gender identity and crosses a line that opens up the tranquilized perfection and so-called stability of gentry life.

Lydia experiences something like orgasmic delight in the titillating adventure of arraying a man in women's clothes, crossing physical boundaries as her hands move over his body, veiling his "real" identity under lavish female apparel: "—Lord! How I laughed! And so did Mrs. Forster. I thought I should have died" (221). She almost "dies" laughing again, and engages in a kind of cross-dressing herself, when she elopes with Wickham. In her goodbye letter to Mrs. Forster announcing her elopement, Lydia can "hardly write for laughing" (291). This image, almost defying representation—does Lydia double over with laughter? shake uncontrollably with the giggles? convulse with merriment?—evokes an instance of the physical almost overpowering the cognitive. If Lydia's laughter "breaks up, breaks out, splashes over," signaling "the moment at which [she] crosses a dangerous line," she significantly does not or cannot acknowledge the transgression she commits, and her apathy about consequences implies that she does not "find herself excluded" from "the cultural demarcation" she has crossed:

> You will laugh when you know where I am gone, and I cannot help laughing myself at your surprise to-morrow morning, as soon as I am missed. I am going to Gretna Green, and if you cannot guess with who, I shall think you a simpleton, for there is but one man in the world I love, and he is an angel. I should never be happy without him, so think it no harm to be off. You need not send them word at Longbourn of my going, if you do not like it, for it will make the surprise the greater, when I write to them, and sign my name Lydia Wickham. What a good joke it will be! I can hardly write for laughing. Pray make my excuses to Pratt, for not keeping my engagement, and dancing with him to night. Tell him I hope he will excuse me when he knows all, and tell him I will dance with him at the next ball we meet, with great pleasure. I shall send for my clothes when I get to Longbourn; but I wish you would tell Sally to mend a great slit in my worked muslin gown, before they are packed up. Good bye. Give my love to Colonel Forster, I hope you will drink to our good journey. (291–292)

Like so many others in the novel, Lydia puts her body in motion; embracing her body's needs, she acts with a man's freedom. With a last lubricious request that they drink to her journey (not to her marriage)—that they imbibe her libidinous joy vicariously—she abandons all, and like nail clippings or strands of hair, leaves behind family, friends, dancing partners, and clothes, specifically one dress with a "great slit." Exultant, she uses the word "laughing" three times and calls her elopement a "good joke." Exclaiming that it would be fun if she were married, she sounds like characters from Austen's early "The first Act of a Comedy": When Chloe sings, "I shall be married to Strephon, / And that to me will be fun," a Chorus of ploughboys answer her with the refrain: "Be fun, be fun, be fun, / And that to me will be fun" (*Minor Works* 173).[8] Lydia's fun alludes to the sexual delight she anticipates with Wickham. The laughter that almost prevents her from writing her elopement letter, not to mention the great slit in her worked muslin gown, suggest that Lydia has already lost her virginity. The word "muslin" carried sexual connotations, as in the following definitions: "a bit of muslin" referred to "a woman, a girl"; "a bit of muslin on the sly" suggested illicit sexual relations (Partridge 545). In leaving this "wound" behind, her letter implies her conviction that elopement will repair the breach as neatly as Sally will mend her gown, and that she will return to her previous condition (hymenally sound), and that there will be no negative consequences to her actions—an assumption that proves largely correct. Rather than reading her conviction that anything can be restored as an indicator of her childlike sense of irresponsibility, I would suggest instead that like Cassandra ("The Beautifull Cassandra") and Eliza ("Henry and Eliza"), heroines from the Juvenilia, she has left her "dress" behind, literally and figuratively, and like a man, anticipates a sexual relationship without fear of repercussions for her respectability.

As the greatest transgressor in all of the novels, Lydia provides the deepest aporia in Austen's oeuvre, representing someone who, as cross-dresser and much else, both exists outside society's rigid gender expectations and embodies social constructions of sexuality. Nietzsche's aphorism in *Thus Spake Zarathustra*, "Not by wrath, but by laughter, do we slay" (41) helps explain why Lydia considers her elopement "a good joke." In a Hobbesian sense, she guffaws with the "sudden glory" her sense of triumph over her unmarried sisters affords her. If she has transgressed the culture's expectations for women, she has also fulfilled them, trumping her sisters (especially Elizabeth, whom Wickham rejected) by marrying first, and she does so without the fear or shame that the same culture inculcates in female minds. How she can neither grasp nor care about the possible repercussions of her behavior is mystifying, in large part because the novel so glaringly enunciates these consequences. Without Darcy's prestidigitation, chances are good that she would have become a workingwoman: that is, a prostitute. The slit in her dress and the reference in that letter to her "*worked* muslin gown" (emphasis added) foreshadows Lydia's possible future, since, as I pointed out, "muslin" was a common metonymy for "a girl"; the phrase that results, "worked girl," combines sex and labor. As I discuss in relation to *Northanger Abbey* and *Mansfield Park*, Austen is alive to the sexual double entendres attached to torn gowns. In making a joke about a "great slit in [Lydia's] muslin gown," Austen uses humor to suggest possible tragic outcomes and, in doing so, she also reveals the complex historical pressures propelling Lydia, the degree of Lydia's own volition in her behavior, and the vulnerability of young women in her culture in general. The novel sets the precedent for reading her letter as a hint of future disaster, since the neighborhood itself expects—in fact, anticipates with pleasure—the denouement of her ruin; as Austen ironically puts it: "To be sure it would have been more for the advantage of conversation, had Miss Lydia Bennet come upon the town; or, as the happiest alternative, have been secluded from the world, in some distant farm house" (309). "Coming upon the town" means a life of prostitution, and "seclusion from the world in some distant farm house" refers to the practice of sequestering pregnant unmarried young women. Roger Sales, suggesting that Lydia resembles the famous courtesan, Harriette Wilson (whose story Austen knew), claims that the "world of organized prostitution is not very far away" from the world of *Pride and Prejudice* (*Janeites* 200). Other allusions to Lydia's alternative career abound: while in London, she and Wickham find lodgings with the help of Mrs. Younge, Wickham's intimate friend and the governess who betrayed Georgiana Darcy by trying to procure her for Wickham. Elizabeth's aunt, Mrs. Gardiner, explains in a letter to her niece that this panderer had a "large house in Edward-street and maintained herself by letting lodgings" (209). If "letting lodgings" is a euphemism for whoremongering, the house address somewhat corroborates the seedy associations: between 1770 and 1779, St. Ann's Parish, Soho contained 21 bawdy houses (by comparison, St. Martin's had 149, Covent Garden had 51, Marylebone had 2 and Bloomsbury had 1) (Trumbach 122).[9]

I have several times now drawn connections between Lydia and various transgressive characters in Austen's earliest writings. These genealogies merit close attention. Parallels emerge, for example, between Cassandra ("The Beautifull Cassandra") (1787–1790) and Lydia Bennet: both run away from home, have an adventure in London, cannot pay for food they order, dress up a man, are met by their respective mothers with love and transport when they return home from committing their crimes, and define "a day well spent" ("Cassandra" 47), as one spent in consumption and dissipation. Both also abuse their bonnets: Lydia exclaims,

"Look here, I have bought this bonnet. I do not think it is very pretty; but I thought I might as well buy it as not. I shall pull it to pieces as soon as I get home, and see if I can make it up any better."

And when her sisters abused it as ugly, she added, with perfect unconcern, "Oh! but there were two or three much uglier in the shop; and when I have bought some prettier-coloured satin to trim it with fresh, I think it will be very tolerable. Besides, it will not much signify what one wears this summer, after the – – – shire have left Meryton, and they are going in a fortnight." (219)

Lydia consumes for the sake of consuming when she purchases a bonnet she dislikes. Her plan to "trim it fresh" was a common activity at the time. Austen writes to Cassandra in December 1798 that "I took the liberty a few days ago of asking your Black velvet Bonnet to lend me its cawl, which it very readily did, & by which I have been enabled to give a considerable improvement of dignity to my Cap, which was before too *nidgetty* to please me" (Le Faye 25). Lydia's plan to retrim the bonnet with yet another purchase, "prettier-coloured satin," mimics how she transforms herself into a commodity for the militia. Her ferocious words, that she "will pull it to pieces," seem overdetermined. In its emphasis on violent refashioning, her remaking of the bonnet is linked to the radical capacity for remaking the self, which itself exists in paradoxical relationship to early-nineteenth-century women's fashions, which were predicated on "the effect of deliberate display ..., supported by the effect of deliberate trouble taken for the purpose—elaborate headwear, difficult footwear, cosmetics, extraneous adornments and accessories, constriction and extension" (*Sex and Suits* 9). Lydia's fashionable redressing of her bonnet strikingly contrasts to the male ideal of fashion during the Romantic period, in which "decorative elements are integrated with the overall scheme, so that nothing sticks out, slides off, twists around, gets bruised, goes limp or catches on anything" (9). Men's clothing, in short, "reflects the modern esthetic principles that were conceived put of Neo-classic aspirations ..., just like modern democratic impulses" (*Sex and Suits* 9).

Her mutilation of the bonnet/self to make it "tolerable" thus reveals less her democratic than her capitalist spirit, one in which she is both the product and the consumer. Lydia always sees herself being seen; she is a "visual transaction [that] is always ideologically organized" (Kaja Silverman 187). Retrimming the bonnet parallels the ambitious way she puts herself forward in the world but also reveals how ideological imprints always compromise (no doubt because they propel) her transgressive acts. As usual, she objectifies herself since whatever she does to the bonnet does not signify given that she (and it) will not have an audience now that the militia will soon leave Meryton for Brighton.

Lydia's rage against the bonnet is foreshadowed in "The Beautifull Cassandra," in which Cassandra "fall[s] in love with an elegant Bonnet," but later uses it to assault the coach driver she cannot pay by "putting [it] on his head and r[unning] away" (45, 6). The impulses generating Cassandra's adventures and perhaps Lydia's stem from terrible constraints on women suggested in the short work's dedication to another Cassandra, Miss Cassandra Austen:

> Madam, You are a Phoenix, Your taste is refined, your Sentiments are noble, & your Virtues innumerable. Your Person is lovely, your Figure, elegant, & your Form, majestic. Your Manners are polished, your Conversation is rational & your appearance singular. If therefore the following Tale will afford one moment's amusement to you, every wish will be gratified of Your most obedient humble servant The Author. (44)

That a story of feminine delinquency would offer "one moment's amusement" to this paragon of womanhood could be ironic, but it could also be apposite, insofar as the "Tale" offers psychic and physical release from the coercive demands placed on women. If Cassandra Austen is a "phoenix," perhaps it is from the ashes of those expectations that she so energetically reemerges as "the Beautifull Cassandra." Austen's listing of these absurd expectations in her dedication parodies the literature found in various lady's magazines, in which just these kinds of catalogues occur and aim to be taken seriously. Though the following poem, published in 1806 in the *Lady's Monthly Museum*, was written after Austen had composed "The Beautifull Cassandra," it offers a clear example of the kind of feminine ideal that Austen wants to satirize and does, through Elizabeth Bennet's voice in *Pride and Prejudice* (1813).

A GOOD WOMAN'S HEART.

Her price is far above rubies;
In her eye is the lustre of heaven:
The law of kindness dwelleth on her tongue;
Her whole exterior is stamped with the virtues of her life
Her manners delineate her heart,
And her heart embraces every ingredient of true worth;

Virtue and Truth;
Simplicity and Piety;
Charity and Benevolence;
Love and Modesty;
Dignity, Elegance, and Delicacy;
Prudence and Economy;
Affability and Politeness;
Humanity and Justice;
Constancy, Chastity, and Honor;
Humility and Good nature;
Sincerity and Friendship;
Compassion and Meekness,
Gentleness and Fidelity;
Industry and Contentment;
Tenderness and Gratitude;
Purity and Patience;
Magnanimity and Mercy.
Happy woman! bless'd with these,
Her's, future hope and present ease;
Happier he whose wife she is,
The richest thing on earth is his. (220–221)

Elizabeth wonders that Caroline and Darcy could know "*any*" such women when they describe the "accomplished" lady as possessing "a thorough knowledge of music, singing, drawing, dancing, and the modern languages, to deserve the word; ... a certain something in her air and manner of walking, the tone of her voice, her address and expressions, ... and to all this she must yet add something more substantial, in the improvement of her mind by extensive reading" (27). Caroline and Darcy's language mirrors the lexicon Austen uses in her "Dedication" to her sister.

Toward the end of the beautiful Cassandra's day, during which she has wandered "thro' many a street" (a phrase that compromises her chastity), the narrative juxtaposes her extensive liberty with the financial, rational, and imaginative deprivation represented by "her freind [*sic*] the Widow, who squeezing out her little Head thro' her less window, asked her how she did?" (46). The widow's "less window"—her narrow point of view and even smaller prospects—exacerbates or perhaps explains the tiny intelligence suggested by her "little Head." This woman's "smallness" portrays an accurate picture of most women's lives, a reality in vivid contrast to Cassandra's. When the heroine feminizes the coachman by placing her bonnet on his head because she cannot pay him, she gestures toward the dis-gendering of male authority and to a different kind of female power than that promised by the acquisition of "accomplishments." Playing "man," she takes freedoms denied to women, especially those who must be paragons of "Virtue and Truth; Simplicity and Piety; Charity and Benevolence; Love and Modesty; Dignity, Elegance, and Delicacy"; and so forth. One could argue that Cassandra and Lydia both "turn round" and "trasvestie" themselves (to borrow Hazlitt's phrase about Byron)[10] insofar as they act out of keeping for their gender and refuse to place any more emphasis on their chastity than a typical man of their age would.

In "Jack and Alice," another story from the Juvenilia, Austen recasts roles assigned to specific genders in order to savor the absurdity of what the age deemed "natural" behavior for women. Lucy, Charles Adams's female admirer, takes the role of the male suitor when she writes a "very kind letter, offering him with great tenderness my hand & heart. To this I received an angry & peremptory refusal, but thinking it might be rather the effect of his modesty than any thing else, I pressed him again on the subject" (*Minor Works* 21). And when he departs, she writes him again "informing him that I should shortly do myself the honour of waiting on him at Pammydiddle, to which I received no answer; therefore choosing to take, Silence for Consent, I left Wales, unknown to my Aunt, & arrived here after a tedious Journey this Morning" (22). Here Lucy, performing the role Mr. Collins will later enact, interprets Charles in terms of social expectations for women—that they dissimulate under the mask of demure reticence: "no" means "yes," but so does silence. This transvestite activity, however, renders Lucy immobile when she falls into a trap set up for poachers and breaks her leg, circumstances anticipating Maria Edgeworth's *Belinda* (1801), in which Harriet Freke disables her leg in a mantrap. A similar breakdown of gender roles occurs in Harriette Wilson's *Memoirs* (1825), in which she takes on the masculine role and solicits a man's "hand"; she sends no less a figure than the Prince of Wales what amounts to an ironic version of a proposal, wanting to know if he "would like to see" her and that he should write her back, if he believes he could make her love him (7).

LYDIA'S SEXUALITIES

The novel knows that sexual pleasure will not sustain Lydia's happiness with Wickham, but assessing her courtship story in such terms hardly exhausts this character's meaning; one can speculate, for instance, that some readers might find a point for identification, even a release in Lydia's riotous insistence on her freedom and physical self-fulfillment.[11] In the Juvenilia, characters such as Cassandra, who resemble Lydia, command respect and create a thrill of anarchic delight. Many readers of *Pride and Prejudice* find instead that the novel inhibits their identification with Lydia Bennet, and that the narrative, in encouraging a judgment against her based on patriarchal demands of women, disables vicarious enjoyment of her pleasure. Her joys simply do not titillate or inspire any desire for imitation: "even the notoriously 'fast' Lydia," Joseph Litvak remarks, "is stuck in a one-joke role" (*Strange* 23). As Johanna M. Smith argues, "why ... does the novel chastise Lydia for wanting the same happy ending the heroines achieve?" (71). By contrast, Harriette Wilson (to return again to the famous courtesan) presents her sexual conquests and a rationale for her "elopement" in a way that fosters sympathy.[12] At the beginning of her *Memoirs* (which caused a near riot when they were first issued, the demand was so great), she explains that one of the inducements for running away from home to become the mistress of the Earl of Craven when she was fifteen years old, was her father's "severity" and that the "very idea of a father put [her] in a tremble" (5, 8).

A psychological reading might suggest that Lydia repulses because she does not risk any real feeling. From this context, Lydia, though an obvious gambler in the game of love and reputation, in truth hazards nothing in her "communications," a phenomenon that, in Bataille's words, takes place "*between two people who risk themselves,* each lacerated and suspended, perched atop a common nothingness" (*On Nietzsche* 21). Unlike Elizabeth and Darcy, pulled centrifugally from their settled positions, Lydia's orientation remains wholly centripetal. In other words, her narcissism prevents her from reaching outward to connect to others (Kristeva, *Powers* 14). Because Lydia does not see or hear anything of "which she chose to be insensible" (205), her remorselessness places her out of the rubric of controlling systems; she is immune to any attempt to break down her fiction of corporeal wholeness. In being unable to suffer, Lydia, in Elaine Scarry's sense, remains outside the "fundamental cultural activity of making a world, of creating artifacts and fictions" (164). Because her decisions lie outside the realm of behavior that could mitigate her actions—she does not run away from a cruel family; she is not a seduced innocent; she does not strive to make a political statement about the double standard—Lydia instantiates instead the abject "leavings" of her culture. She is a force of disorder in the system, an excess which threatens the sparkling, the tidy, and the wholesome, an object lesson in the voracious nature of female sexuality, a force that must be contained. Along those lines, one could argue that Austen reforms the "civic body" of the novel by jettisoning its libido onto Lydia Bennet and then transporting her and her vim to the north of England.

Reading Lydia as a homily, however, does not interest me. I am intrigued by the way in which she, though a rule-breaker, fulfills polymorphic cultural constructions of female sexuality. Inspired by her "high animal spirits," Lydia could be interpreted as acting from female instincts *if* those same reckless carnal impulses did not also embody her mother's desperation to get her married. Though wild, Lydia, like Charlotte (her unlikely double), epitomizes the panic induced when a society thinks unwed women are worthless. As Fay Weldon points out, Mrs. Bennet is the only character "with the slightest notion of the sheer desperation of the world" (76)—and perhaps Lydia should be included with her mother in intuiting that truth. Her decisions thus arise from multiple and often conflicting impulses, a point that is less psychological than it is historical. How does history illuminate Lydia? First, how is she related to—how might she dramatize—the shift from an understanding of women as inordinately sexual to the belief that they were fundamentally passionless?

As I discuss throughout this study, Austen explores in subtle terms such a turn in medical discourse throughout her work. Her writings draw from ideologies that span the continuum of the mid-eighteenth to early nineteenth centuries, and in *Pride and Prejudice* competing discourses are at play—as, no doubt, they were at play throughout her lifetime. For example, Wickham tries to seduce two adolescent girls, both fifteen. One of them, Georgiana Darcy—the innocent, shy, reserved victim of his ambitious, heartless machinations—best resembles the later demure ideal of intrinsic innocence, while Lydia, erotically charged, partakes of the earlier prototype of woman, assumed to be sexual and responsive to amatory texts. The cross-dressing episode provides evidence that Lydia warms to sexually stimulating material.[13] As I discussed in chapter 1, earlier eighteenth-century courting was characterized by heavy petting, but no intercourse, for fear of pregnancy; while later in the century, the "London" style was to get pregnant, and then married. By any eighteenth or nineteenth-century standards, Lydia transgresses the rules. The particular ways she embodies various expectations and prohibitions concerning the female body's agency and mobility, however, complicate any secure definition of what her transgression is. She could be seen as simultaneously embodying the earlier model of the young woman encouraged to be sexual in order to win a husband and thereby conceive *after* marriage and the later, fashionable trend of using pregnancy as a courtship strategy to get married, a plan that her words to Darcy imply: "She was sure [she and Wickham] should be married some time or other, and it did not much signify when" (323). Trumbach argues that "the new male heterosexuality encouraged men to seduce young women whom they had no intention of marrying, and that the young women usually consented in the belief that sexual intimacy was a prelude to marriage" (230)—a calamitous recipe for women who played this high stakes game and lost.

Lydia's pleasure always takes precedence over self-interest, but again, there is more to understand about her character than this fact. Shrewd enough to know that the only way to keep Wickham is to remain in his orbit and that to return home without him would be to have failed at the grand goal of marriage, Lydia "absolutely resolve[s] on remaining where she [is]" (322). Here, embodying the reluctance of a massive object to change its motion, she fulfills Newton's third law. Because Lydia is "untamed, unabashed, wild, noisy, and fearless" (315), the force acting upon her must be stronger than society's censorship, and given Lydia's limited intellect and self-knowledge, that force could only be another kind of censorship—the shame of being unmarried—or another kind of encouragement.

When Lydia refuses to leave Wickham, it is possible to see the impact of an alternate ideological imperative, one advanced by the discourse of sensibility—that it was "natural" to remain with a man she loves. Much has been written about Marianne Dashwood as a parody of sensibility; Lydia, though, functions as a parody of the Enlightenment's assumption that nature had so designed human nature as "to follow pleasure, that sex was pleasurable, and it was natural to follow one's sexual urges" (Porter, "Mixed Feelings" 4). In this sense, Lydia, like Sophia and Laura in Austen's *Love and Friendship*, iterates a one-pronged aspect of sensibility insofar as she isolates from the movement only its sexual discourse. That she is one of those "soft, plump, tender melting, wishing, nay, willing Girls," to quote Colonel Britton from Susanna Centlivre's *The Wonder* (6), a play the young Austens performed (Nokes 94),[14] suggests that Lydia follows advice from the popular *Aristotle's Master-piece*, a text that did not "stain sex ... with stigmas of sin, decadence, libertinism, enslavement to passion, or psychological disturbance" nor decree that it should be "sublimated, suppressed, or sentimentalized. Rather it was viewed as an agency of nature" (Porter 15–16). *Aristotle's Master-piece* explains that "'Tho' the great Architect of the world has been pleased to frame us of different sexes, and for the propagation and continuation of mankind, has indulged us in the mutual embraces of each other, the desire whereof, by a powerful and secret instinct, is become natural to us ..." (26). The matter-of-fact way in which Lydia guiltlessly pursues her pleasure suggests this text's influence—or at least of those cultural forces reflected in it; as her elopement letter explains, "I should never be happy without [Wickham], so think it no harm to be off" (291). Lydia recalls "Aristotle's" demystifying explanation that "to some[,] nature has given greater desires after enjoyment than to others"; the author follows this statement with an account that both exonerates a woman who technically may not be a virgin although offering a kind of primer (though he qualifies it) for those women seeking pleasure: "tho' they abstain from enjoyment, yet so great is their lust and desire after it, that it may break the *Hymen* or *Claustrum Virginale*" (35–36).[15]

To sum up, Lydia could be fulfilling any number of roles: as the stereotype of the sexually voracious woman—a kind of Wife of Bath—a type recognizably alive at least in the earlier eighteenth century, when Pope said that every woman was at heart a rake; as the cipher of her mother's view that a woman signifies nothing without a husband; as a devoted follower of the fad for pregnancy as the inducement for marriage; as the avid consumer of the epistemology that sexuality, the guarantor of generation, is the agency of nature; as a believer in the sexual imperative at the heart of some theories of sensibility, one that liberates her native libido. In that last role, like Fanny Hill, Lydia is aware of "how powerful are the instincts of nature, and how little is there wanting to set them in action" (Cleland 98). All of these possible readings have their force. I want to emphasize, though, the way in which Austen breaks down the idea that Lydia's behavior is "natural" or that she deserves to be rebuked. In the fantasy world of pornography, Fanny Hill may be "guided by nature only" (25), but Lydia's "shamelessness"—a strikingly immovable force in this novel of mobility—arises from multiple causes and reveals that she crystallizes various and competing ideas about the female body. Lydia may lack an inner moral barometer, but she also labors under the burden of ideologies that pose as moral ideas.

Lydia allows Austen to examine one of the most popular, indeed ubiquitous, and charged subjects of her day: the fallen woman. Markman Ellis, analyzing the period's many narratives of redeemed prostitutes and unwed mothers, points out that these texts "have a distinct moral and political purpose: an ideologically correct reformulation of the seduction convention giving it, through repentance, a happy ending" (178). Austen's treats this subject in other ways: with the exception of *Sense and Sensibility*'s Marianne, who marries happily (though that is debatable), the author provides sorrowful endings for these disgraced women, but not because she takes an unforgiving stance. Claire Lamont argues that when the married Maria Bertram elopes with her lover, she "offends against her creator's view of how responsible autonomy in a woman might manifest itself. Jane Austen may have 'a good eye at an Adulteress,' but it was not [Austen's] purpose to make a heroine of one" (79).[16] Austen obviously does not make Lydia and Maria heroines, but she reserves her scorn for those who castigate the fallen. She satirizes Collins's egregious response to Lydia's folly, a reaction that is, in the words of *Clueless*'s Cher, "Way harsh": the clergyman contends that Lydia's death "would have been a blessing in comparison"; that her "licentiousness" is the family's fault, and yet, on the other hand, that her disposition is "naturally bad"; that this "false step" will keep the other daughters unmarried; all of which make him relieved that he did not marry into the family (297). Through such a satire of his "solemn, specious nonsense" (Le Faye 203),[17] Austen shows how ideology dehumanizes women, denying them the independence to think for themselves, all the while expecting that they will nonetheless embody virtue.

Like many writers of the Romantic era, Austen "identif[ies] the social factors that drove women to their destruction" (Ellis 164), but she does not do so in any way that leads her to sentimentalize the fallen woman. She topples the contention that a disgraced woman's reclamation in a marriage such as Lydia Bennet's was better than nothing and that an empty ritual that could guarantee neither happiness nor fortune is better than scandal, than prostitution, than destitution. Further, the novels endorse Mary Wollstonecraft's point that "many innocent girls become the dupes of a sincere, affectionate heart, and still more are, as it may emphatically be termed, *ruined* before they know the difference between virtue and vice:— and thus prepared by their education for infamy, they become infamous. Asylums and Magdalenes are not the proper remedies for these abuses. It is justice, not charity, that is wanting in the world!" (71). Characters from their respective novels admit that an inadequate education has led to Maria and Lydia's ignominy. In *Mansfield Park*, the cosmopolitan Mary Crawford lacks Wollstonecraft's philosophical eclat; however, she offers here an alternative to exiling the ruined: a social solution based on group effort that in spirit, if not in particulars, resembles what occurs in *Pride and Prejudice*: she suggests that once Henry has been persuaded to marry Maria Bertram, the adulteress, and once "... properly supported by her own family ... she may recover her footing in society to a certain degree. In some circles, we know, she would never be admitted, but with good dinners, and large parties, there will always be those who will be glad of her acquaintance; and there is, undoubtedly, more liberality and candour on those points than formerly" (*Mansfield Park* 456–457). Mrs. Bennet requests and wants for Lydia, her disgraced child, the same kind of institutional markers that Mary Crawford does for Maria, the material foundations that will provide the "body" of a respectable marriage (201). To this purpose, in contrast to the neighborhood's fantasies of disciplining Lydia, the mother conjures up happy endings for her daughter about "elegant nuptials, fine muslins, new carriages, and servants"; she rejects possible houses because the "drawing-room" is too small or the "attics are dreadful"; and, believing that without wedding clothes, Lydia's marriage will be invalid, she expects Mr. Bennet to offer his daughter money for such finery, which he refuses to do.

Whether Lydia deserves her trousseau, however, is inconsequential; what is significant is that because Mrs. Bennet has no say over the family finances, she must depend on her husband for his good will, just as she had to do at the novel's beginning when he taunts her by refusing to visit the new and eligible bachelor, Bingley. Mrs. Bennet's lack of financial and decision-making power and her subsequent displacement of her ensuing frustration into nervous fits, angry sulks, and her emphasis on "frivolous" items such as clothing, constitute more typical and trivial ways of rebelling against female constraints than Lydia's elopement; but they also reveal ironically how the more effectively women embody those regulations—and Mrs. Bennet's name leads all the rest—the more they lead to self-destructive behavior. The novels satirize the culture's obsession with controlling the female body: by using humor to show how such constraints lead to rebellion and pathology, Austen can both canvass the wild girl/woman and critique the ideology that leads to her destructive behavior.

UNBECOMING DOUBLES

In this novel and the others, Austen breaks down the binary opposition between the good and the bad woman, the champion of ideology and the rebel against it. She accomplishes this by establishing links between the women characters and by showing the ways in which, for all their variations, they duplicate each other. Doubling Lydia to Elizabeth, Charlotte to Elizabeth, and Lydia to Charlotte enables Austen to concentrate on how ideology affects women, rather than on making moral judgments or on establishing an inflexible hierarchy among the characters.[18] Because the doubled characters differ, however, Austen can accentuate individual divergences and thereby allow the possibility for some agency, while also revealing the common denominators that govern their behavior.[19] As Paul Gordon argues in *The Critical Double*, "to be double is to be different and the same ... to be therefore *both* one and two" (19). Lydia, then, is more than just a "wild animal" and Elizabeth is liberated from the narrow definition of having only a "quiet [autonomy that] invites the conventional female reader to identify with unconventional energies but commits her to nothing more" (Newton 79–80). Austen demonstrates the variety of ways expectations can crystallize in individual lives while revealing the power of those expectations by analyzing their influence in characters as diverse as Elizabeth and Lydia— the princess and the prostitute.[20] As Katherine Canning argues, "subjects ... are not simply the imposed results of alien, coercive forces; the body is internally lived, experienced and acted upon by the subject and the social collectivity" (88).

My argument, I believe, counters the claim that *Pride and Prejudice* exploits the focus on an individual woman and her marriage because Austen has an interest in denying potentially disruptive female bonds, and that the happy ending's emphasis on the fate of an individual such as Elizabeth, combined with its rendering of the pleasures of marriage, means that the novel endorses patriarchal values, including a denial of real alliances among women.[21] For example, Judith Lowder Newton, addressing the novel's conservatism, claims that "if there is any punch ... in Elizabeth's resistance to Darcy's traditional assumptions of control, it is certainly diminished by our continuing awareness that the rebellion itself works in the interests of tradition" (79). In other words, Elizabeth acquiesces to custom, and if she does resist, she does so within conventional parameters: by flirtatiously resisting Darcy, an act that leads to marriage, she fulfills the fantasy (and demand) for romantic closure.

I argue, instead, that doubling illuminates how ideology, like transference, manifests itself in infinite ways, although stemming from the same roots. Thus, as I pointed out above, a culturally determined desperation to compete for and win a husband drives both Lydia and Charlotte to self-destructive choices. No one could doubt that Elizabeth and Charlotte inhabit different universes, a fact that has led to conclusions such as Judith Lowder Newton's that Charlotte Lucas's marriage functions to show "on the one hand, the perverting force of women's economic lot," while it "prevent[s] us, on the other, from feeling that force as a reality in the universe of Elizabeth Bennet" (72). But instead of polarizing these characters, I would suggest that recognizing their doubleness reveals how their converging worlds allow Austen to critique "women's economic lot" in subtle ways.

Elizabeth acknowledges her link to Lydia when she admits that they share similar sentiments about Wickham's fleeting interest in the heiress, Mary King: Lydia asserts "'I will answer for it he never cared three straws about her. Who *could* about such a nasty little freckled thing?' Elizabeth was shocked to think that, however incapable of such coarseness of *expression* herself, the coarseness of the *sentiment* was little other than her own breast had formerly harboured and fancied liberal!" (220). Elizabeth here locates her sentiments in her body—her breast—reinforcing the novel's emphasis on the corporeal intellect, as she acknowledges the way the need for a husband shapes both herself and her sister. Their expressions of joy also link them. Lydia can hardly "write for laughing" as she euphorically prepares to elope. Elizabeth, on the verge of marriage, exclaims that, "I am the happiest creature in the world. Perhaps other people have said so before, but not one with such justice. I am happier even than Jane; she only smiles, I laugh" (382–383). William Deresiewicz analyzes Elizabeth's happiness as revealing an emphasis on pure mind, as he argues that "bliss belongs to Jane; to Elizabeth belongs the blessing of awakened consciousness" (529).

Indeed, she experiences an awakened consciousness, but the singing out of joy and triumph that Elizabeth's laugh arises from an aroused body-mind rather than a disembodied intellect. Jane's smile activates only the muscles of her face, and bespeaks a certain restraint; Elizabeth's laugh, like Lydia's, animates her whole system. A transporting mental and physical bliss belong to the heroine; her "psychical corporeality" (Grosz 22) unhinges the need to declare the superiority of reason at the expense of the flesh. In another instance of doubling, occurring at varying times in the novel, the daughters's transgressions lead Mrs. Bennet to hector Elizabeth and Mr. Bennet to bully Lydia with threats of expulsion from the family. Elizabeth hears her mother say, "*I* shall not be able to keep you—and so I warn you.—I have done with you from this very day" (113). Mr. Bennet echoes these words, when he says of Lydia and Wickham, "Into *one* house in this neighborhood, they shall never have admittance" (310). That neither young woman faces final exile does not obviate the threat; rather, sending the same warning to contrasting sisters reinforces the reality of such punishment in the culture, and its possibility undercuts the idea that Elizabeth inhabits a fantasy world quarantined from systems that pressure and tattoo women sexually and economically.

If the sisters are thus intertwined, how can whatever is abject in Elizabeth be purified?—that "wild manner" in which she is "suffered to" "run on ... at home" (42); her "blowsy! hair" and "petticoat, six inches deep in mud" (36); the woman who will "pollut[e]" "the shades of Pemberley" (357); the firebrand of a radical who accuses Caroline of conflating Wickham's "guilt and his descent" (95). One solution is to expel Lydia. But that symbolic purification, that kind of ritual separation of the abjected from the good one who remains, serves only to underscore their deep connection. Unlike Maria Bertram in *Mansfield Park*, Lydia remains in play till the novel's ending, a fact that works to project her presence in its afterlife: when Lydia asks for money, Elizabeth "endeavoured ... to put an end to every intreaty and expectation of the kind. Such relief, however, as it was in her power to afford, by the practice of what might be called economy in her own private expences, she frequently sent them" (386–387). "Defilement," as Kristeva, following Mary Douglas, argues, "is what is jettisoned from the '*symbolic system*'" (*Powers* 65). Though Darcy jettisons Lydia, she leaves her mark on the symbolic system through Elizabeth, who secretly contests her husband's will (the embodiment of the system) by helping to support her sister and brother-in-law.[22] Because Lydia embosses her signature on the Darcy family, because Elizabeth rebels privately by acknowledging that imprint, and because she can only help her sister in secret, I disagree with Mary Poovey's argument that *Pride and Prejudice*'s ending "disguise[s] the inescapable system of economic and political domination" (237). Closer to the mark is Karen Newman's point that in Austen's endings "we find an ironic self-consciousness that emphasizes the contradiction between the sentimentality of Austen's comic conclusions and the realism of her view of marriage and of women's plight" (704). Lydia, though earlier snubbing "social rationality, that logical order on which a social aggregate is based" (Kristeva, *Powers* 65), now makes use of it while also flaunting its rules: in a sentence that suggests that she disregards her wedding vows while also exploiting the safety they promise, the novel explains that Lydia, "in spite of her youth and her manners, ... retained all the *claims* to reputation that her marriage had given her" (387, emphasis added). Austen laughs both at and with women who break rules governing gender and sexual behavior.

CONCLUSION

Few readers would agree with Austen's famous remark that *Pride and Prejudice* sparkles too lightly and brightly, since that "too" suggests something amiss, and most readers of the novel love it precisely because it is so deliciously high-spirited:

> Your letter was truely welcome & I am much obliged to you all for your praise; it came at a right time, for I had had some fits of disgust;—our 2d evening's reading to Miss Benn had not pleased me so well, but I believe something must be attributed to my Mother's too rapid way of getting on—& tho' she perfectly understands the Characters herself, she cannot speak as they ought.—Upon the whole however I am quite vain enough & well satisfied enough.—The work is rather too light & bright & sparkling; it wants shade; it wants to be stretched out here & there with a long Chapter—of sense, if it could be had, if not of solemn specious nonsense—about something unconnected with the story; an Essay on Writing, a critique on Walter Scott, or the history of Buonaparte—or anything that would form a contrast & bring the reader with increased delight to the playfulness and Epigrammatism of the general stile. I doubt your quite agreeing with me here—I know your starched Notions. (Le Faye 203)

This passage is a mock depreciation, and Jane Austen hardly reveals dissatisfaction with her work here, since her comic examples (a history of Buonaparte added to *Pride and Prejudice* or any of Austen's novels is, indeed, nonsense)[23] are, themselves—in being witty, pointed quips—playful and epigrammatic. Instead, she takes pleasure in her creation, so much so that her mother's misreading gives her "fits of disgust."[24] Austen is right: not that the novel "wants shade," but that what might be called the "shady" material unravels in as much sparkle as the light. The same rapier style that fleetingly solidifies the glittering princess fantasy also describes such turbid matter as seduction, flogging, prostitution, and marriage for hire, events that in a hierarchical cosmos would constitute the novel's underworld—its umbra. Instead, they appear in just as rococo a style as the beguiling occurrences: the "playfulness and Epigrammatism of the general stile" diminishes bold contrasts between shadow and light, and these opposing events and characters, far from remaining safely cordoned off, remain always deeply linked.

Notes

1. John Wiltshire argues that we "glimpse, in the violence of [Mrs. Bennet's] emotions, in the volubility of her discourse, in the unnuanced, coarse vibrations of her presence, a great deal of ... sexual energy" (183).

2. Nokes points out that Austen "found some amusement in all the scandalous stories surrounding [Lord] Nelson's relationship with Lady Hamilton" (295). See also the discussion of Emma Hamilton's "attitudes" in relation to Austen in Honan (163–164).

3. For a different interpretation of this scene, see O'Farrell, who focuses on what she calls the "erotics of embarrassment," and sees a kind of pleasure in Elizabeth's "mortification" (21–22).

4. This phrase comes from Austen's *Lesley Castle*, in a scene in which Margaret describes her sister-in-law, who had so "openly violated the conjugal Duties" by eloping with "Danvers & dishonour" (110). Nokes says that the "prospect of marriage had clearly brought Cassandra none of those gloomy apprehensions of domestic dullness and 'conjugal duties' that Eliza so dreaded" (164).

5. Perry may be correct that sexual disgust was an eighteenth-century invention, but Austen's novels provide evidence that the female characters experience this phenomenon. In *Sense and Sensibility*, Marianne exhibits disgust for Brandon, and Elinor physical repulsion for Robert Ferrars while she watches him pick out a toothpick case; in *Mansfield Park*, Fanny Price reacts to Crawford and Maria Bertram to her husband with revulsion.

6. Contrast my reading to Julia Prewitt Brown's point that in *Pride and Prejudice*, "we have only the disembodied voices of wife and husband clashing in an empty space" (66).

7. For the association between the pen and penis, see Judith Mueller, who discusses *The Case of Impotency, As Debated in England*; this was the "best-selling 1719 reprint of the early seventeenth-century trial in which the Lady Frances Howard sued her husband, the Earl of Essex, for divorce on the grounds of impotence. There, the Lord Chamberlain speculates, 'That, perhaps, the Father's Sin' (the older Earl had been beheaded as a traitor) 'was punish'd upon the Son: [and] That it was Truth, that the Earl had no Ink in his Pen'" (Mueller 87).

8. Austen's use of the name "Strephon" recalls a popular song, "The Shepherdess *Lerinda's* Complaint," by Walter Overbury: Lerinda complains that Strephon is dull until she is "kind" to him, then "Such strange alteration as will her confute, / That *Strephon's*

transported, that *Strephon's* transported / That *Strephon's* transported and grown more acute" (VI 85). This song is reprinted in *Wit and Mirth: or Pills to Purge Melancholy*, a facsimile reproduction of the 1876 reprint of the original edition of 1719–1720. Thus, though the song is from an earlier era, its reprinting history suggests that these songs remained popular for over 150 years.

9. Once bribed, Mrs. Younge reveals Wickham's and Lydia's address, which the novel never discloses.

10. Hazlitt uses this phrase in *The Spirit of the Age* (1825): "From the sublime to the ridiculous [in *Don Juan*] there is but one step. You laugh and are surprised that any one should turn round and *travestie* himself" (241).

11. For an excellent reading of the interrelated issues of Lydia, embarrassment (or its lack), and sexuality, see O'Farrell, who discusses how "the text that engenders embarrassment offers and teaches as a pleasure indulgence in mortification's textually modulated pain" (20).

12. Harriette was a mistress to Lord Craven, the patron of Tom Fowle, Cassandra Austen's fiancé. Whether Austen had met Harriette Wilson is unclear; Tom Fowle's cousin, Eliza Fowle, did and told her about it: Eliza "found [Lord Craven's] manners very pleasing indeed.—The little flaw of having a Mistress now living at Ashdown Park, seems to be the only unpleasing circumstance about him" (Le Faye 71).

13. Austen may be making an ironic joke when she names the shy Miss Darcy after the cosmopolitan Georgiana Cavendish, Duchess of Devonshire. See Stephen Derry, "Two Georgianas: The Duchess of Devonshire and Jane Austen's Miss Darcy."

14. This passage occurs in a section that addresses whether a man can tell if a woman is a virgin; this example gives the woman the benefit of the doubt.

15. Eliza de Feuillide took the lead role. Nokes points out that "Eliza loved [the character of] the lascivious officer, Colonel Britton, who lusted after a nunnery full of 'soft, plump, tender, melting, wishing, nay, willing girls'" (95).

16. Here Lamont refers to Austen's famous letter of May 12, 1801, in which she records having seen an adulteress (actually her cousin) at a party (Le Faye 85).

17. February 4, 1813. This is the famous letter (quoted in its entirety at the end of this chapter) in which Austen describes *Pride and Prejudice* as "light & bright & sparkling" (203).

18. My point differs somewhat from Mary Poovey's suggestion that the strategy of doubling allowed women writers the "opportunity not only to dramatize the negative counterparts of the heroine's perfect qualities but also play at different roles, to explore ... direct actions forbidden to the more proper lady" (43). She suggests that, in Austen, "apparent polarities" give way to "myriads of possible combinations, each understood in terms of costs and benefits, sacrifices and opportunities" (44).

19. Contrast this to Galperin, who (without using the word) discusses a kind of doubling between Elizabeth and Lydia (representatives of individual expression) and Darcy and Lady Catherine (aristocrats, and upholders of a conservative order). For Galperin, these parallel characters frustrate the attempt to find a stable ideology in the novel, since each pair contains a representative who makes their ideology look good, and one who makes it look bad (*Historical* 136).

20. On seeing Lydia as a decoy see e.g., Claudia Johnson, *Jane Austen*, 76.

21. For a slightly different point, see Mary Poovey: "Jane Austen unintentionally echoes the values of individualism when she assigns to individual women the task of correcting the moral wrongs of an entire class if not of society as a whole. However, her heroines's limited accomplishments and the fairytale quality of her novels' conclusions suggests that Austen senses, at some level, the futility of this 'solution'" (28).

22. Susan Staves's research on pin money explains why a woman's use of her independent resources was politically fraught insofar as laws controlled what a wife could do with them. She quotes Samuel Richardson who complains in Johnson's *Rambler* (97) about pin money, which "makes a wife independent, and destroys love, by putting it out of a man's power to lay any obligation upon her, that might engage gratitude, and kindle affection" (2:158). See Staves's *Married Women's Separate Proper in England, 1660–1833* (159). Elizabeth remains both independent and affectionate.

23. Waldron makes the excellent point that this letter reveals how the novel is "primarily an experiment in new possibilities in fiction rather than the vehicle for any moral or didactic purpose" (60).

24. See Joseph Litvak who argues that Austen's "fits of disgust" also refer to her repugnance at the novel's conformity to the ideological expectations of heteronormative romance: "For if the novel functions discreetly and thus all the more efficaciously as a kind of conduct book, the good manners and good taste it works to implant operate in the service of a eugenic teleology of *good breeding*: that is, of the marriage plot, whereby the traditional novel idealizes heterosexuality and its reproduction" (22).

ASHLEY TAUCHERT

Pride and Prejudice: *'Lydia's Gape'*

In the face of the two possibilities which might seduce the imagination—
an eternal summer or a winter just as eternal, the former licentious to
the point of corruption, the latter pure to the point of sterility—man
must resign himself to choosing equilibrium and the periodicity of the
seasonal rhythm. In the natural order, the latter fulfills the same function
which is fulfilled in society by the exchange of women in marriage and
the exchange of words in conversation, when these are practiced with
the frank intention of communicating, that is to say, without trickery or
perversity, and above all, without hidden motives.
                    —Claude Lévi-Strauss, 'Incest and Myth'[275]

The simplest way out of the sacrificial situation, for the story-teller, is
the Proserpine solution.
                    —Northrop Frye, *Secular Scripture*[276]

8.50 am
Mmm, Wonder what Mark Darcy would be like as a father (father to
own offspring, mean. Not self. That would indeed be sick in manner of
Oedipus)?
            —Bridget Jones, *Bridget Jones' Diary: The Edge of Reason*[277]

From *Romancing Jane Austen: Narrative, Realism, and the Possibility of a Happy Ending*, pp. 73–92.
© 2005 Palgrave Macmillan.

Terry Castle asked us recently to look seriously at the question: 'How bad are most of the novels produced by English women writers in the decades before Jane Austen?'[278] Since Jane Spencer demonstrated that Austen did not emerge fully formed from the mists of women's pre-literate history, we have been rightly preoccupied with documenting the relatively long and complex history of women's writing prior to Austen. Perhaps this has drawn our attention from acknowledging the specific nature of her achievement in the context of that history.

Castle finds in women's narrative writing prior to Austen a literary 'autism' which leads the reader to lose 'faith in the shaping consciousness behind the fiction'.[279] She finds evidence of a 'psychic compartmentalization', 'splitting up', or 'psychic trauma' in women's narrative writing prior to Austen. Her conclusion is that while of course socially 'empowering', women's historical acquisition of literacy 'inevitably brings with it self-division, ambivalence, and an infantile element compounded of fear and rage: fear that one's words may offend those who own writing already, rage at being cut off from discourse for so long'.

Austen 'somehow' overcomes this literary 'autism', which manifests as precisely that 'murderous, estranging hostility to parental figures' or 'Oedipal rage' evident in Wollstonecraft's work. It is in the absence of an aesthetic failure common to women's writing preceding Austen, that Castle identifies the 'miracle about which we know little': she 'invariably looks her reader in the eye'. But Castle's sense of what was specific to Austen and enabled such a literary 'miracle' to arise is provocatively discreet: 'the touch of grace, the inability to feel frightened, either of past or future', which has 'something' to do with her father. She answers her own question with an image of idealised father–daughter relations: 'the admirable Reverend Austen, whose love for his brilliant daughter shines forth in all of her compositions, had something to do with this grace', and we can only conclude that he 'did something well enough to make writing seem the most natural thing in the world'.[280]

This seems to be a turn to nostalgic biography to account for Austen's miraculous transcendence of literary distortions otherwise apparent in eighteenth-century women's literary narrative, and as a result easy to take lightly. The point remains, however: Austen is quite unique in her abiding status as the first 'great' woman novelist. She not only captures a moment of self-consciousness in the unprecedented evolution of women's (particular) narrative tradition, but also stands as a defining figure in the 'canon' of 'English Literature' itself, and more specifically the history of 'the Novel'. Castle's point is an odd one, since autism as a condition is widely believed to be an extreme form of masculinity, and the mother's positive contribution to her daughter's literary consciousness is sidelined.[281] However, the point remains that Austen achieves a narrative transcendence unavailable to her literary predecessors, and as a woman writer this *does* seem to indicate the absence of an otherwise common foreclosure of literary intelligence, which would seem to be associated with paternal power. Women writers' early attempts to achieve literary expression could be expected to have incorporated a cultural encoding of masculinity over femininity. Austen overcomes this tendency.

In the new Millennium, Austen's star continues to rise. The year 2002 witnessed the landmark opening of Chawton House Library: a unique and beautiful, material and scholarly resource to further the study of women's writing; purchased, renovated, and maintained by a private patron in Austen's name. *Pride and Prejudice* topped a poll to find women's favourite novel, and was runner-up in the recent poll to find 'the Nation's favourite literature' (The Big Read). Mr Darcy emerged triumphant, as if from Pemberley lake in a wet shirt, in a recent BBC vote to find the most fancied fictional figure of women's desire—leaving James Bond and all his bedroom skills and gadgets in second place. These three very contemporary examples of Austen's exponential appeal, within which her particular appeal to women readers is central, document the high and rising market asset of her Regency fictions, which exists in parallel to an abiding academic fascination with the highly specific aesthetic achievement the work represents. One way to appreciate the sheer scale of Austen's historical and aesthetic achievement is by contrast with her famous near-contemporary, Mary Wollstonecraft.

Mary Wollstonecraft's writing life overlaps with Austen's: Wollstonecraft lived from 1759 to 1797, Austen from 1775 to 1817. Wollstonecraft was 16 when Austen was born: the year she seems to have first made friends with Fanny Blood, who became her most intimate female companion, and whose death provoked Wollstonecraft to write her first novel (*Mary, A Fiction*, 1788). Austen had just finished the first draft of 'First Impressions', which would later become *Pride and Prejudice*, and was about to begin revising 'Elinor and Marianne' into *Sense and Sensibility*, when Wollstonecraft died in September 1797, and—according to Tomalin's biography—would have probably heard of Wollstonecraft's attempted suicide in the Spring of 1796 through a mutual family friend (Sir William East).[282] We can assume that Austen, as an intelligent literate woman, and not averse to a scandal, would in any case have become aware of Wollstonecraft's radical writings, unusual life story, and unseemly death. There is also internal evidence for considering that Austen's narratives incorporate a response to the very questions that Wollstonecraft was famous for making conscious: questions concerning women, reason, and—of course—writing.

Austen seems to refer to Wollstonecraft's work in *Pride and Prejudice* in particular.[283] This work initiated around October 1796, and was sent to Cadell publishers by Austen's father in November 1797. Rejected for publication, the manuscript was substantially rewritten around 1810–12 (Tony Tanner notes that its chronological structure is analogous to the 1811 almanac), and published in 1813. Rachel Brownstein has shown how Elizabeth Bennet echoes the tone of Wollstonecraft's *Vindication of the Rights of Woman* (1792) when she insists that her rejection of Mr Collins's proposal of convenient marriage is the utterance of 'a rational creature speaking the truth from her heart'.[284] The middle Bennet sister—Mary—is bookish and theoretical, and may figure an early version of Wollstonecraft as younger intellectual woman, living through her bookshelves: 'What say you, Mary? For you are a young lady of deep reflection I know, and read great books, and make extracts'.[285]

Mr Collins attempts to read aloud from James Fordyce's *Sermons to Young Women* (1761) for the Bennet sisters, but is undercut by Lydia's tremendous 'gape' and outburst of trivial gossip. Collins remarks in turn that it 'amazes' him 'how little young ladies are interested by books of a serious stamp, though written solely for their benefit'.[286] This scene echoes Wollstonecraft's open scorn of Fordyce's proclamations in her own 'book of a serious stamp', also written for the 'benefit' of those very young ladies. Wollstonecraft's critique of Fordyce sounds very much like one of Mary's moralising discourses: 'Dr Fordyce's sermons have long made a part of a young woman's library; nay, girls at school are allowed to read them; but I should instantly dismiss them from my pupil's, if I wished to strengthen her understanding.'[287] Wollstonecraft's sheer disdain of Fordyce's moralising strictures on female behaviour, shared by the feminist critical tradition which follows from her work, is dramatically embodied by Lydia's 'gape'.

These references to Wollstonecraft allow us to consider Austen's narrative work as a response to questions concerning women, reason, and writing that Wollstonecraft's life and work embodied. As a writing woman, I find these questions compelling, and still largely unanswered. Austen's unprecedented literary 'greatness', and her continuing popularity with women readers inside and outside the cloistered debates of the academy, begs us to consider her particular answers, as well as their longevity, carefully in our own consideration of those questions. The aesthetic 'failure' of Wollstonecraft's novels can be read as an unconscious realisation of the 'failure' of women's historical subjectivity. Wollstonecraft's narrative anti-romances offer an inverted version of the relationship of content to form exhibited by Austen. Wollstonecraft's radical argument for women's 'independence' ends in the misery, madness and/or death of her own fictional heroines, Mary and Maria. Read historically, Wollstonecraft's brilliantly broken novels capture the logical anxiety that arises when women make direct claim to reason—including a narrative claim—in the already masculine context of eighteenth-century literary culture.

Cora Kaplan has come to identify the 'instability of "femininity"' as both 'a specific instability, an eccentric relation to the construction of sexual difference', and as a marked encounter with the 'fractured and fluctuant condition of all consciously held identity, the impossibility of a will-full, unified, and cohered subjectivity':

> Rather than approach women's difficulty in positioning themselves as writers as a question of barred access to some durable psychic state to which all humans should and can aspire, we might instead see their experience as foregrounding the inherently unstable and split character of all human subjectivity.[288]

Wollstonecraft's painful self-definition in her theoretical writing rests on the disembodiment of her rational self, in order to avoid effeminisation in the work. Femininity is explained away as a false consciousness specific to women: a humiliating dependency and resulting lack of subjective autonomy that maps onto Lacanian ideas of 'castration' as well as Kant's notion of active and passive citizenship. The articulating 'female subject' is left with no choice but to dis-identify with femininity in order to become an intelligible subject of discourse. This dis-identification reveals itself as a primary contradiction in her claim to reason, and can be traced in some detail through the fault-lines of Wollstonecraft's self-identification as a 'rational' woman.

Austen, by contrast, seems to enter signification *sans lack*, suffers no apparent symptoms of the 'humiliation' attendant on her embodiment, and makes a unique and powerful intervention in the emerging generic form of modern capitalism (the Novel). She manages this without deviating from a feminocentric style and content, and apparently without breaking sweat. The point is not so much that Austen was a better writer than Wollstonecraft, or that Austen's harmonious aesthetic implies a healthier model for female subjectivity, but that her aesthetic achievement avoids the pitfalls of cultural masculinisation. Something that is broken in Wollstonecraft's encounter with narrative remains untouched in Austen's.

If most women really do still want what Austen made Elizabeth Bennet realise she wanted two hundred years ago, as recent polls indeed imply, then as serious readers of Austen it behoves us to sit up and listen. This may not simply mean that what we/they want is Colin Firth in a Regency wet shirt (although I can think of worse ways to spend a Sunday evening).

Both Wollstonecraft and Austen could be said to be engaging the problem that is rational female subjectivity under less than ideal social conditions. Wollstonecraft's theoretical paradigm tends finally towards a repudiation of the humiliations attendant on femininity under 'capitalist-patriarchy', and results in the claim to a problematically disembodied rationality for woman. This position is inevitably plagued by the 'eternal return' of the repressed feminine-maternal, which can be read as a hysterical symptom operating as counter-rhythm to the theoretical text claiming rationality for the female subject. Austen's work indicates an (admittedly unfashionable) alternative *narrative* route to rational autonomy.

Austen's six complete novels offer tantalising glimpses of the subtle range of feminine agency within the lesser or greater material and proprietal constraints of domestic existence. These narratives work through variations on the harmonic realisation of domestic tableaux disordered by the social demands of courtship, as experienced and understood through the consciousness of a young woman between adolescence and marriage. It is significant, given her eye for living detail and her realist tone, that Austen gives all her mature heroines a happy ending. The problem of the Austen happy ending for autonomous female subjectivity is pronounced in feminist interpretation. As Rosalind Coward reminds us, Austen's work situates itself in a field of reference 'where significant events may happen, after which [the heroine's] choices and identity are lost for ever'.[289]

Or are they? Under the revision of 'choices' offered by the dialectical structure of Austen's narrative work, we are brought to consider plausible routes towards positive agency, embodied in female characters, to reform and transform the otherwise degraded social context. The happy ending, after all, is only satisfactory if it offers the heroine rational autonomy as well as domestic bliss. Emma Woodhouse, Elizabeth Bennet, Anne Elliot, Catherine Morland, Elinor and Marianne Dashwood, and even Fanny Price, epitomise recognisable characteristics of rational female subjectivity finally unmarked by 'hysteria' or 'neurosis'. Their respective engagements in negotiation of the dangerous waters of possible outcomes, once faced with a common rite of passage from daughter to autonomous subject, map out abstract routes for positive resolutions of the social fate of women in the necessary transition from child to adult: a feminocentric focalisation of the 'quest' narrative.

Critical frustration with Austen's happy endings seems founded in a belief that the heroine can only be a heroine in isolation, or at best in female community. But Austen's narrative model of the possibility of objective freedom for autonomous feminine subjectivity, unmarred by hysteria or neurosis, is embedded in a conclusion centred specifically on her desire to be wed. The marital ending registers an overcoming of difference, a meeting of minds, a breach—through love—of the terms of individuation and sexual difference that otherwise seem to govern realist representation.

The common resolution offered to Austen's heroines, providential marriage, works explicitly to align individual and social destiny. Elizabeth and Darcy's union at one and the same time signals the positive reform of the female character, of the male suitor, and of the social world in which they figure. Austen's marriages consistently satisfy the conditions for narrative closure by harmonising otherwise contradictory demands on the novelistic field of reference: the heroine's need for rational autonomy, self-regulation, and freedom from undue restraint (which demands at some level a satisfactory exit from the realm of the family); the male partner's need for (re)connection to the affective domain signalled by the ethics of love (mutuality, moderation of desire, and open communication of feeling); the unbending material determinants (represented as precise—'concrete'— economic forces determining the happy endings) that must mediate the union; as well as the formal literary determinants of the romance paradigm. Each parallel series must find its proper completion before conditions make the happy ending necessary, sufficient, and hence inevitable.

By far the most popular example, *Pride and Prejudice* (1813), presents these competing demands as incommensurate, but shows them brought into harmonious relation as the key characters approach their union. Elizabeth Bennet, when forced to speak on the subject late in the narrative, makes a startling declaration of autonomy: 'I am only resolved to act in that manner, which will, in my own opinion, constitute my happiness, without reference to you, or to any person so wholly unconnected with me'. This scene famously inverts Elizabeth's earlier refusal of Darcy's unexpected first proposal of marriage, when he asserts that she 'must allow me to tell you how ardently I admire and love you'.[290] The narrative route offered by Darcy's first proposal, if then accepted by the heroine, would doubtlessly have answered her material and perhaps—eventually—her romantic needs. But at this point in her narrative sequence, the proposal is directly against her will; she does *not* wish to allow him to tell her.

The narrative turn between first and second proposals, during which Elizabeth and Darcy are both awakened to new perceptions of their situations, allows precisely for the conditions attendant on her autonomy of will to be established. 'You could not have made me the offer of your hand in any possible way that would have tempted me to accept it', is finally shown to have precluded the one possible way of offering and receiving that the narrative then makes possible.[291] Between Elizabeth's arch rejection of the first proposal and easy acceptance of the second, Austen simply reverses the context. The first proposal illuminates a scene in which what we might call

Wollstonecraft's paradigm dominates, where marriage is oppressive and in spite of the heroine's will. The second illuminates an alternative that testifies to the healing agency of 'love', as represented through the providential marriage, which—as the culmination of 'full identity'—reaches the limit of narrative representability: 'removed from society so little pleasing to either, to all the comfort and elegance of their family party at Pemberley'.[292] It is easy to assume that the heroine has undergone a great change in character to allow for this reversal, but her stance in both scenes is identical with regard to her claim to autonomy. The specific difference illuminated by reversal between the parallel scenes is in her perception of Darcy, now a collaborator in her narrative of possible freedom.

The heroine's threatened absence of freedom is narrated through the sequence of unwilled or imposed proposals, painfully observed in Mr Collins' truly creepy assertion that 'now nothing remains for me but to assure you in the most animated language of the violence of my affection'.[293] Elizabeth's only available action here is to insist that her own will must be consulted: 'Accept my thanks for the compliment you are paying me. I am very sensible of the honour of your proposals, but it is impossible for me to do otherwise than decline them.'[294] This assertion is overlooked by Collins, and interpreted by Mrs Bennet as 'headstrong', then highlighted as beside the point by her further plea to Mr Bennet: 'come and make Lizzy marry Mr Collins, for she vows she will not have him'.[295]

Mr Elton's proposal to Emma, and Thorpe's to Catherine, underline the same 'logical anxiety' of absence of feminine desire in an economically or sexually approvable union. Mr Collins' proposal also answers the founding narrative anxiety posed by the 'entail' on the Longbourne estate, and would elevate Elizabeth to her mother's place as Lady of the house. In fact Charlotte Lucas takes this place in an ironic recasting of Mrs Bennet's own conquest of her husband. A similar solution is posed to Anne Elliot, when Mr Elliot offers her the opportunity to revive her mother by marrying the heir to her own estate, otherwise lost to an entail. The heroine's strongest action in these narratives, given the codes of civility that prevent a sharp knee to the groin, is to assert her will by saying 'no'. This rejection preserves the condition of her availability to the providential marriage that connotes her happy ending. The heroine's negation seems to be the hinge on which the narrative transformation that establishes the conditions for a happy ending turns.

More dangerous yet are instances where the heroine's will is temporarily inclined to say 'yes' to the wrong suitor; exhibited in Elizabeth's open attraction to Wickham, as well as Marianne's 'passion' for Willoughby, Emma's flirtation with Frank, and Anne's close encounter with Mr Elliot.

Each present a fork in the heroine's narrative path, or a near-miss, that—if taken—would have found her relatively well-married, or relatively free, but lost to her own final salvation or objective freedom.

For Barthes, these near-misses illuminate the narrative sequence as 'made up of a small number of nuclei' which 'always involves moments of risk'. 'At every one of these points, an alternative—and hence a freedom of meaning—is possible.'[296] The heroine's avoidance of the wrong marriage is as important to her happy ending as her final recognition and acceptance of the right one. When the heroine finds herself positioned within a narrative sequence leading to a mistaken marriage, her only available agency is negation. The denials and refusals uttered at these moments forge a break between the redeemable and the delusional, subject to correction later in the narrative. In Frye's analysis, these moments of denial represent the 'recognition of the demonic and its separation from the progressive or surviving elements'.[297]

Marriage in spite of female will is as dangerous to Austen's heroines as it is to Wollstonecraft's, and always connotes rape. But Austen goes on to propose a reinterpretation of marriage as an appropriate object of a rational feminine desire, and a reinterpretation of rational femininity that is centred on the possibility of love. *Pride and Prejudice* contextualises the providential marriage of Elizabeth and Darcy against the incomplete conditions of a range of unsatisfactory unions. Mr and Mrs Bennet's marriage, founded on Mrs Bennet's 'youth and beauty', is warped by the absence of her husband's '[r]espect, esteem, and confidence'; Charlotte Lucas accepts Mr Collins, and wins a relative domestic truce, but at the sacrifice of intimacy; Elizabeth is warned off 'an affection [for Wickham] which the want of fortune would make so very imprudent'. Most dramatically, Lydia demonstrates the dangers of female will unrestrained by 'the periodicity of the seasonal rhythm', regulated by civility, in allowing herself to be abducted by the same man.[298]

This last pairing is particularly contrasted with Elizabeth and Darcy's providential union, at a moment when that union seems most unlikely: 'But no such marriage could now teach the admiring multitude what connubial felicity really was. An union of a different tendency, and precluding the possibility of the other, was soon to be formed in their family.'[299] The providential marriage is carefully marked out by its negation in these examples of inadequate relations. Lydia's tremendous gape in response to Mr Collins' attempt to read from Fordyce's *Sermons*, which aims primarily to teach young ladies the importance of modesty, takes on a remarkably sexual connotation in the light of her subsequent 'licentious' marriage.[300]

> If the female sex thus represents, in Sartre's words 'the obscenity
> ... of everything which gapes open', then men seem to be justified
> in their instrumental attitude to women and to everything,
> including nature, which has been 'feminised' and which must
> therefore be distanced, controlled, aestheticised, subdued.[301]

Elizabeth and Darcy's 'frank' exchange of words in conversation, by contrast, establishes their union as a site of moderated exchange conducive of 'equilibrium'. This argument is usefully inverted in Arielle Eckstut's brilliant imagining of Austen's 'lost sex scenes':

> Both were in the throes of desire; and desire had outstripped
> sense. Elizabeth took advantage of their weakened state and
> pulled Mr. Darcy down to the ground. A quick glance over her
> shoulder confirmed that the Gardiners were deep in conversation
> with a cow at least a mile off. She arranged him on the grass and
> with an unexpected gesture sat square on his middle with her
> muslin gathered round her knees. With leisurely determination
> she advanced her hands up his chest. She slowed and prolonged
> the anticipation of their first kiss to a near halt until at last her
> lips just brushed his.
>   'I hope the weather has not been too wet for you while at
> Rosings, Mr Darcy?' The warm breath of each of Elizabeth's
> words was felt upon his lips.
>   'No, I am rather partial to all things wet, Miss Bennet. It
> makes going inside all the more pleasant.'[302]

This return of the repressed during the fateful visit to Pemberley is imagined specifically under conditions of the absence of the usual terms of their intense conversation: 'They did not speak for some time, and both luxuriated in the pleasant and, to them, unique sensation that nothing at all needed to be said: that the only necessity was to restore the appearance of their clothes, which had been so enthusiastically disturbed.'[303]

Darcy's two proposals mark his own split identity: divided between the objective weight of 'claims of duty, honour, and gratitude', and a more unfamiliar, subjective, inclination inspired by the heroine, and expressed in terms of 'feelings' and 'inclination'. Darcy's 'feelings' literally breach the demands of social and familial 'duty'; they 'will not be regressed', leading him to blurt 'how ardently I love and admire you', in spite of his 'sense of her inferiority—of its being a degradation—of the family obstacles which judgment had always opposed to inclination'.[304] Elizabeth is rational enough to find this scene at the time 'gratifying'—but it is only in the context of a narrative reinterpretation of her autonomy of will, simultaneous with a narrative reinterpretation of Darcy's 'abominable pride', that she can maintain her rational autonomy and accept his second proposal: 'her sentiments had undergone so material a change, since the period to which he alluded, as to make her receive with gratitude and pleasure, his present assurances'.[305]

Her 'sentiments', because the context for Darcy's proposal has by now reversed: where her autonomy was under the earlier conditions preserved by the virginal 'no', now it can be realised through the bridal 'yes'. This is the Proserpine solution of Frye's account of the Romance: while marriage has been convincingly demonstrated by the narrative to work against the relative claims to freedom of its female characters (Wollstonecraftian hell), it might *also* offer an image of specifically Austenian freedom, but only when Elizabeth has realised that union with Darcy is her own will after all.

Darcy has meanwhile shifted seamlessly, through the eyes of Elizabeth whose vision we are invited to share, from representing a possibility of relative material well-being for the heroine, a preoccupation since the novel's famous opening scene, to acting as agent of 'vertical transcendence'. Georg Lukács understands the 'irony of the novel' as 'the self-correction of the world's fragility: inadequate relations can transform themselves into a fanciful yet well-ordered round of misunderstandings and cross-purposes, within which everything is seen as many-sided'.[306] Elizabeth experiences a transformation of consciousness, which allows for a reinterpretation of her context: she literally sees things differently by the time of Darcy's second proposal. Darcy is both the catalyst for that transformation, and the transformed object of its new vision. Since the reader is given access to the heroine's consciousness, a successful reading experience will be one that shares in this transformation of 'no' into 'yes'.

A key moment in the narrative transformation of consciousness occurs through Elizabeth's reading of Darcy's letter, which follows his rejected proposal and reviews the narrative events to date from a new perspective. We read the letter with Elizabeth; it is reproduced directly and forms a long digression. She shifts, under the burden of reinterpreted evidence it presents, from 'a strong prejudice against everything he might say' to her recognition that 'I have courted prepossession and ignorance, and driven reason away, where either were concerned. Till this moment I never knew myself'.[307] This is Frye's restoration of memory, where partial perception gives way to complete knowledge: 'The theme of restoring the memory is, naturally, often an element in the recognition scene itself, as the action then normally returns to the beginning of the story and interprets it more truly than the previous account has done.'[308] The 'more true' understanding of events seems to imply the overcoming of subjective prejudices, or partiality, in the heroine's view of her object and the world in which he figures.

While Bingley is generally applauded for being a 'single man of large fortune; four or five thousand a year', Darcy offers transcendence of materiality itself with his perfectly aestheticised status as land-owning gentry. His first introduction to the narrative is as Bingley's friend: 'another young man' with his 'fine, tall person, handsome features, noble mien; and the report which was in general circulation within five minutes after his entrance, of his having ten thousand a year' and a 'large estate in Derbyshire'.[309] The full narrative significance of Pemberley remains indistinct until reinterpreted as the proper, and inevitable, context for the heroine's freedom, at which point it takes on the aura of a world governed by 'authentic value':

> The park was very large, and contained great variety of ground. They entered it in one of its lowest points, and drove for some time through a beautiful wood, stretching over a wide extent.... They gradually ascended for half a mile, and then found themselves at the top of a considerable eminence, where the wood ceased, and the eye was instantly caught by Pemberley House, situated on the opposite side of a valley, into which the road with some abruptness wound. It was a large, handsome, stone building, standing well on rising ground, and backed by a ridge of high woody hills;—and in front, a stream of some natural importance was swelled into greater, but without any artificial appearance. Its banks were neither formal, nor falsely adorned. Elizabeth was delighted. She had never seen a place for which nature had done more, or where natural beauty had been so little counteracted by an awkward taste. They were all of them warm in their admiration; and at that moment she felt, that to be mistress of Pemberley might be something![310]

As experience and reflection correct the false perceptions of pride and prejudice in all the parties, the heroine's marriage can finally be offered as an event that harmonises and heals the degenerate world in which she has found herself, as well as healing her own partial and mistaken knowledge:

> She began now to comprehend that he was exactly the man, who, in disposition and talents, would most suit her. His understanding and temper, though unlike her own, would have answered all her wishes. It was an union that must have been to the advantage of both; by her ease and liveliness, his mind might have been

softened, his manners improved, and from his judgement, information, and knowledge of the world, she must have received benefit of greater importance.[311]

The social healing of the union is figured as the moral reform of key characters, achieved by the resolution of mistaken narratives and misperceptions of character between Elizabeth and Darcy: 'But think no more of the letter. The feelings of the person who wrote, and the person who received it, are now so widely different from what they were then, that every unpleasant circumstance attending it, ought to be forgotten. You must learn some of my philosophy. Think only of the past as its remembrance gives you pleasure.'[312] Austen's heroines display a dialectical self-consciousness which transforms objective problems into subjective solutions of negation or acceptance. The heroine's transformation from fallen (degraded) subject via 'vertical transcendence' to objective freedom is clearly marked, but in terms that remain recognisable as belonging to the world of plausible reality. The union that forms the apex of the heroine's transcendence is also the smallest possible unit of collectivity, signalling a harmonisation of irreducible difference. Frye notes how 'original identity' is figured in romance by 'symbolism of the garden of Eden', in which the 'social' is 'reduced to the love of individual men and women within an order of nature which has been reconciled to humanity'.[313] It is interesting, then, that the bold adaptation of this narrative into contemporary Bollywood represents Elizabeth and Darcy's relationship as analogous to colonised/coloniser under postcolonial conditions.[314]

The impact of the marriage, once settled, and its causal history thoroughly reviewed by Elizabeth and Darcy, is detailed character by character in the last three chapters following the proposal. These chapters follow the impact of the news of the marriage on widening circles of characters, repeating the moment of reinterpretation in the light of its fact through various scenes of Elizabeth re-narrating the story of their mutual shift from mistaken dislike (pride and prejudice) via revelation to love: first Jane, then Mr Bennet, then Mrs Bennet, Mrs Gardiner, Lady Catherine, Mr Collins, Miss Darcy, Miss Bingley, Sir William Lucas and finally Wickham and Lydia, are shown in their respective reactions to the news of the marriage, and judged in the light of it, according to their acceptance of the 'authenticity' of its value in spite of the apparent mismatch it formerly represented. The reader's own relief at news of the marriage implies that the reinterpretation of 'world', characters, and events, made possible by this providential union, extends beyond the confines of the fiction and into the consciousness of the reader. This direct engagement of readerly desire might explain why a member of the BBC panel discussing the shortlist of the 'Big Read' poll recently described *Pride and Prejudice* as 'better than Prozac'. It might also contextualise the fact that Austen's novels have been dispensed as therapy for shell-shocked soldiers in times of war.

Narrative is argued to hold a privileged relationship with identity, and the movement of romance narrative comprises a pattern oscillating between loss, forgetting, or confusion of identity and regaining, remembering, or understanding of 'original identity'. 'Identity' has, since Freud at least, been understood within a frame of reference adapted to abstract masculinity. The quest narrative that seems to underlie narrative formations is centred on a hero searching for a lost object, of which he remains unconscious, but in perpetual search of which he is driven by an unnamed, or displaced, desire. This narrative is captured in the Oedipal myth, and as Barthes notes: 'without wanting to strain the phylogenetic hypothesis, it may be significant that it is at one and the same moment (around the age of three) that the little human "invents" at once sentence, narrative, and the Oedipus'.[315]

The question begged by Austen's narratives is, at its most abstract, 'how might things change for the better?' Jameson returns to the romance as a past genre of providential causality, externalised residue of 'necessity', through which we can glimpse something significant about the present. He notes that Frye's religious frame of reference aligns with the Marxist notion of 'final determination':

> any comparison of Marxism with religion is a two-way street, in which the former is not necessarily discredited by its association with the latter. On the contrary, such a comparison may also function to rewrite certain religious concepts—most notably Christian historicism and the 'concept' of providence ... as anticipatory foreshadowings of historical materialism within precapitalist social formations in which scientific thinking is unavailable as such.[316]

For Jameson, romance 'does not involve the substitution of some more ideal realm for ordinary reality', but 'a process of transforming ordinary reality'. As a result, the quest that centres romance narrative form is 'the search of the libido or desiring self for a fulfillment that will deliver it from the anxieties of reality but will still contain that reality'.[317] Austen's novels turn on just such a 'magical' transformation of misery into joy, separation into union, limitation into freedom; and without sacrificing the terms of 'realist' verisimilitude and mimesis.

The subjective desire initiated and satisfied by Austen's narratives is specifically and decidedly feminine; and apparently still recognisable to contemporary women. Is this really desire for a Regency gentleman to come and make it all better that has endured feminist analysis of the 'false consciousness' of women's romance fantasies? A real dream of sexual harmony? Another bloody ideology? We might rather consider it a manifest desire for the transformation of an 'ordinary reality'.

Raymond Williams understands 'the realist tradition in fiction' as work which 'creates and judges the quality of a whole way of life in terms of the qualities of persons'. The key works of this tradition subordinate neither individual nor social context, but maintain a vision that allows us to consider 'a whole way of life, a society that is larger than any of the individuals composing it' without losing sight of the creative agency of 'human beings who, while belonging to and affected by and helping to define this way of life, are also, in their own terms, absolute ends in themselves.' Crucially, 'neither the society nor the individual, is there as a priority', and 'society is not a background against which the personal relationships are studied, nor are the individuals merely illustrations of aspects of the way of life.' It is precisely the interpenetration of individual and collective consciousness, then, that centres the narrative tradition in which Austen figures: '[e]very aspect of personal life is radically affected by the quality of the general life, yet the general life is seen at its most important in completely personal terms'.[318]

Jane Austen is not the first writer to centre this cultural ambition on a female individual. Samuel Richardson and Daniel Defoe are famous for focalising novelistic consciousness through a socially marginal female character (Pamela and Moll Flanders), and Austen clearly builds on the earlier narrative work of Frances Burney in particular. But Austen's work offers certainly the most successful—in terms of complete—alignment of feminine subjectivity and narrative consciousness in the Anglophone tradition. The individual in society is the 'content' of the novel as a literary mode. Put simply: if the individual is feminine, then the 'quality of the general life' exhibited cannot be straightforwardly generalised to the level of the human, without a transformation in the definition of 'human' that goes well beyond gender.

If 'a substantial work of literature is always about how one way of life is yielding to another', we can read the world of characters and problems presented in Austen as a literary swansong.[319] The intensity of these narratives is centred on a subjective transformation, or yielding, which produces a distinctively happy ending for the heroine. This internal, narrative transformation does not, however, align with external, social, factors known to be the context for Austen's writing. In fact, it reverses the movement, so that optimism is restored to the reader in spite of the irreversible decline of the world she celebrates as well as satirises (or celebrates in satire). This is why Austen never really fits the history-of-female-oppression model that is the bedrock of feminist analysis, but also why she is considered a 'great' novelist. Her work is not so much of mournful retrospective, although taken up as exemplary heritage literature: rather, a narrative study of the novels reveals a striking trajectory for feminine consciousness, which implies a social agency outside of the familiar rhetoric of 'oppression' and 'struggle'.

It has become axiomatic that women in the affluent West are progressing through a chronology from greater to lesser 'oppression': emerging slowly from social conditions which have generally denied them full access to educational, economic, material, sexual, and cultural forms of agency and self-expression. Rosi Braidotti identifies herself writing 'as a woman' in terms of writing as 'a subject emerging from a history of oppression and exclusion'.[320] The implications of this argument for the literary critic are clear: remove these forms of oppression, as tending to social exclusion, and women can achieve levels of aesthetic and social expression previously only seen in the work of men. The point can lead to Austen's biography to find what was different about *this* particular woman: if the argument concerning women's historical oppression is correct, then Austen simply should not have been able to do what she seems to have done. The problem with this argument seems to be that it positions aesthetic realisation itself as a craft, or skill, to be acquired under specific material conditions which women have traditionally been denied. In a more positive light, Terry Castle's suggestion that 'women always lag about a century behind in the history of major cultural shifts', allows us to consider a similar 'lag' in their incorporation by an increasingly totalised system of ideology. Women might turn out to have known more than should by now be known, and be hiding it as well as they can. The romance seems a good place to begin to look for this otherwise lost knowledge.

The historical oppression-of-women argument identifies 'patriarchy' as the overarching context for women's aesthetic work. The concept of patriarchy has been defined as 'a strategy which will eliminate not men, but masculinity, and transform the whole web of psycho-sexual relations in which masculinity and femininity are formed'.[321] More recently, patriarchy has become the context for feminist cultural analysis and activism:

> Feminists have taken up the struggle over the production, distribution, and transformation of meaning in a number of specific cultural practices as a focus of political intervention and

opposition in order to challenge the forms of representation
which constrain and oppress them.[322]

Patriarchy, it could be argued, oppresses feminists more than anyone else,
in the way that capitalism particularly oppresses Marxists: both concepts
certainly oppress me when I stop to think about them. The 'oppression'
of women under 'patriarchy' has been evidenced in a myriad of ways since
women 'seized the means' of literary and social criticism. Everywhere
I now turn to think through the questions posed by women's writing, I
am reminded that I am of an historically oppressed sex, and should feel
humiliated and angry at my oppression, often in language raised to incite
oppositional 'struggle':

> On every side we see women troubled, exhausted, mutilated,
> lonely, guilty, mocked by the headlined success of the few. The
> reality of women's lives is work, most of it unpaid and, what is
> worse, unappreciated. Every day, we hear of women abused;
> every day we hear of new kinds of atrocities perpetrated on the
> minds and bodies of women; yet every day we are told that there
> is nothing left to fight for. We have come a long way, but the
> way has got steeper, rockier, more dangerous, and we have taken
> many casualties. We have reached a point where the way ahead
> seems to have petered out. The old enemies, undefeated, have
> devised new strategies; new assailants lie in ambush. We have no
> choice but to turn and fight.[323]

Everywhere, that is, but in the romance: where the struggle is between
subjective desire and objective determinants, and one which can only be
resolved by an apparently impossible, or empirically implausible, synthesis
between these. One question raised by the persistence of Austen's romance,
then, is whether—given the apparently ongoing alienation of feminine
consciousness—we should spend our remaining energies in a struggle with
oppressive material conditions, or in a struggle with our own 'ideological'
desires. Neither struggle seems particularly conducive to a peaceful life
at the level of the individual or the collective. The point is not so much
that artistic synthesis is preferable to political struggle, but that political
struggle *participates* in social disharmony, and that true harmony—social
or aesthetic—cannot really be founded on struggle, except perhaps
the struggle to awaken from a nightmare. Synthesis depends on a true
relationship between the subject and its objects; struggle has nothing to do
with this truth.

Austen's narratives of the triumph of feminine consciousness do not treat of oppression as much as of liberation: the resurrection over the cross, the comedic over the tragic, the happy ending in spite of carefully designated empirical odds. Romance is in Austen's hands a comedic formation: wish-fulfilment towards restoring the fallen world otherwise apprehended in myth. It cannot be avoided that the feminine romance tends to represent this wish for restoration, the quest of myth itself, in figures of idealised courtship.

Women's particular, and lasting, contribution to the novel is to embody the hero of the mythic quest for the sheer possibility of an unfallen world, in which social necessity is shown to give way to objective freedom, in figures of feminine agency. But if feminine romance is recognised only as outmoded fantasy, subjective wish-fulfilment, 'false consciousness', which has to give way to the more tragic forms of 'social realism' as a more appropriate and accurate mode of narrative representation, then this tendency remains a curiosity. I want to claim instead that Austen's narrative art manifests the kind of power described by Adorno:

> the greatness of works of art lies solely in their power to let things
> be heard which ideology conceals. Whether intended or not,
> their success transcends false consciousness.[324]

Recent critical thought understands the structural position of the feminine subject as inherently ambiguous. This ambiguity is productive of significantly different truth claims which would be expected to contradict—or at least speak back at—social hegemony, understood from this perspective as 'patriarchy'. Feminine romance, then, might claim an epistemic specificity, but only after considerable work:

> Perhaps the central paradox running through the [debate
> concerning female epistemology] has been that any attempt to
> define a feminist epistemology requires an acknowledgement
> that we seek recognition of a gendered identity that has itself,
> in Patricia Waugh's words, 'been constructed through the very
> culture and ideological formations which feminism seeks to
> challenge and dismantle'.[325]

So we cannot claim that Austen's work embodies a peculiarly female 'stimmung', without acknowledging that the very concept of 'femaleness' on which this claim rests has been externally defined, or 'constructed', and cannot really evidence anything but its own necessarily false consciousness.

Accepting this, it remains nonetheless that the happy-ending-in-spite-of-empirical-odds common to Austen's mature narrative work, when understood as a 'socially symbolic act', can take us someway towards apprehending a particular tension between material determinants (captured at the level of realist content) and feminine desire (captured at the level of 'romance' form). Expressed another way: we love Austen because she effectively mediates the gap between the feminine imaginary and the masculine symbolic, in such a way as to suggest that things may not turn out as badly as current coordinates might seem to threaten.

Austen's particular 'substitution' for the 'magical causality' available to Medieval romances is a knowing narrative providence that works through form to harmonise discord between desires and their objects; in the process converging the various levels of determination towards the 'happy ending' that emerges in spite of realist obstacles and interruptions.[326] Austenian providence speaks back at the 'necessity' of her social context, and the work continues to speak of a providential consciousness to an enthusiastic audience. But there is less religious than economic determination in Austen's work, perhaps because her faith has been displaced onto narrative causality itself. Mr Bennet responds in a characteristically interesting way to Mrs Bennet's excitement for 'our girls' on news that '[a] single man of large fortune' is moving into their neighbourhood:

> 'How so? How can it affect them?'
> 'My dear Mr Bennet,' replied his wife, 'how can you be so tiresome! You must know that I am thinking of his marrying one of them.'
> 'Is that his design in settling here?'
> 'Design! Nonsense, how can you talk so!'

Jane is described to Charlotte Lucas by Elizabeth as 'not acting by design' in her relationship with Bingley, and Charlotte suggests that she might add a little design to her actions if she means to catch him in the end.[327] 'Design' is an interesting term in both cases, with possible connotations ranging through 'intention', 'meaning', 'planning' to 'creation', it implies a narrative consciousness of 'design' as providential in the hands of the narrator, but as wilful manipulation in the hands of human agents.

Each novel waits on the moment of self-consciousness in the heroine before the degraded perception of a fallen world and its objects turns (back) towards the paradisal: we never see beyond this indication of direction, the unfallen world is crucially not subject to direct representation. The lesson is in the turn itself. Elizabeth and Darcy recede from our view under cover of the narrative summary which sees them released to 'all the comfort and elegance of their family party at Pemberley'. Their union signals the beginning of something beyond the terms of narrative representability. Richardson, in going beyond this point and documenting Pamela's marital experiences, following her miraculous conversion of Mr B, maintains her at the status of mere wife, rather than allowing her to ascend to the realistically impossible terms of the romance heroine. Austen's work, by contrast, incorporates the 'generic message' of the structural principles of romance as 'a mediatory or harmonizing mechanism' in itself. This move effectively appropriates the comedic potential of the romance for feminine consciousness.

The 'romance' mode is shown by Austen to be structurally conducive to feminine wish-fulfilment. This alignment of what we might term abstract 'femininity' with the distinct narrative mode recognisable as 'romance' displaces the tragically inclined tropes demanded by a realism already solidifying in the fires of industrialisation. The feminisation of romance? But the form itself has always had the potential to gather into its representational content material conducive to feminine self-representation, as both Frye and Doody demonstrate in different ways.[328] Austen's specific intervention in this long narrative tradition is to make explicit the mediation of the plausible with the nonetheless possible. The 'truth' universally denied remains an unreasonably romantic desire.

Notes

275. Lévi-Strauss, 'Incest and Myth', in David Lodge (ed.), *Twentieth-century Literary Criticism*, p. 550.

276. Frye, *Secular Scripture*, p. 87.

277. Fielding, *Bridget Jones' Diary: The Edge of Reason* (London: Picador, 2004), p. 5.

278. Terry Castle, 'Sublimely Bad', *Boss Ladies, Watch Out! Essays on Women, Sex, and Writing* (London and New York: Routledge, 2002), p. 137.

279. Castle, p. 140.

280. *Ibid.*, pp. 141, 142, 143.

281. Simon Baron-Cohen, 'The extreme-male-brain theory of autism', in H. Tager-Flusberger (ed.), *Neurodevelopmental Disorders* (Cambridge, Mass.: MIT Press, 1999).

282. Claire Tomalin, *Jane Austen: A Life* (Harmondsworth: Penguin, 2000), p. 160.

283. Min Wild has drawn to my attention the strains of Robert Bage, *Hermsprong: or Man as He is Not* (1796) in Austen, and Claire Tomalin mentions the fact that Austen owned a copy of the novel (p. 125). Bage was an admirer of Wollstonecraft's work.

284. Rachel Brownstein, '*Northanger Abbey, Sense and Sensibility, Pride and Prejudice*', in Edward Copeland and Juliet McMaster (ed.) *The Cambridge Companion to Jane Austen* (Cambridge, 2002), p. 53.

285. Austen, *Pride and Prejudice*, p. 47. But I have been reminded by Jane Spencer that Mary is not particularly 'Wollstonecraftian' in her proclamations, particularly when she comments on Lydia's elopement: 'we must stem the tide of malice, and pour into the wounded bosoms of each other, the balm of sisterly consolation' (*Pride and Prejudice*, p.

298). Mary's tone here seems to derive from an allusion to Mr Tyrold's epistolary conduct advice to his daughter in Frances Burney, *Camilla* (1796). See also Fordyce's *Sermons to Young Women*, the relevant sections of which are included in Appendix B to Irvine's edition of the novel; and Hannah More's *Strictures on the Modern System of Female Education, with a view of the principles and conduct prevalent among women of rank and fortune* (London: T. Cadell Jun. and W. Davis, 1799), pp. 53–5 (included in Irvine's edition, Appendix D).

286. Austen, *Pride and Prejudice*, p. 103.

287. Mary Wollstonecraft, *Vindication of the Rights of Woman* (London: Everyman, 1995), p. 105.

288. Cora Kaplan, 'Speaking/Writing/Feminism', in Kemp and Squires (eds), *Feminisms*, p. 42.

289. Rosalind Coward, 'The True Story of How I Became My Own Person', in Catherine Belsey and Jane Moore (eds), *The Feminist Reader*, p. 37.

290. Austen, *Pride and Prejudice*, p. 210.

291. *Ibid.*, p. 214.

292. *Ibid.*, p. 382.

293. *Ibid.*, p. 137.

294. *Ibid.*, p. 138.

295. *Ibid.*, p. 141.

296. Barthes, 'Structural Analysis of Narratives', pp. 273–4.

297. Frye, *Secular Scripture*, p. 145.

298. Austen, *Pride and Prejudice*, p. 250, 172.

299. *Ibid.*, p. 318.

300. *Ibid.*, p. 103.

301. Patricia Waugh, 'Modernism, Postmodernism, Gender: The View from Feminism', in Kemp and Squires (eds), *Feminisms*, p. 211. She is quoting from Jean Paul Sartre, *Being and Nothingness* (New York: Philosophical Library, 1956).

302. Arielle Eckstut, *Pride and Promiscuity: The Lost Sex Scenes of Jane Austen* (Edinburgh: Canongate Books, 2003), pp. 25–6.

303. Arielle Eckstut, *Pride and Promiscuity*, p. 29.

304. Austen, *Pride and Prejudice*, pp. 210–41.

305. *Ibid.*, p. 366.

306. Georg Lukács, *The Theory of the Novel* (tr.) Anna Bostock (London: Merlin Press, 1971), p. 75.

307. Austen, *Pride and Prejudice*, pp. 223, 227.

308. Frye, *Secular Scripture*, p. 145.

309. Austen, *Pride and Prejudice*, p. 49.

310. *Ibid.*, p. 259.

311. *Ibid.*, p. 318.

312. *Ibid.*, p. 368.

313. Frye, *Secular Scripture*, p. 149.

314. *Bride and Prejudice* (Dir.) Gurinder Chadha, Miramax Films, 2004.

315. Barthes, p. 295.

316. Jameson, *Political Unconscious*, p. 285.

317. *Ibid.*, p. 110.

318. Raymond Williams, 'Realism and the Contemporary Novel', in David Lodge (ed.), *Twentieth-Century Literary Criticism*, p. 584.

319. John Peck and Martin Cole, *A Brief History of English Literature* (Houndmills: Palgrave, 2002), p. 149.

320. Rosi Braidotti, 'Cyberfeminism with a difference', in Kemp and Squires (eds), *Feminisms*, p. 523.

321. Sally Alexander and Barbara Taylor, 'In Defence of "Patriarchy"', in Mary Evans (ed.) *The Woman Question: Readings on the Subordination of Women* (Oxford: Fontana Press, 1982), p. 80.

322. Elizabeth Wright, 'Thoroughly Postmodern Feminist Criticism', in Kemp and Squires (eds), *Feminisms*, p. 180.

323. Germaine Greer, *The Whole Woman* (London: Anchor, 2000), p. 19.

324. T.W. Adorno, 'Lyric Poetry and Society' (trans.) Bruce Mayo, *Telos*, 20 (Spring 1974), p. 58.

325. Kemp and Squires, 'Epistemologies', in Kemp and Squires (eds), *Feminisms*, p. 145. See Patricia Waugh's excellent piece in the same collection, 'Modernism, Postmodernism, Gender: The View from Feminism', pp. 206–12: 'The concept of a "woman's identity" functions in terms both of affirmation and negation, even within feminism itself. There can be no simple legitimation for feminists in throwing off "false consciousness" and revealing a true but "deeply" buried self. Indeed, to embrace the essentialism of this notion of "difference" is to come dangerously close to reproducing that very patriarchal construction of gender which feminists have set out to contest as *their* basic project of modernity' (pp. 206–7).

326. Jameson, *Political Unconscious*, p. 131.

327. Austen, *Pride and Prejudice*, pp. 44, 60.

328. And as Jane Spencer reminded me in a corridor conversation—the return of romance, rather than its inauguration at this moment.

Chronology

1775	Jane Austen is born on December 16 in the village of Steventon, Hampshire, to George Austen, parish clergyman, and Cassandra Leigh Austen. She is the seventh of eight children. She and her sister Cassandra are educated at Oxford and Southampton by the widow of a principal of Brasenose College, and then attend the Abbey School at Reading. Jane's formal education ends when she is nine years old.
1787–1793	Austen writes various pieces for the amusement of her family (collected in the three volumes of *Juvenilia*), the most famous of which is *Love and Freindship*. She and her family also perform various plays and farces, some of which are written by Jane, in the family barn.
1793–1797	Austen writes her first novel, the epistolary *Lady Susan*, and begins the epistolary *Elinor and Marianne*, which will become *Sense and Sensibility*.
1796–1797	Austen completes *First Impressions*, an early version of *Pride and Prejudice*. Her father tries to have it published without success. Austen begins *Sense and Sensibility* and *Northanger Abbey*.
1798	Austen finishes a version of *Northanger Abbey*.
1801–1802	George Austen retires to Bath with his family. Jane possibly suffers from an unhappy love affair (the man in question is believed to have died suddenly), and also probably becomes engaged for a day to Harris Bigg-Wither.

1803	Austen sells a two-volume manuscript entitled *Susan* to a publisher for £10. It is advertised, but never printed. This is a version of *Northanger Abbey*, later revised.
1803–1805	Austen writes ten chapters of *The Watsons*.
1805–1806	George Austen dies. Jane abandons work on *The Watsons*. She, her mother, and her sister live in various lodgings in Bath.
1806–1809	The three Austen women move to Southampton, living near one of Jane's brothers.
1809	Jane, her sister, and her mother move to Chawton Cottage, in Hampshire, which is part of the estate of Jane's brother Edward Austen (later Knight), who has been adopted by Thomas Knight, a relative. Edward has just lost his wife, who died giving birth to her tenth child, and the household is now in the care of Jane's favorite niece, Fanny.
1811	Austen decides to publish *Sense and Sensibility* at her own expense, and anonymously. It appears in November in a three-volume edition.
1811–1812	Austen revises *First Impressions* extensively and begins *Mansfield Park*.
1813	*Pride and Prejudice: A Novel. In Three Volumes. By the Author of "Sense and Sensibility"* is published in January. A second edition of it, as well as a second edition of *Sense and Sensibility*, comes out in November.
1814	*Mansfield Park* is published anonymously and in three volumes. It sells out by November. Austen begins *Emma*.
1815	Austen completes *Emma* and begins *Persuasion*. *Emma* is published in December, anonymously, in three volumes, by a new publisher.
1816	A second edition of *Mansfield Park* is published.
1817	A third edition of *Pride and Prejudice* is published. Austen begins *Sanditon*. She moves to Winchester, where she dies, after a year-long illness, on July 18. She is buried in Winchester Cathedral. After her death, her family destroys much of her correspondence in order to protect her reputation.
1818	*Persuasion* and *Northanger Abbey* are published posthumously together, their authorship still officially anonymous.

Contributors

HAROLD BLOOM is Sterling Professor of the Humanities at Yale University. He is the author of 30 books, including *Shelley's Mythmaking, The Visionary Company, Blake's Apocalypse, Yeats, A Map of Misreading, Kabbalah and Criticism, Agon: Toward a Theory of Revisionism, The American Religion, The Western Canon*, and *Omens of Millennium: The Gnosis of Angels, Dreams, and Resurrection. The Anxiety of Influence* sets forth Professor Bloom's provocative theory of the literary relationships between the great writers and their predecessors. His most recent books include *Shakespeare: The Invention of the Human*, a 1998 National Book Award finalist, *How to Read and Why, Genius: A Mosaic of One Hundred Exemplary Creative Minds, Hamlet: Poem Unlimited, Where Shall Wisdom Be Found?*, and *Jesus and Yahweh: The Names Divine*. In 1999, Professor Bloom received the prestigious American Academy of Arts and Letters Gold Medal for Criticism. He has also received the International Prize of Catalonia, the Alfonso Reyes Prize of Mexico, and the Hans Christian Andersen Bicentennial Prize of Denmark.

STUART M. TAVE has taught at the University of Chicago and is the author of *The Amiable Humorist: A Study in the Comic Theory and Criticism of the Eighteenth and Early Nineteenth Centuries* and *New Essays by De Quincy*.

CHRISTOPHER BROOKE is a fellow at Gonville & Caius College, part of the University of Cambridge. He has authored several titles, including *The Medieval Idea of Marriage* and *Saxon and Norman Kings*.

MARY JANE CURRY is an assistant professor at the University of Rochester. She is a lifetime member of the Jane Austen Society of North America and author of *Teaching Academic Writing*. She has also written many articles as well as book chapters and book reviews. She has also been an editor and translator.

JOHANNA M. SMITH is Associate Professor of English at the University of Texas at Arlington; she teaches eighteenth- and nineteenth-century British literature and women's studies. She authored *Mary Shelley*, was the editor for a book of Mary Shelley's, and coedited *Life-Writing by British Women 1660–1815*.

JOE BRAY lectures in literary stylistics at the University of Stirling, Scotland. He is the author of *Epistolary Novel: Representation of Consciousness* and a coeditor of *Ma(r)king the Text: The Presentation of Meaning on the Literary Page*.

ALEX WOLOCH is Professor of English at Stanford University, where he focuses on the history of the novel and literary theory. He is the coeditor of *Whose Freud? The Place of Psychoanalysis in Contemporary Culture*.

CAROLE MOSES is Professor of English at Lycoming College. In addition to her writings on Jane Austen, she has published *Melville's Use of Spenser* and *Process, Purpose, Practice: A Basic Writer's Guide*.

EMILY AUERBACH is a professor at the University of Wisconsin, Madison. She has interviewed a wide variety of Austen scholars for her public radio series, *The Courage to Write*. In addition to writing about Jane Austen, she has published *Maestros, Dilettantes, and Philistines: The Musician in the Victorian Novel* and other titles.

DARRYL JONES is a lecturer in English at Trinity College, Dublin. He is the author of *Horror: A Thematic History in Fiction and Film* and coauthor of *Studying Poetry*.

JILLIAN HEYDT-STEVENSON is Associate Professor of English at the University of Colorado, Boulder, and Executive Director of the university's Center for British and Irish Studies. She is the author of *Austen's Unbecoming Conjunctions: Subversive Laughter, Embodied History* and associate editor of *Last Poems of William Wordsworth*.

ASHLEY TAUCHERT has been Senior Lecturer at the University of Exeter. She has published *Mary Wollstonecraft and the Accent of the Feminine* and coauthored *Gender, Teaching and Research in Higher Education*.

Bibliography

Bloom, Harold, ed. *Jane Austen*. Philadelphia: Chelsea House, 2004.

Bonaparte, Felicia. "Conjecturing Possibilities: Reading and Misreading Texts in Jane Austen's *Pride and Prejudice*." *Studies in the Novel* 37, no. 2 (Summer 2005): 141–161.

Clark, Robert. Sense and Sensibility *and* Pride and Prejudice—*Jane Austen*. New York: St. Martin's, 1994.

Clifford-Amos, Terence. "Some Observations on the Language of *Pride and Prejudice*." *Language and Literature* 20 (1995): 1–10.

Deresiewicz, William. *Jane Austen and the Romantic Poets*. New York: Columbia University Press, 2004.

Damstra, K. St. John. "The Case against Charlotte Lucas." *Women's Writing* 7, no. 2 (2000): 165–174.

Gray, Donald, ed. Pride and Prejudice: *an Authoritative Text, Backgrounds and Sources, Criticism*. New York: Norton, 2001.

Greenfield, Susan C. "The Absent-Minded Heroine: Or, Elizabeth Bennet Has a Thought." *Eighteenth-Century Studies* 39, no. 3 (Spring 2006): 337–350.

Hall, Lynda A. "Jane Austen's Attractive Rogues: Willoughby, Wickham, and Frank Churchill." *Persuasions: Journal of the Jane Austen Society of North America* 18 (December 1996): 186–190.

Irvine, Robert P. *Jane Austen*. London; New York: Routledge, 2005.

Jenkyns, Richard. *A Fine Brush on Ivory: An Appreciation of Jane Austen*. Oxford; New York: Oxford University Press, 2004.

Jones, Vivien. *How to Study a Jane Austen Novel.* Houndmills, Basingstoke, Hampshire: Macmillan, 1997.

Knox-Shaw, Peter. *Jane Austen and the Enlightenment.* Cambridge, UK; New York: Cambridge University Press, 2004.

Littlewood, Ian, ed. *Jane Austen: Critical Assessments.* Mountfield: Helm Information, 1998.

Looser, Devoney, ed. *Jane Austen and Discourses of Feminism.* New York: St. Martin's Press, 1995.

Macpherson, Sandra. "Rent to Own; or, What's Entailed in *Pride and Prejudice.*" *Representations* 82 (Spring 2003): 1–23.

Marsh, Nicholas. *Jane Austen: The Novels.* New York: St. Martin's Press, 1998.

Miller, D. A. *Jane Austen, or, The Secret of Style.* Princeton, N.J.; Oxford: Princeton University Press, 2003.

Morris, Ivor. "Elizabeth and Mr. Bennet." *Persuasions: The Jane Austen Journal On-Line,* 25, no. 1 (2004 Winter) [no pagination].

———. *Jane Austen and the Interplay of Character.* London; New Brunswick, N.J.: Athlone Press; Somerset, N.J.: distributed in the United States by Transaction Publishers, 1999.

Morrison, Robert, ed. *Jane Austen's* Pride and Prejudice: *A Sourcebook.* New York: Routledge, 2005.

Moses, Carole. "*Pride and Prejudice,* Mr. Collins, and the Art of Misreading." *Persuasions: The Jane Austen Journal On-Line* 23, no. 1 (Winter 2002) [no pagination].

Neill, Edward. "'Found Wanting'? Second Impressions of a Famous First Sentence." *Persuasions: Journal of the Jane Austen Society of North America* 25 (2003): 76–84.

Parker, Jo Alyson. *The Author's Inheritance: Henry Fielding, Jane Austen, and the Establishment of the Novel.* DeKalb: Northern Illinois University Press, 1998.

Poplawski, Paul. *A Jane Austen Encyclopedia.* Westport, Conn.: Greenwood Press, 1998.

Rigberg, Lynn R. *Jane Austen's Discourse with New Rhetoric.* New York: P. Lang, 1999.

Ruderman, Anne Crippen. *The Pleasures of Virtue: Political Thought in the Novels of Jane Austen.* Lanham, Md.: Rowman & Littlefield Publishers, 1995.

Shields, Carol. *Jane Austen.* New York: Viking, 2001.

Southam, Brian. "Sir Charles Grandison and Jane Austen's Men." *Persuasions: Journal of the Jane Austen Society of North America* 18 (December 1996): 74–87.

Stovel, Bruce, and Lynn Weinlos Gregg, eds. *The Talk in Jane Austen.* Edmonton: University of Alberta Press, 2002.

Swisher, Clarice. *Readings on* Pride and Prejudice. San Diego, Calif.: Greenhaven, 1999.

Tandon, Bharat. *Jane Austen and the Morality of Conversation.* London: Anthem, 2003.

Tauchert, Ashley. "Mary Wollstonecraft and Jane Austen: 'Rape' and 'Love' as (Feminist) Social Realism and Romance." *Women: A Cultural Review* 14, no. 2 (Summer 2003): 144–158.

———. *Romancing Jane Austen: Narrative, Realism, and the Possibility of a Happy Ending.* Basingstoke, England; New York: Palgrave Macmillan, 2005.

Todd, Janet, ed. *Jane Austen in Context.* Cambridge, UK; New York: Cambridge University Press, 2005.

Tuite, Clara. *Romantic Austen: Sexual Politics and the Literary Canon.* Cambridge, U.K.; New York: Cambridge University Press, 2002.

Wenner, Barbara Britton. *Prospect and Refuge in the Landscape of Jane Austen.* Aldershot, England; Burlington, Vt.: Ashgate, 2006.

Werker, Anke. *By a Lady: Jane Austen's Female Archetypes in Fiction and Film.* Tilburg, The Netherlands: Tilburg University Press, 1998.

White, Laura Mooneyham, ed. *Critical Essays on Jane Austen.* New York: G.K. Hall; London: Prentice Hall International, 1998.

Wilson, Jennifer Preston. "'One Has Got All the Goodness, and the Other All the Appearance of It': The Development of Darcy in *Pride and Prejudice.*" *Persuasions: The Jane Austen Journal On-Line* 25, no. 1 (Winter 2004).

Acknowledgments

"Pride and Prejudice" by Christopher Brooke. From *Jane Austen: Illusion and Reality*, 74–84. © 1999 by Christopher Brooke. Reprinted with permission of Boydell & Brewer Ltd.

"'Not a Day Went by Without a Solitary Walk': Elizabeth's Pastoral World" by Mary Jane Curry. From *Persuasions: The Jane Austen Journal* 22 (2000), 175–186. © 2000 by the Jane Austen Society of North America. Reprinted with permission.

"The Oppositional Reader and *Pride and Prejudice*" by Johanna M. Smith. From *A Companion to Jane Austen Studies*, edited by Laura Cooner Lambdin and Robert Thomas Lambdin, 27–40. © 2000 by Greenwood Press. Reproduced with permission of Greenwood Publishing Group, Inc., Westport, CT.

"The Source of 'Dramatized Consciousness': Richardson, Austen, and Stylistic Influence" by Joe Bray. From *Style* 35, no. 1 (Spring 2001): 18–33. © 2001 by *Style*. Reprinted with permission.

"The Double Meaning of Character" by Alex Woloch. From *The One vs. the Many: Minor Characters and the Space of the Protagonist in the Novel*, 50–56. © 2003 by Princeton University Press. Reprinted with permission of Princeton University Press.

"Jane Austen and Elizabeth Bennet: The Limits of Irony" by Carole Moses. From *Persuasions: The Jane Austen Journal* 25 (2003), 155–164. © 2003 by the Jane Austen Society of North America. Reprinted with permission.

"The Liveliness of Your Mind: *Pride and Prejudice*" by Emily Auerbach. From *Searching for Jane Austen*, 128–165. © 2004 by The Board of Regents of the University of Wisconsin System. Reprinted with permission.

"*Pride and Prejudice*" by Darryl Jones. From *Critical Issues: Jane Austen*, 93–112. © 2004 by Palgrave Macmillan. Reproduced with permission of Palgrave Macmillan.

"The Anxieties and 'Felicities of Rapid Motion': Animated Ideology in *Pride and Prejudice*" by Jillian Heydt-Stevenson. From *Austen's Unbecoming Conjunctions: Subversive Laughter, Embodied History*, 69–102. © 2005 by Palgrave Macmillan. Reproduced with permission of Palgrave Macmillan.

"*Pride and Prejudice*: 'Lydia's Gape'" by Ashley Tauchert. From *Romancing Jane Austen: Narrative, Realism, and the Possibility of a Happy Ending*, 73–92. © 2005 by Palgrave Macmillan. Reproduced with permission of Palgrave Macmillan.

Every effort has been made to contact the owners of copyrighted material and secure copyright permission. Articles appearing in this volume generally appear much as they did in their original publication with few or no editorial changes. In some cases foreign language text has been removed from the original essay. Those interested in locating the original source will find bibliographic information in the bibliography and acknowledgments sections of this volume.

Index